BIRTH
AND
BEYOND

Sally Williams

B🌿XTREE

First published in Great Britain in 1994 by
Boxtree Limited, Broadwall House, 21 Broadwall, London SE1 9PL

10 9 8 7 6 5 4 3 2 1

ISBN 1 85283 509 5

The glossary was compiled by Dr Essie Menson
Cover design by Robert Updegraff
Cover photograph: The Image Bank
Author photograph: Henry Thomas

Typeset by SX Composing, Rayleigh, Essex
Printed and bound in Great Britain by
Butler and Tanner Ltd, Frome, Somerset

A CIP catalogue entry for this book is available from the British Library

Printed and bound in Finland
by Werner Söderström Osakeyhtiö

To my mother

Contents

Acknowledgments

This book is based on interviews with and questionnaires from recent mothers. In the spring of 1993 I placed a letter in regional newspapers countrywide and some nationals asking for recent mothers interested in talking about their experiences of motherhood. To those who replied I sent out questionnaires, which I then followed up with interviews. Approximately 120 women filled in questionnaires and I interviewed about 70 of them. The women are from all parts of the country, backgrounds and ages. They were self-selecting in that they chose to reply to my letter, but they had no idea of the questions or aspects of motherhood I was going to ask them about. I have changed the names of all the interviewees to preserve confidentiality. Many gave me long and frank answers and this book could not have been written without their help and, while I cannot name them I would like them to know how grateful I am.

I would also like to thank Jack Dominian, Christine MacArthur, Christopher Clulow, Lesley Page, Mel Parr, Sally Marchant and Keith Hobbs for talking to me; Sarah Lutyens, James Fergusson and Lucy for helping make it possible; and Sara Menguc for her work on my behalf.

Finally, special thanks to Henry, Lily and Fergus without whom none of this would have happened.

Introduction

This is the book I wanted to read after I had my first baby: a book about mothers not babies. Pregnancy and birth are well documented, as is every aspect of babies from feeding to development; but mothers, the mother's wellbeing, the mother's emotional and physical health are not. Women are pregnant for nine months, give birth in hours, but are mothers for life. I felt the focus of the books to be all wrong. The really big changes happen after birth, not before. Becoming a mother is the single most life changing event for a woman. Her body, identity, self-image, relationships with family and friends, work – everything is affected but, because of the lack of information, motherhood can be a shock. Even your own mother will not tell you the full story. While it is impossible to anticipate exactly what happens after having a baby, knowing a little of the realities would help women understand just how profound a business motherhood is. Babies are wonderful, but they carry a price. New mothers at first tend to feel more tired than ever before, have less time for partners, be a bit depressed and go off sex, as well as feeling fulfilled and satisfied. It might all sound gloomy, but it is a normal part of becoming a mother. Children bring losses and gains, and an awareness of the full spectrum is important if women are not to feel let down as the real experience inevitably falls short of the fantasy.

Flying in the face of political correctness, the term husband is used in its broadest sense and sometimes includes unmarried partners. Likewise a father's family are referred to as in-laws, whether legally so or not.

Lastly, I am no expert. I have no theories or dogma to promote. I am a recent mother who had a lot of questions after my first baby and for me this book has answered them. I hope it does for other mothers too.

Birth

Being prepared

No matter how old, a mother always remembers the birth of her children. Whether wonderful or horrible or a mixture of both, childbirth is one of the most overwhelming of human experiences. Compared with other rites of passage – kissing, periods, sex, marriage – pushing a baby, a whole baby into the outside world is probably only beaten in terms of physical and emotional intensity by death. The Elizabethans described an orgasm as *le petit mort* (the little death), but the person who thought that up was obviously male; he would have thought again if he had been through labour. Of course, unlike death, mothers do more than just live to tell the tale – they move into a whole new way of life. Babies change everything and the woman who is awaiting the birth of her first child is facing an unparalleled transition.

Birth is both a big event and an unknown quantity; and mothers-to-be, almost from the first missed period, turn to the experts to prepare themselves. From *Spiritual Midwifery*, Gordon Bourne, Sheila Kitzinger, Miriam Stoppard, Mothercare Books, BBC Books to *Practical Parenting* magazine, they read up on birth, watch videos and 'breathe' through ante-natal classes. While nine months might seem a long time to plan for something that is, after all, a fairly set procedure, women soon discover it takes that long just to absorb all the information and options that are available. Hi-tech, low-tech, at home, in hospital, on a 'birthday bed', listening to music, knocked out, in water, with a midwife, husband or the whole family – the only thing that is fixed about birth in the 1990s is the outcome. There has never been so much choice, and getting ready for birth has never involved making so many decisions.

Having a baby used to be much more like it or lump it. Women had little control over what happened and choice did not go much beyond what nightdress to wear. Childbirth education was unheard of and the only preparation was listening to the experiences of family and friends. When "their time came", many were paralyzed with fear, expecting black holes of terror, howling, screaming and bedpost-gripping. Or, worse, they were told nothing at all. Edie had her baby in the 1930s: "I never dreamt it would have come from there! I remember at the very last minute I suddenly realized where it was coming from. It shook me. I was so shocked. No, I didn't know before. I don't know what I thought. But suddenly, knowing that this child would have to come out of there. I knew the size of a . . . Oh, I was so shocked and frightened."[1]

The days of the stork, total ignorance and old wives' tales are long gone. Birth has been stripped of its mystery. Information and preparation are central. Women today not only know where babies come from, but are technical experts in the mechanics of birth, contractions and pain control, fetal monitors, forceps and birthing pools. They are trained for labour and this is largely down to the natural childbirth movement.

Birth: a history

As little as 70 years ago, a woman facing birth knew that she might also be facing death. Childbirth was the greatest hazard. At times and in certain places it killed as many as fifteen or even twenty mothers out of every one hundred.[2] In the 17th century John Donne, the poet, referred to the womb as the 'house of death'. 'Death in childbirth' was a fact that was widespread.

With the threat of death, a 'life experience' was a low priority, getting through it was enough. Women prepared for labour by wearing amulets, saying prayers, putting their trust in God and hoping for the best. Women gave birth at home and were attended not by professionals, but by 'the handywoman' or the 'woman you called for'. An older woman and respected member of the community, she was in effect a midwife, but midwives were not officially recognized as professionals until 1902. When birth was straightforward all was well, but if anything began to go wrong, without the benefit of today's technology there was only so much that could be done.

Forceps

Obstructed labour and malpresentations were a particular problem. Forceps were not invented until 1588, by Peter Chamberlen, an English obstetrician, and were not widely used until the 18th century. Without forceps there were no live deliveries of births presenting unusual difficulties. Instead, to save the woman's life, a barber surgeon was called and he would remove the baby with his tools. Alternatives were manual intervention by the 'midwife', who would pull on any part of the baby that presented itself (almost always a disaster) or, if more skilled, she would try to turn the baby. If all failed, the labouring woman would be left to her fate.

Caesareans

Many believe that the term Caesarean derives from the birth of Julius Caesar, who was cut out of his mother's womb. Others point out that since Caesar's mother survived in an era long before the development of techniques to preserve the life of both mother and baby, this must be incorrect. They claim the true derivation is from the Latin *caesura*, a cutting. Either way, the practice of cutting into dead or nearly dead mothers to save the baby is many centuries old. In Ancient Rome the law required that every woman dying in advanced pregnancy should be so treated; likewise in 1608 the Senate of Venice made it a criminal offence for any practitioner to fail to perform this operation on a pregnant woman thought to be dead. The first known Caesarean birth in which both mother and child survived was in 1500 when Jacob Nufer, a pig gelder operated on his wife after the doctors had given her up as a lost cause. Miraculously, she survived and went on to have four more children vaginally. Other women had to wait nearly 400 years before the operation became more commonplace. Doctors were reluctant to do it as, even if a live baby could be produced, the mother nearly always died from infection or haemorrhage. In 1882, Max Sanger, a German doctor, performed the first modern version of the caesarean, using a 12 inch vertical incision rather than the neat bikini line cut of today. By this time anaesthetic was available, and the causes of infection and use of antiseptic techniques well known. Even so, caesareans continued to be a hit-and-miss affair with high maternal death rates until antibiotics were developed between the two wars. Only then did caesareans become a safe option for baby and mother.

Haemorrhages

Even with the safe delivery of her child the dangers to the mother were not over. She could still face danger from haemorrhage. Once the placenta is delivered and following an initial flow of blood, the uterus usually contracts and the blood vessels are closed off. In some instances however, the uterus does not contract automatically, and then haemorrhage can occur. The causes are many: anaemia, prolonged labour, previous deliveries, large placenta (from, for example, a large baby or twins) or incomplete removal of the placenta. It is one of the main reasons why many obstetricians say that no delivery is 'normal' until it is finished. Until the discovery of ergometrine and the perfection of blood transfusion techniques in the 20th century, there was little that could be done to stop the bleeding. In cases of placenta praevia (where the placenta is completely or partly implanted over the cervix so that the baby cannot get out), death from haemorrhage was inevitable.

Eclampsia

Another ever-present danger was from convulsions or eclampsia. The first real symptoms are a swelling of the body tissues, particularly the wrists and ankles. Then, without warning, a fit can begin from which a woman would often die. These fits occurred perhaps once in every 600 deliveries.[3] There was no real remedy for convulsions until the late 19th century, and it was only in the 20th century that it became possible to control it properly.

Infections

Women have suffered from infection following birth throughout history. Although it might start a few hours after birth, childbirth or puerperal fever often does not appear until a week later. The symptoms are a high temperature combined with some kind of pain or swelling of the abdomen. The infection, if unchecked, spreads quickly through the body and can be fatal. The disease was known to the ancients, including Hippocrates, but became particularly common after the development of dirty, crowded towns. Between 1652 and 1862 there were 200 epidemics of the disease. The worst ones happened in the Lying-in Hospitals which were founded in the 17th and 18th centuries, supposedly to help women. Thanks to ignorance and dirty conditions – infected and healthy patients would share the same bed and doctors would do internal examinations fresh from doing post-mortems on disease victims – they proved to be breeding grounds for the fever. In 1660, it killed two-thirds of the women confined in the Hotel Dieu in Paris. By the end of the 18th century, the cause of the fever began to be understood, but it was not until the end of the 19th century and the introduction of antiseptic that mortality rates fell; the discovery of antibiotics this century has meant that childbirth fever is no longer a mortal threat.

General health

Tuberculosis, diphtheria and typhoid were rampant for many centuries. The childhood disease rickets was another cause of complications in delivery. Rickets occur when the bones do not harden properly and as a result grow crooked. It is caused by lack of vitamin D and it affects both men and women. But it represented a particular danger to women because of the damage it could cause to the pelvis. A pelvis deformed by rickets meant that the baby could not pass through unassisted by instruments. As recently as 1920 one working-class urban woman in four suffered a delay in labour because of the disease.[4]

Pain relief

Nobody bothered much with the pains of childbirth. Mandrake plants were widely used as an anaesthetic from the Middle Ages until the 16th century, and alcohol or opium were sometimes used by surgeons of the 18th and 19th, but not for labouring women. After Queen Victoria turned the tide of male religious prejudice, chloroform remained in use for the following 100 years. Next came 'Twilight Sleep': invented by Carl Gauss, a German obstetrician, it was a mixture of morphine and scopolamine (a powerful hallucinogenic and amnesiac) and was popular in the 1920s, embraced by campaigners as the answer to pain-free labours. But not for long: it turned into a 'twilight nightmare'. It supposedly made women forget their labour, but most reported hazy memories of having felt like an animal howling in pain.[5] It was not until very recently, when pethidine was introduced in the 1950s and Entonox and epidurals in the 1960s, that a relatively safe, pain-free labour became a possibility.

The natural childbirth movement

"Women are herded like sheep through an obstetrical assembly line, are drugged and strapped on tables while their babies are forceps-delivered," was one woman's experience of a hospital birth in the late 1950s. Another said, "I was immediately rushed into the labour room. A nurse prepared me. Then, with leather cuffs strapped around my wrists and legs, I was left alone for nearly eight hours, until the actual delivery." A third said, "Far too many doctors, nurses and hospitals seem to assume that just because a woman is about to give birth she becomes a nitwit, an incompetent, reduced to the status of a cow (and not too valuable a cow at that). I was strapped to the delivery table on Saturday morning and lay there until I was delivered on Sunday afternoon. When I slipped my hand from the strap to wipe sweat from my face I was severely reprimanded by the nurse. For 36 hours my husband didn't know if I was living or dead. I would have given anything if I could have just held his hand."[6]

Traditionally women gave birth at home, but from the turn of the century, encouraged by the promotion of hospitals as the key to a safe, pain-free delivery, the growth of the welfare state and the National Health Service, more and more women chose hospital. In 1927, 15 per cent of women gave birth in hospital, by 1974 it was 96 per cent; today it is 99 per cent. As the move to hospital increased, so did routine intervention. Shaving, enemas, episiotomies, forceps, painkillers and being strapped down was standard for *all* suffering from the 'illness' of childbirth, high or low risk. By the late 1970s almost one in two women could expect to be induced.[7]

For the obstetricians, prevention made medical and humanitarian sense as it reduced the kinds of damage feared by mothers, both for themselves and their babies: prolapsed uteri, vesico-vaginal fistula or sagging perineums, babies with epilepsy or cerebral palsy. But for the women, physical wellbeing was achieved at considerable emotional cost. Founded by mothers who were fed up with the factory-belt system, routinely being shot up with drugs, shaved and treated like 'nitwits', the National Childbirth Trust was formed in 1956, but really gained momentum in the 1970s.

The founding fathers
The NCT attacked obstetricians and hospitals, criticised routine intervention and condemned a process which turned women into pieces of meat. Men and technology had hijacked birth from mothers and midwives, rang the battle cry; women should fight back and reclaim birth as theirs. And fight back women did and do, with the help of a philosophy based on the teachings of a man – in fact, several men. The NCT was founded on the ideas of the high priest of natural childbirth, Dr Grantly Dick Read. A British obstetrician and author of *Childbirth without Fear* (1930), his view was that labour pains did not actually hurt; women, tense and fearful, *imagined* they hurt. Awareness, relaxation and correct breathing methods could break the fear-tension-pain cycle and ease the pain. Dr Ferdinand Lamaze, a French doctor and author of *Childbirth without Pain* (1956) took a similar stand, stating that birth was a natural process which should not cause pain if the woman knows how to behave. Prenatal instruction in the dynamics of pregnancy and labour, limbering up exercises and breathing techniques were prescribed. Dr Robert Bradley, author of *Husband-coached Childbirth* (1965), pioneered the hands-on involved birth partner, but unfortunately rather blew his credibility with women when he remarked, "Let's face a fact: they [pregnant women] are nuttier than a fruitcake."[8] Dr Frederick Leboyer, a French obstetrician and author of *Birth without Violence* (1975) was another who had little sympathy for the labouring woman. He cares more for the babies – the 'tortured prisoners'. He recommends quiet, dark and placing the baby immediately on the mother's abdomen to reduce the baby's, not the mother's, separation anxiety. Then there is Dr Michel Odent, another French obstetrician, and champion of the birthing pool. He encourages women to spend their pain-relief free labours in a bath or to give birth squatting or standing.

The first woman to have a major influence on the natural birth movement was Sheila Kitzinger, an anthropologist and author of *The Experience of Childbirth* (1962) as well as more than twenty other books on childbirth. She looks to primitive woman for inspiration, questioning the assumption that hospital was the safest place for birth, and focusing on birth as an experience that involves a women's whole being. She is largely responsible for the humanization of most British hospitals and the outlawing of routine shaving, enemas and strapping women into stirrups. For Kitzinger, labour is a potentially sexual act. She claims it can be "passionate, intense, thrilling and often completely irresistible and for some women it is the nearest thing to overwhelming sexual excitement"[9] This is a feeling shared by Janet Balaskas, high priestess of active birth, founder of the Active Birth Centre in London, and author of *New Active Birth* (1989), who wrote, "Many women say that the moment of birth was like the greatest orgasm they have ever experienced. Women talk of great ecstasy and bliss, of the deepest feelings of joy and love."

What is natural childbirth?
Definitions of natural childbirth have changed over the years, but broadly speaking, based to varying degrees on the teachings of the founding fathers (and the odd mother or two), the idea is that birth is not an illness and that active medical management is inappropriate for what is essentially a normal event. Most women are capable of giving birth without intervention, given the right conditions and support. Control and choice are important, and women should be educated to know what is happening to them, to be aware of alternatives and to be prepared. They should be able to choose where they have their babies and how they have them. Drugs are not magic bullets, they have side-effects and take away not only the pain but some of the emotional dimension to labour. A drug-free labour is a more fulfilling, almost mystical experience, and is healthier for both mother and baby.

Classes, books and magazines – women in training
Whether hardline or diluted, the teachings of the natural childbirth movement have been absorbed into most childbirth education. Private classes – NCT, active birth etc, – and hospital classes may vary in emphasis, but they cover basically the same ground: they both aim to provide emotional support and friendship in pregnancy, information on technical and 'natural' ways of handling pain, and preparation for childbirth. NCT classes tend to be smaller, have more beanbags and are taught by childbirth educators who are mothers; while hospital classes are taught by midwives and might have the added bonus of a trip around the labour ward and

'parentcraft' lessons – learning how to bath and change a baby. But the thrust of both types of class, information and preparation, is the same.

Since the first ante-natal classes were launched by the NCT in the 1950s, childbirth education has grown in importance and is now big business. Most mothers-to-be now read up on pregnancy and birth and attend ante-natal classes, if only to meet other women and "learn how to breathe". Women are now informed. They prepare and train for birth as they would for an athletics event. From the first missed period, mothers-to-be are locked into a calendar, a timetable of weeks for training. Week 15 is the time to book ante-natal classes; week 17 to start limbering up for labour with yoga and swimming; week 27 to start thinking about pain relief; week 31 to drink raspberry leaf tea to make contractions stronger; week 32 to start rubbing the perineum with oil; week 34 to practise squatting, to start your classes, to learn how to breathe etc. etc.

Books and magazines with their week-by-week guides to "You and Your Pregnancy", ante-natal care with its appointments set for specific weeks, ante-natal classes with their week-by-week preparation programmes, and Birth Plans where women record their idea of the perfect birth – all underline the feeling that far from pregnancy being a preparation for motherhood (certainly hours of self-absorption and being the centre of attention has little to do with what comes after), it is really a nine-month, 40-week build up for D-day – delivery day. Birth is the big hurdle and life after something to be dealt with once the hurdle is safely cleared. Ask any pregnant woman how pregnant she is and she will answer in weeks, weeks gone and weeks to go before IT happens. And IT is not the baby.

The concentration on labour is so intense that the actual birth can seem more important than the product. Gone are the days when birth was something to be got through, instead it is a time of intense emotion which is ideally to be enjoyed in itself. Conveyor-belt obstetrics neglected the mind for the body, so psychology and anthropology were drawn upon to put the balance right. The mind and the spirit are now high on the agenda and birth today is much more than just a physical event. Women prepare for labour expecting not only a baby, but a Positive Life Experience. Apart from feeling, as one mother described, that "Once I'd had the baby and we were driving back from the hospital in the car, I felt that I'd done my bit, done what I'd set out to do – give birth – and I wasn't sure what I was supposed to do next", months of preparation can heap expectations and challenges on women which are not realistic. To focus on the process of birth and to try and do it 'right' can provoke all sorts of emotions when the birth has not gone to plan.

The fantasy and the reality

One of the first jobs for the new mother, according to psychologists, is to square the fantasy of childbirth with the reality.[10] If one follows the other, as it did with Wendy, aged 24, the mother is psychologically strong at the end of it and is ready to greet her baby. Her daughter is six-and-a-half months old. "The labour was just as I wanted it to be. I had really wanted a natural labour and that's the way it turned out, in the GP unit at the hospital, with no technology, dimmed lights, music and a rocking chair. It was a wonderful, very moving experience." But if the actual birth is very different from the imagined one (and first-time mothers have greater discrepancies than second timers[11]), if mothers felt overwhelmed, abandoned and betrayed, they are in no shape psychologically to start mothering. Studies in one Toronto hospital[12] showed an increase in post-natal neuroses and even psychoses in women who had participated in over-aggressive childbirth classes that had influenced them against hospital procedures and undermined their confidence in hospital staff.

Am I in labour?

'A woman always knows when she's in labour,' say the books. No, they do not. Some women arrive at hospitals five minutes before birth wondering what that backache is all about, and others arrive two weeks early with nerves. Hannah, aged 36, whose daughter is now nearly one, had been having contractions for 12 hours when she went into hospital. She was on the Domino Scheme and phoned her midwife who told her to come in. "They [the contractions] were three minutes apart. I had been sick, which I thought was a sign that I was in transition, and I was sure it was going to happen soon. The midwife examined me and said, 'Look, I think you should go home because there is nothing happening, you haven't dilated at all.' I thought, 'I've got it all wrong. How stupid of me to have thought I was in labour and I am not.'" For some women especially first-timers, labour can be a very long-drawn-out affair. The early stages can rumble on for hours before anything really happens, although it feels as though *everything* is happening. Labour does not officially start until you are 3cms dilated, and being told after a night of walking around and breathing through contractions that you are not even in labour can be very dispiriting. As Hannah said, "I thought, what sort of mother am I going to be, when I can't even tell whether I'm in labour or not."

Labour is divided into three stages

Mary, aged 39, said, "The stages of labour have never been as clear-cut as I imagined them to be. I've had three children and I can honestly say that the stages have not been as they are described in the books. They do not have a beginning and an end – they all blur into one." Squaring reality with images from classes, books and television can cause problems of recognition. Just as some mothers-to-be who have studied the books cannot imagine their baby as anything other than a diagram, others think of labour as being divided into three neat, distinguishable phases. The term itself is very misleading – stage implies a definite period. Books and magazines set them out in different sections or chapters with separate headings. Like a starter, main course and pudding, each stage is dealt with as a separate entity, specific signs are described for each, different positions and different breathing suggested and transition is a fleeting state before the main course comes along. Of course, books are not the whole truth and nothing but, as women find out, but it is not surprising that, when contractions come fast and furious, or she is being sick or shaking (often seen as a sign of transition) every half an hour, that women, trying to match symptoms with the relevant chapter, get confused. "Despite going to NCT classes, weeks of ante-natal information shoved down my ears and reading endless books", said Kerry, aged 35, who had a daughter five months ago, "I was not prepared for what happened. It was 3 am and contractions started every two minutes, not every forty minutes, make a cup of tea, a meal, have a bath, relax etc. The impression I was given was that you would have plenty of time to prepare yourself; it would be a slow build-up, and you would have time to get used to the idea that you were in labour. I did try to have a bath and a cup of tea, but it all got too much. I couldn't get over the pain from the first before the second one came, I couldn't pace myself properly." Despite the contractions it took a long time for Kerry to dilate. After 20 hours, pethidine, an epidural, episiotomy and forceps – a 'full house' and three shifts of midwives – her daughter was born. "I was then sick." It was not so much the hi-tech birth itself that bothered her – she was "easy-going" and would "play it by ear" – but that, "you read all these books, you watch all the videos and gear yourself up as best you can and then it doesn't happen like you were told it would."

Pain

The Romans did not call childbirth *poena magna*, 'the great pain', for nothing. And it has not stopped hurting just because Dr Dick Grantly Read thought up some breathing exercises. Labour is painful. It is ranked above all other pain except amputation of a digit or pain from a nerve injury.[13] It is true that a few women, 9 per cent, feel little pain.[14] Laura is 29 and has a seventeen-month-old son. "I'd always been very frightened of giving birth, right from an early age. I used to wake up with really bad nightmares. And I always wanted to know, like when Mum's friends had babies, what the pain was like – all the gory parts. I had always said that I would have an epidural because I didn't want the pain, but when it happened, it was so much easier than I had imagined. It was amazing, almost as if someone up there had said, 'She's suffered enough – we'll make this easy.' It was wonderful." Other women are not so lucky: 60 per cent[15] reported that labour pain was the most intense pain they had ever experienced.

Because women no longer see other women in labour, they have lost touch with the pain of childbirth. As with death and dying, birth is mostly hospitalized and anaesthetized out of sight, and women have lost an awareness that the beginning of life is both marvellous and horrible. Caroline, aged 35, whose son was born eighteen months ago, said, "It was so painful. I was not prepared for such intense pain. Other people I've come across had labours that went on for hours and hours, but they seemed to manage to be in control, even though it was painful. But when it came to me, I was totally out of control. I'd done all the reading and the breathing and thought I would cope. All I did was scream my head off." Caroline had a very long labour, the last four hours of which were excruciating, because the baby got stuck. She asked for an epidural, but was told it was too late. She was eventually delivered with the help of forceps. "I didn't know you could go through that much pain and not die. I suddenly realized how women died of childbirth. I thought, if this goes on, just let me die."

Beverly, aged 27, who has a son aged six months, said, "The labour was much more painful than I imagined. I actually felt in a state of shock afterwards at how painful it had been – I hadn't anticipated it. A lot of people had said to me that it was just like bad period pain and I suffer from those, so I thought, 'I can cope with that'. I hadn't intended to have any pain relief apart from gas and air, but I found myself screaming for pethidine. Later, I demanded an epidural which I had convinced myself I wouldn't want, but it was too late. I suppose I feel slightly ashamed of myself – that I had given in when I hadn't intended to."

The influence of the natural childbirth movement has meant that women approach labour with two very worrying ideas: first, that a relaxed, relatively painless childbirth is available to any woman who knows how to breathe properly, and second, that it is good to do without pain relief. Intended or not, this is the message which many women get from ante-natal classes and the books they read. Women believe that by refusing pain relief, they are exercising choice and control. A 'good birth' is pain relief free, a 'bad birth' is where women 'succumb'. Women who do not have pain relief feel proud that they did it by themselves, are congratulated and admired. There is nothing wrong with that, but those who do have pain relief feel as if they have failed.

Women today are being encouraged to reject something that our mothers and grandmothers fought for. According to the Bible (Genesis, chapter three, verse 16): "In sorrow shalt thou bring forth children", women were supposed to suffer in childbirth. When Dr James Young Simpson, Professor of Midwifery, Edinburgh University, discovered the anaesthetic properties of chloroform in 1847, the Church of England was united in its opposition to the use of it in childbirth. It was condemned as a "decoy of Satan, apparently offering itself to bless women; but in the end it will harden society."[16] It was Queen Victoria who gave the concept of pain-free labour a big boost. She used "that blessed chloroform" during her eighth confinement and the opposition was withdrawn. Now, here we are again. Women are being told once more, but this time not by the Christian church, that female pain is good and that it is good to suffer.

"It is important to realize", says Janet Balaskas, "that the pain involved is only part of the great variety of intense feelings one experiences. If one cuts out the pain, one generally cuts out, to some extent, the other feelings too."[17] "Contractions", says Sheila Kitzinger, "are *not* pains. They are tightenings which may be painful, especially when they are being most effective. There is an art to approaching each new contraction thinking 'splendid! Here's another one!' and later, as you approach the end of the first stage, when they are at their biggest, 'oh, this is a really good one!'"[18] Margaret Jowitt says that "Women are led to believe that labour will be painful and it becomes so. But contractions are not intrinsically painful."[19]

Contractions *are* intrinsically painful. It is true that some aspects of pain are in the mind and that learning how to breathe does help to take away some of the pain. Studies have shown that women who went to ante-natal classes and knew how to breathe had lower levels of 'affective' pain – the horrible, distressing and frightening qualities of pain.[20] "The breathing really helped" was something that women said again and again. But that still leaves the other side of pain – the plain old painful physical side. What Dick Read *et al* did not spell out was that pain is not *all* in the head. The different amounts of pain experienced from woman to woman and from birth to birth are not simply to do with breathing or pain thresholds. There are basic obstetric factors which cause pain, for example the strength of uterine contractions and the precise size and position of the baby relative to the dimensions of the birth canal. Induced labours or artificially rupturing the membranes can cause a more painful labour, and labour is more painful for women giving birth the first time, partly because of psychological reasons – it is unknown territory and therefore more frightening – but also because of the physical fact that muscles are being used that have never been used before. Second-timers find the first stage less painful because they are not so frightened, but the second stage as painful because delivery is more rapid and therefore physically more traumatic.[21]

At the end of the day, a natural pain relief free labour does not necessarily equal a 'good birth'. Cathy, aged 37, has two children, aged five-and-a-half and two-and-a-half. Her second labour was better than the first, despite her having an epidural and it nearly being an emergency caesarean. "The first was quite a shock. I went to active birth classes and NCT ante-natal classes, but it still came as a shock as to how intense and painful birth was. I didn't want any drugs; on my birth plan I put down that I didn't want drugs – just gas and air. I wanted to do it as naturally as possible. Looking back I don't know why it was so important to me. I think it had something to do with the ante-natal classes I'd been to. There was a very strong ethos towards no drugs. The more you coped without them the better, and if you coped without gas and air you got a gold star! For me an epidural was definitely the best way to do it second time around. I remember saying, 'I'm not going to do that again, I don't want to go through that pain.' I felt that I'd been pushed to the limit and beyond with the first birth. One thing that made me really cross the second time around was that I went back to my ante-natal group, as everyone did, to tell your story, and when I told everyone that I'd chosen to have an epidural, nobody wanted to know."

Sandra, aged 34, has two children, aged six years and four-and-a-half months, and was equally shocked by her natural birth. Her oldest had been born with the help of an epidural, forceps and an episiotomy, but her second was very different. "I wasn't averse to pain relief. The epidural had been brilliant the first time, but I knew each labour was different and I went into it with an open mind. It all happened so quickly. Before I knew it the midwife said I was ready to push, and it was all over. I was so shocked. I was shaking all over. I didn't want to hold the baby after. I can't believe that now, looking back. He was laid in a cot at the end of the bed and I was looking at him and my husband said, 'Do you want to hold him?' and I said 'No,' I feel quite guilty about that now, but there had been so much pushing and shouting and it had happened so quickly. I never thought in a million years that I could go through childbirth without pain relief."

Control

Control and choice are important if a woman is not to feel violated by birth. Helen is 21 and her son was born 18 months ago. Two months before Sam's birth she separated from her husband. "My son was born in a teaching hospital and everything that they could do to me they did. A natural birth wasn't important to me, but I thought I would be consulted about pain relief, that someone would ask what I wanted. Instead, they just gave me an epidural and didn't really explain what was going on. I felt disappointed with the whole labour, not just the epidural. It felt as though it was all taken out of my hands. I hated the whole thing. I think maybe if I'd been a bit more assertive things would have been a bit different. From the minute I had the epidural, with the blood pressure monitor and the drip, I couldn't move around, I couldn't sit down, I just had to lie there and they made all the decisions. They decided whether it needed topping up or not, they decided that my waters needed to be broken, they decided that an internal monitor was necessary. I didn't feel up to arguing. I wish I had done now as I feel that I was pressurized into everything. I wasn't happy with the whole experience. I hated that feeling of being out of control."

Perhaps if Helen had been older or if labour had happened at a less vulnerable time she might have felt more able to argue, to assert herself. At the end of the day she might have had exactly the same obstetric intervention, but she probably would have felt happier about it. Control and choice are not so much about what actually happens or does not happen – although obviously that is connected – it is more about how the woman perceives what has happened. The definition of control is very subjective. It can mean conquering pain and controlling the actual delivery. Some women said: "I feel so proud. I can say I did it. I endured the pains" "It was the most exciting experience. It was the greatest high" and "People have always been there helping me, but this I did alone. It was great to feel I did it by myself. I feel more confident now, more self-assured." Or control can mean not screaming, not being grouchy and being able to socialize normally – a control which comes from pain relief. Sophie, aged 37, who has one daughter aged twenty-two months, said, "The pain was too great. I heard myself asking for an epidural. It was wonderful. I have pictures of Nelly's birth. I have a huge grin on my face".

It does not matter how hi or low-tech a birth has been; if a woman feels she has controlled it, she will more likely feel OK about it. Fran, aged 37, has a daughter aged twenty-two months. "My labour was quite a long one and I ended up having forceps and an episiotomy. They were very careful to explain to me why it was necessary and although I didn't want a hi-tech birth, they explained to me the way my daughter's head had turned and I felt satisfied that they were doing everything according to my wishes, even though it wasn't the original plan. It was necessary and I understood why. I still felt in control although I had the forceps and everything. I didn't feel let down by it."

Classes and childbirth education fail to emphasize that there is a lot about

14

labour that cannot be controlled, both with the experience itself and the hospital environment. Many women think that if they have been to classes, understood what is going to happen, understood the way their body works, cooperated with the midwives and the midwives have cooperated and supported them, then they should have a pretty good time. The equation is not true. To give birth is to give up control; you have to go with your body. Some women are terrified of this almost primeval feeling. Their genitals are exposed to strangers, they are often being sick, sometimes defecating, they can do nothing with their bodies. Women today can control their weight by dieting, they can control their careers by switching jobs, and they can control their lifestyles by choosing when to have a baby; they can also chose their partner and leave him if it does not work out. But when it comes to giving birth women have to let go. Mandy, aged 25, whose son was born seven months ago, said, "I had everything I wanted. I gave birth at home, it was all straightforward, the midwife was nice and Mike was there, but I hated it. I felt like an animal. It was all so degrading."

Labour is a very dynamic process. "I had a healthy pregnancy. I am fit. I had done all the swimming and yoga – nothing led me to believe that I wouldn't have anything other than a straightforward labour", underlines a common misconception – that the investment will pay off and one will automatically lead to the other.

Georgia is 33. Her son was born three years ago and her labour has "completely changed my spiritual and emotional life." She wanted a home birth. "I thought I was a normal woman, fitter than most, who'd have a normal labour, twelve hours maximum, hard work, but no need for pain relief, ending with the birth of a healthy baby and a peaceful, romantic cuddle in bed with John. What happened was forty-six hours, a seemingly endless, completely exhausting endurance test." It ended with Barney swallowing two lungfuls of meconium in the last hour and being born hardly breathing. Within half an hour they were both in hospital in the special care unit with a very sick baby. "At the time death from brain damage seemed inevitable." Barney stayed in special care for two weeks and is now fine, but the experience has stayed with Georgia. "I had a big control thing. I wanted to do it myself and it fitted in with being into homeopathy and having an independent midwife and being at home. I was so sure that I would produce a baby without too much fuss. I thought I could do it no matter what, that I was in control. I really thought I was going to die of exhaustion; I was so extremely not in control." Georgia suffered from depression after the labour. "It made me feel very inadequate. I did a lot of denying. I went around acting as if it had been fine, as if I was fine, and he was fine and that we were heroes. I wouldn't admit that we had been in danger." It has taken three years and the birth of a daughter ("at home, on the bed, on all fours, with the sun streaming through – all the things I wanted first time") for Georgia to come to terms with what happened. "It's only very recently that I've relaxed about it all, now that Barney's OK and I can start enjoying some of it. I consistently had to say that what we had done was right – and I don't know if I can say that."

Trisha, aged 27, has three children, aged fourteen weeks, eighteen months and four years. Her first was an emergency caesarean. She had been in hospital, in labour for eight hours. She was not dilating and they noticed on the monitor that the baby was in distress, the heartbeat was not picking up. "That was it, they just whisked me down to theatre. It all happened so fast. I felt very let down afterwards, very annoyed with the parentcraft classes; they were just a joke. Our way of coping with pain was for our partners to squeeze our ankles. They led me to believe that if you breathe properly you'd have a good labour. I don't think they discussed anything going wrong, they just talked about normal births. They might have touched on the possibility of caesareans, but I never imagined it would be me. It was wonderful to have this baby. But even though I knew he had been in real danger, I felt very disappointed in myself at not being able to have a normal birth. I thought therefore that I wasn't a good mother. The feeling of failure lasted a long time, about seven or eight months. I felt very jealous when I was speaking to women who had had a more straightforward birth. A vaginal delivery is referred to as a 'normal delivery', so I felt quite abnormal because I hadn't done it right."

High blood pressure, herpes, long labours, premature babies, overdue babies, distressed babies, can all lead to intervention. Routine intervention, unnecessary inductions or caesareans – women are right to resist. But some obstetric interventions are not an optional extra, they can mean the difference between a live baby and a dead one, a damaged baby or a healthy one. The emphasis on uncomplicated labours and delivery means that some women build up an unrealistic idea of how much control they will have. They are very definite about how they want labour to be, have specific goals which they want to achieve. Birth is black and white – it is only with experience that women become aware of the grey. Georgia still hates hospitals, but 'the hi-tech medical establishment saved Barney's life. In another time he would have died immediately. I still think natural birth at home is best, but I do now completely respect women's right to chose, which I never would before.' Frances, aged 34, whose son was born ten months ago, had wanted a natural labour at home, but because her son was breach, she ended up in hospital. "I was really pleasantly surprised. In fact, I wrote to the midwives in the hospital thanking them, because I was so pleased at the way

16

I was treated. I had a lot of misconceptions – about being bossed about, not being able to do what I wanted. I thought it would be very much a shop-floor, factory process, but it was very much a good experience. I was very prejudiced, so it would have taken a lot for me to change my mind. I think for baby number two I would go to hospital".

The problem is that childbirth is irrational. Flora, aged 39, whose twins were born by caesarean section a year ago, said "It's not much to do with the brain at all." Flora's caesarean had been almost totally painless. One of her twins was breach, the other transverse and she could see at the time that a section was the most sensible thing to do. But she admits, "I was totally screwed up about the whole thing. I didn't want a section. I'd been to all my NCT classes and had got into the idea of natural birth and felt that I was missing out, that I'd let myself down in a way, by not experiencing contractions, by not doing it naturally. I know it's not a sensible thing to feel, but there is this feeling that you want to do it for yourself, by yourself. It's an accomplishment – it's something you should be able to do because you're female. I distinctly remember a very strong feeling of failure, but it's totally irrational."

The environment

One of the other flaws in the control ideal is the hospital environment itself. Women being in charge of their labours presupposes that hospitals and hospital procedure will fit in with the women's expectations. A birth in the low-tech 'mothers suite' presumes that there will be room, a birth in the birthing pool supposes that it will be empty and discussion about pain relief presupposes that there will be midwives available to have a discussion with. Unfortunately, shortages in money, space and staff can mean that often women's expectations fall flat, not because of the dynamics of the labour itself, but because of the lack of wider facilities. Heather is 33 and has two children, aged two years and seven months. Her first baby was nearly born in a side ward rather than the delivery suite. "The hospital was operating on a forty-eight hour discharge and the attitude seemed to be, 'Do we care'. I arrived late at night and it was a case of, 'Humph, you're only just starting to dilate, lie there and do it quietly.' I thought I would be able to discuss pain relief with them. They didn't want to discuss anything. They just shoved me in a side ward with three other women, also in the early stages of labour. It wasn't what I imagined at all. There wasn't even enough room to walk around in. As for breathing and building myself up, I didn't want to make any noise because the new mothers in the main ward were trying to sleep. I wanted gas and air, but was told to forget it, that was only available in a delivery room, and then they whacked some pethidine in my leg and left us alone." Labour progressed very quickly and the baby was about to be born, "I couldn't even find a buzzer to get some assistance. In the end I yelled at the top of my voice and we ended up legging it down the corridor, in between contractions, to get to the delivery room. I can laugh about it now, but it was horrible at the time. I was really quite astounded afterwards, it was all so different from what I was led to expect."

Hospital and hospital policy has changed enormously since the high intervention days. Things are much more tailored to women's needs. Most hospitals aim to be more homely, to hide the hi-tech apparatus behind floral curtains, to have beanbags and birthing pools and sympathetic midwives available, recognizing that the environment, the atmosphere within which labour occurs is very important. In an ideal world, women would have whatever they wanted when they wanted but, sadly, the ideal is not always available. Labour is sometimes inhibited by poor facilities and facilities are the luck of the draw. The same is true for midwives.

One of the biggest shocks to some labouring women is that midwives work on a shift system. Childbirth education today emphasizes the importance of support – both physical – rubbing backs and holding hands and moral encouragement – and metaphorical back-patting. A supportive midwife can make a labour good, an unsupportive one can make it bad. They can be invaluable, but they are also only human – they have to eat, they may have families and, as dedicated as they may be, their shift will end, more often than not mid-labour. For the woman, who has been encouraged and rubbed through many hours, it is like a lover walking out. Ann, aged 36, whose daughter is two, did not have the same midwife throughout her labour. "It was unfortunate. The midwife I started with finished her shift at 9 pm and Amanda didn't come for another hour and forty minutes. But at 9 pm she had to go. She had been marvellous, absolutely wonderful and was in tears at having to leave. She said, 'I just can't stay today.' It was Saturday night, so presumably she had made some arrangements. The next two who came in were totally different. They kept talking about the price of meat and their holidays across my feet and only stopped when I had a contraction. One kept going on and on about Tescos and bumping into people in Tescos. I thought, God, I'm going crazy. The other one had been so marvellous and quiet and had given us both (me and my husband) so much confidence. I felt I was doing everything properly, even if I wasn't. I had coped much better than I thought I would and I'm sure that was down to the first midwife. If it had been with the other two I don't know what I would have been, they were so impersonal. We both got so tense and it just spoilt the last hour and a half. I felt a bit cheated. Obviously I didn't expect her to extend her shifts just for me, but shifts never crossed my mind when I imagined how labour would be."

The birth partner

Gone are the days when husbands dropped off their wives at the hospital and were not expected back until the baby was born. Men have been moving into the delivery rooms since the 1950s and what started out very alternative, is an established part of the childbirth experience – about 90 per cent of all deliveries are now attended by fathers.[22] Since families have become more isolated, couples have generally become more emotionally dependent on each other, and fathers have taken the place of the female friends and relatives who used to support women through labour. They were welcomed by the childbirth experts as a comforting presence which makes labour easier and, after initial resistance by medical people, partners were accepted. After all, if the father is there, you do not need so much nursing care. Again, in theory fathers are a nice idea – in practice, not always.

Jane is 25. Her husband left her just before her son, now aged two, was born. Although the pregnancy was planned, Jeff, her husband, started to change, "He was boozing, staying out late and spending too much money. He got violent a couple of times and I gave him an ultimatum." A few weeks before David was born he left. When labour pains started, Jane went to hospital alone. She found labour traumatic and frightening. "I had been bleeding and everyone was panicking. I didn't get any answers. I was wheeled down into the delivery room, and one of the nurses turned out the light and I was left in the dark by myself having contractions. It seemed like ages. The lights were switched back on and it was action stations. I would have coped so much better if I'd had someone there. I felt so alone, so frightened. I shall never forget it. I was in pain, in the dark, by myself, I shall never forget that."

As Margaret Jowitt says, "Fathers are probably the most appropriate people to massage the pain away in childbirth"[23], but that depends on the sort of father whose doing the massaging. Nancy is 31. Her daughter was born ten months ago and her husband, Stephen, was not that helpful. "There wasn't a chair for him to sit on, so he had to stand the whole time and he kept fidgeting and yawning. When I needed help with the pushing he wasn't really there. I think he was a bit embarrassed about the whole thing." Some fathers rub backs and breathe deeply with their women, others faint, cry, rush around with video cameras or sit in the corner with a newspaper, sandwich and a mobile phone. It is not the man's fault. The pressure for them to be there is enormous. So much so that, unless they are involved with everything that happens, it is assumed they must be 'bad' husbands and fathers. They are not really given a choice, never really asked if they want to be there. And when they are they get shouted at by irritated wives, put on the spot when their partner, who insisted she did not want an epidural, is screaming for one, made to feel extraneous, and sometimes witness a major operation – all of which can have a serious effect on the relationship. Women can feel let down and betrayed; men, watching their partner suffering, can sometimes blame the baby or, by realizing that there is nothing they can do, feel shut out and rejected. Beverly said, "It would have made much more sense if Mum had been there. At least she would have known what it was all about. It was great having a familiar face around, but next time, I'd like it to be Mum's."

Good labours/bad labours

A 'good' labour depends on control and expectations. If a woman expects one thing and does not get it, she is more likely to feel disappointed. If she feels out of control, even if she gets what she wants, she is more likely to suffer stress. The emotions brought to birth can also affect the experience. The more a woman wants a baby, the less her experience of labour pain.[24] The fact that it had taken Dorothy, aged 37, five years to conceive her daughter, now aged nine months, coloured her view of pregnancy. "I gave up work straight away and was delighted to be throwing up every day for fourteen weeks as it meant I *was* pregnant". Although Julie was born by caesarean, "I still found it a very rewarding experience. I didn't really care how she came into this world, just as long as she was here. I know all babies are special, but she was very precious to me."

Rachel is 27 and has four children, three boys and one girl aged from four years to three months. Her fourth labour was overshadowed by the death of her mother. "My baby was due five months after my mother's death. It was going to be the first labour where I would be without my partner as he had to stay to look after the other children. During labour, I became very emotional over the loss of my mum. I must have suppressed it when she died. I am the strong one of the family. I had to look after my dad and my brothers. All the feelings I'd been trying to hide came flooding out and when the midwife said it was a girl after three boys I just cried my eyes out." Birth is about letting go and for some women emotions which have been hidden surface along with the baby.

Definitions of good and bad labours used to be much simpler. Denied the luxury of our mother and baby mortality rates, a good labour was when both mother and baby survived; a bad, where either one or both died. Confidence in the survival of mothers and babies is the basis of modern childbirth and is essential to virtually all ideas about it. Nearly everything that is written, said or thought about childbirth now takes it for granted that nobody dies. Yet it is only in recent years that this confidence has been possible.

Birth today

It seems that our memories are short. No sooner has the lesson been learnt than there are pressures to forget it. Women campaigned for the right to have hospital births, now they are campaigning against them. The wheel has turned again. Childbirth has been made so safe that we tend to forget that it was ever dangerous. Natural used to mean a strong possibility of death, now 'natural', the advertiser's dream word (Hovis, real ale, yogurt, muesli) sounds so appealing, so healthy. In many ways, a natural birth is healthier than a hi-tech delivery. Epidurals are associated with backache and headaches after labour,[25] and tend to lead to other interventions – the forceps and episiotomies, both of which, in turn, can lead to long-term bruising and soreness. Pethidine crosses the placenta and can leave both mother and baby feeling drugged for some time after birth.

Given those options, it is not surprising that many women try to do without pain relief, but natural is not all sweetness and light. Recent research has shown that longer second stages (often connected with more natural labours where intervention to speed up the second stage is resisted) are associated with higher levels of piles and stress incontinence.[26] Natural too is puerperal fever and the gynaecological ailments that afflict Third World women who do not always give birth like shelling peas or have the same standards of care as the West. To give birth at home with just a midwife can be very satisfying, but scientific and historical evidence is strong: nature tends to be very wasteful of life, however healthy the mother.

The natural birth movement has undoubtedly done much to educate women, outlaw blind fear and panic, humanize birth, prevent routine intervention and make it more woman-controlled, but it has also created unrealistic expectations. A natural birth remains the ideal which most women aim for, but, according to one study, few actually achieve. A survey at St George's Hospital, London, showed that out of 4,000 women who give birth each year, just 6 per cent of first timers and 11 per cent of mothers having second babies managed without pain relief.[27] Having a natural labour is more to do with pot luck than preparation, more to do with babies being in the right position, the strength of contractions and the length of labour, than breathing or high pain thresholds.

While it is important to help women maintain a positive attitude to birth, they should also be prepared for the disappointment they may feel if everything does not go smoothly. In an attempt to get across a more realistic idea of what the experience may be like, the NCT is now trying to introduce couples who have recently had a baby to those who are soon to have one. But one of the fundamental problems is that women can never really be prepared for birth, never really understand how painful or how overwhelming giving birth can be. The only thing that can prepare them for childbirth is childbirth itself. Also, given that birth lasts about a day and motherhood for the rest of your life, it gets a disproportionate amount of attention and fuss. All the information, the factions, the dogmas, the natural vs hi-tech, the hospital vs home, the 'don't do it like that, do it like this', has turned birth into a big event. It is, but not half as big or as life-changing as what comes after.

2

Revelations

Never the same again

Birth may only take a matter of minutes; but the consequences last a life time. Becoming a mother is more than a change of job, it is a change of personality. A woman's life-style, feelings about herself, her family, her friends, the world – all alter. In the past, marriage was the biggest rite of passage and change in status for a woman; today it is motherhood. With the relaxing of sexual morals, more and more couples living together and marriage no longer marking the end of an independent life outside of the home, there is little difference between single and married women. This is not the case with women who have had children and women who have not.

In some cultures the change is celebrated. New mothers alter the way they dress or do their hair, and are treated with greater respect. In England feeling, looking and behaving exactly as before is something that colleagues, friends, partners and even the mothers themselves expect once the baby is born. Few women can actually anticipate the responsibilities of motherhood, and this is made harder by lack of information. Would-be mothers are fed romance, not reality: soft lamplight, lacy white nighties, smiling chubby babies have little to do with real life – the hard work, the change in self-image and the intense highs and lows. The stress on soft-focus is so great that when a 'real' image does make it through, like the August 1991 Benetton poster of a perfectly normal baby just after birth, it is met with outrage; there were 800 complaints in the first week the poster was displayed.[1]

Women are not prepared for how they will feel. Having a baby automatically turns a woman into a mother, but acting and feeling like one deep down can take months. One woman said, "It wasn't until I filled in 'mother' on my passport that it really hit home."

First encounters

"I was amazed it was a baby. He was lifted up and the consultant handed him to me and said, 'Here's your lovely boy' and I just couldn't believe it. It's such a stupid thing to say, because you're pregnant and obviously going to have a baby, but he was there and was so perfect and so like my husband – another human being. It was the best moment of my life. It's very . . . abstract before. It's a bump. It hasn't got features and doesn't look like you. Suddenly it's something else – a real baby. It's a lovely moment, really lovely." Looking back and recapturing the moment when the baby first appears, is for many, like Camilla, an amazing moment of revelation. Towards the end of pregnancy, many women long to see their child and hold it and yet, particularly for first-time mothers, the idea of actually having a baby, *their* baby, is so abstract. Scans can help to make it more real, but like the babies in books, it is two-dimensional, monochrome and fuzzy. Pregnant women often dream about giving birth, but not always to babies (pears, chicken drumsticks and tiny brooch-size clip-on babies featured in the dreams of some of the women interviewed). Ann thought all newborns were "wizened, purple and grey – like little old women". She was surprised to find that they can be plump, pink, and alert. "It was like an emotional dam burst." There was so much pain and then suddenly it stopped, there was this silence before she let out an angry cry. The world changed in a moment."

Bonding

Once the baby is born, the pressure is on to 'bond', a mysterious process that happens just after birth when mothers come to love their newborns. Past generations had thought "for the first few months baby should be treated like a small machine"[2] and that he or she was too underdeveloped to interact with parents; so babies were whisked off to hospital nurseries. But in the 1970s, experts studied animals, in particular goats, and observed that if a kid is taken away from a mother goat for two hours after birth, she will not accept the kid as her own when it is brought back. Similarly, when goslings hatch they will follow the first large moving object, mother, dog or whatever.[3] If the attachment mechanism is disturbed in other mammals – sheep, dogs, deer, zebra, cows and buffalo – the young will develop abnormally The period after birth, the experts concluded, particularly the first 45–60 minutes, is a very sensitive period[4], a make or break time during which mother and child are either mystically glued together in a lifelong loving relationship, or fail to connect, in which case maladjusted behaviour could result. To avoid unnecessary separation, babies were no longer taken away from their mothers after birth and mothers keeping their babies with them and tending to their needs became common practice in maternity hospitals.

The only flaw in the argument is that women are not goats. Women have brains and spirits as well as bodies, and the intensity of response varies from woman to woman. Some mothers do fall in love with their babies on first sight, but not all. Much like any developing relationship, for some it's like a light switch – they give birth and pow! For others it happens more slowly; it takes time for the attachment to grow. Different women have different time-scales, and human bonding, unlike goat bonding, is not something that either happens or does not in the first few hours after birth. It is an ongoing process which can take months.

Despite the accumulation of evidence and a growing awareness that there are many dimensions to nurturing children[5], the bonding myth still flourishes. Mothers, no matter how exhausted, can feel guilty if they do not exhibit some sort of bonding type behaviour straight after birth and sometimes even before the child is born. In the States, failure to 'care' for an unborn infant carries more than just guilt – 'foetal abuse' is a legal offence. One man successfully sued his wife for taking antibiotics while pregnant which discoloured the child's teeth.

Instant response
"To be honest", said Megan, "I'm not a baby sort of person. But I was amazed that the instant I saw her I thought, Oh good God, wonderful." According to Desmond Morris, babies' big eyes, round cheeks and small nose, are designed to stimulate protective and loving care. Many mothers spend the first hours just staring at their babies and this mutual gazing marks the beginning of their feelings of love. Alexandra who has two daughters, aged two years and eight months, remembered very clearly the first night after her eldest was born. "I was tired. I had her at 2.50pm and I hadn't slept the rest of the day as I was just so excited. I fed her for most of the time until she crashed out for five hours. I put her in bed with me and wedged her in with pillows. I had my arm around her and I just lay there and looked at her for five hours. There was so much excitement in my stomach. It was just like when you're in bed with a new lover."

A mother's desire to care for her newborn can be very strong, overriding any pain and discomfort which she may be in. After Lyn's son was delivered by caesarean section she said, "I was in the recovery room and I had this nurse with me as I was quite ill afterwards and I remember looking up and seeing her feed him and I didn't want her to. I got so jealous. When she finished she put him right over the other side of the room from me. I said, 'Can't you bring him over here?' and she said, 'I suppose so', so she wheeled him over. I said 'Can't you put him right next to me?' She said, 'I suppose so.' And I put my hand in the cot and held his hand for the rest of the night. When she came to feed him again, I said, 'No, I'm doing it.' She said, 'I don't think that's wise.' I said, 'I don't care, I'm doing it.' I had all these machines – blood pressure and heart monitor and everything; it was so awkward. But I thought, he's my baby, I'm doing it."

Delayed response
Despite initial problems, the relationship between Lyn and her son flourished. This is not always so; labour and the actual delivery can dramatically interfere with a mother's feelings towards her child. A short rapid labour can make it more difficult for a woman to accept that the event has occurred; a long, difficult labour may leave her exhausted and unable to show any enthusiasm for her newborn child, and as discussed earlier, unfulfilled expectations may mean that she blames her baby for her perceived 'failure' and pain. Helen said, "I didn't bond with Sam until he was six months old and I think it was connected with the labour. I thought it was going to be wonderful – soothing music and soft lights and after, me wearing a white nightie, holding a perfect clean baby. But it was all so horrible. I left him at the end of the room until I went into the ward and then I just wanted to sleep, I didn't want to pick him up. I felt that there should be this tremendous rush of love, but it was like looking at someone else's baby."

Labour is not the only thing that can cause problems. If the baby is very different from a new mother's fantasy image, she will often refuse to accept the real infant. Sophie's son was born with a large friction bump on his head caused by his position in the womb. "They told me it would go in about six weeks. I think that contributed to the fact that I didn't really love him until the end of the first year. I felt so awful. I've seen other mothers and their beautiful baby albums, and I've hardly got any pictures of when he was young, I just didn't want any taken." Unlike the romantic image, some babies are born blotchy and wrinkled with spots and rashes and, contrary to popular wisdom, not all mothers love their babies warts and all. Sophie thought both the labour and the baby would be "lovey dovey". Neither worked out as expected and the rejection of her son had more to do with dashed fantasies than physical imperfections.

Some babies are marked by their entrance into the world. Forceps and ventouse deliveries can sometimes cause bruising and affect the shape of the baby's head. Although this is short-lived it can be alarming, particularly as during the actual delivery there might not be enough time for doctors to explain and prepare mothers for the fact that their baby might have an odd-shaped head. In a forceps delivery, the pressure of the forcep 'spoons' on the baby's head as it is pulled out and sometimes rotated can cause bruising. The suction cup of the ventouse, placed on the baby's head, can cause a bump or 'chignon'. Very occasionally the forceps (or the pressure and position of the baby against the pelvis) can temporarily damage the facial nerve which runs along the baby's cheek causing temporary paralysis down one side, so that when the baby smiles or cries only one side of the face will move. This again tends to resolve itself within the first few weeks, but can nevertheless be very distressing. Like Sophie mothers often avoid having pictures taken or letting people visit.

While it may seem fickle to reject a baby for having the wrong coloured hair or a gummy eye, the real reason is often more complicated. Julie's first son was "too big, too heavy and too ugly. He was 8lbs 11oz which was a horrible shock. My first [a stillborn] was 2lbs and my friend had just had one that was 3lbs 5oz. I was used to tinies, I wasn't used to big ones. His head touched the top of the goldfish bowl cot and his feet touched the bottom and he was grey and bloody and I thought, ugh – that did not come out of me. He didn't look like a baby. All the others had cute babies and I had this blob lying there." Birth can stir up unresolved feelings and the loss of Julie's first child played its part in her not feeling an immediate bond with her son. Jane, whose husband had left her just before her son was born, did not automatically love her baby. "I hated his father so much. David was a boy and the spitting image of his father. I felt it was sod's law." Coming to terms with the loss of a wanted child can be as simple as it being the 'wrong' sex: Maggie really wanted a girl and it turned out to be another boy. "I did feel sad. I didn't really have a name for a boy. I only had one boy's name I liked and I used that on the first one." Her disappointment was eased by the fact that the birth had been straightforward and that he was a less demanding baby than her first. "He is a really affectionate child, which made loving him easier."

Mothers who do not feel an immediate love for their babies often find that the baby itself, by being loving, or responsive, or by seeming so vulnerable encourages the relationship to develop. When Helen's son "finally stopped screaming and said 'Mummy' for the first time", the relationship improved. "You just felt that you were getting a bit more in return for all the hard work." This can be especially true for mothers who like Maggie do not really like newborn babies. "I'm not one of those who when the baby cries, even if they're half a mile away, leaks milk. It must help to make you feel special if you are, but I find babies too demanding. They just *take*. I find that once they start to move around and talk and become characters, I relate to them better."

Maternal instinct

The attachment between mother and child is one of the most powerful relationships in the animal kingdom. The baby is born defenceless and totally helpless, and the mother is impelled to protect, cherish and feed it. The relationship is about caring and survival and, for the baby, it is the basis for an emotional and physical development and future attachments. Whether this relationship is unique to women who are not only biologically but emotionally designed for the job, and instinctively know how to do it, or if, birthing aside, men could do it just as well, is an ongoing debate. In one study[7] three-fifths of mothers-to-be believed in maternal instinct before their babies were born. Less than half did so after.

Whether you are a believer in maternal instinct or not, there are three stages of attachment in the early months. Firstly, the mother learns how to care for her baby, and the baby makes it plain, by sleeping, crying less and eating, that the mother is doing good job. This in turn boosts the mother's confidence. Secondly, the baby becomes more responsive – smiling and laughing, rewarding the mother for her hard work. Thirdly, the baby begins to demonstrate a dependence on the mother which makes her feel she is necessary to the baby. It also starts to recognize her which helps to make her feel that she is doing a worthwhile job. Gradually, the baby's personality unfolds. The baby comes to terms with life outside the womb and mother comes to terms with baby.

A baby's survival depends on the interest the mother shows in him or her. But the timetable – how long it takes for that interest to develop – and how intense that feeling is varies from woman to woman.

Breastfeeding

Feeding dominates the early months, partly because it is all that the baby seems to do, and because feeding and weight are so bound up with how women are seen to be doing as mothers. The scales are the focus of clinic visits and a good weight gain spells confidence; a poor one, anxiety. Breastfeeding in particular is the most intimate and time-consuming of the many mothering activities of the first year. For Rebecca, breastfeeding was one of the most important aspects of being a mother. "Before you have your baby that's the one clear image of motherhood, from the Virgin Mary right through. It would have felt like a big gap in the early months if I hadn't been able to do it. It forced me to sit down with him. He would stare into my eyes and I'd stare into his. I really loved it."

Breastfeeding is encouraged today not only for nutritional reasons, but also for its bonding potential because it involves the physical contact between mother and baby. Despite the initial pain and problems getting started, for many breastfeeding is a very pleasurable, almost passionate experience. They enjoy the cuddles, the extended closeness, the sense of doing something right and useful. Kate said, "I loved the quiet I had with Thomas and the noises he would make, the hmmm hmmm hmmm. He used to put his hand very lightly on my breast, little light touches, and look at me with his big eyes. When he finished, his hair would be damp and he would look drunk and satisfied. It was magical, so magical." Frances said, "It's almost like a love affair, that's the only way you can describe it – it's like a love affair without the sex part." Like Frances, many welcome the feeling of dependency which the baby has on them (and which the mother has on the baby – bosoms fill up and need to be emptied, the dependency is mutual). "I really like the fact that it was only me who could do it. It just gives you that feeling of protectiveness, even now that she is fifteen-and-a-half months old and very independent, when she curls up next to me and she's tired out and she stares at me." Frances said.

Nipples may be tugged and stretched like udders, clothes may be restricted to easy access buttons, and time away from the baby fitted in around the two hourly feeds, but for many, the closeness, the sensuousness, the fact that they alone are able to quieten a crying baby in seconds, that they alone are responsible for the baby growing and thriving and that they are so needed, is very satisfying. So much so that weaning can be seen as a real physical loss. Carol Weston, when she came to wean her daughter, wrote, "I was about to have my body back. Would I welcome it? I could soon start drinking again. Did I want to? My blouses would no longer be misbuttoned and I could start wearing dresses instead of just separates. Did I care? My daughter could not even talk and I was already nostalgic. Because letting go begins with weaning. Because letting go never really ends."[8]

For others, breastfeeding is not so wonderful. Some feel like a cow on tap, and find breastfeeding a humiliating and constricting experience. More women start off breastfeeding than bottle feeding, but within six weeks 60 per cent are using the bottle and today 25 per cent less women breastfeed six weeks after the birth than three years ago.[9] Fiona who has a daughter, aged five months said, "Deep down, I never felt very happy with the idea of breastfeeding. After a couple of days I gave up, even though I had plenty of milk. I felt happy and relieved to turn to bottle feeding. And it was great to know that someone else was able to feed Charlotte. As feeding and sterilizing equipment has vastly improved, it's all so much easier now." Thomasina who has twin daughters said, "The idea of breastfeeding has always made me feel uncomfortable and embarrassed, and being pregnant didn't change that.

What really put me off was the emphasis on demand feeding – it seems that it's not enough just to breastfeed, you have to do it all day long. I decided to bottlefeed because I wanted to impose my own routine, rather than have one imposed on me." The dependency that breastfeeding cultivates can for some seem unhealthy. Caroline said, "I have images of these women who want their children to be dependent on them, who want to tie them to them. Me weaning her was a way of breaking with the child and saying, my body is mine now and you've got to get on with it." A child that is totally dependent for its survival can be quite terrifying. It is a responsibility which is probably more shocking for women today than in earlier history when people were much more dependent on each other anyway. Now food does not have to be grown, it can be bought in a shop. Women do not have to produce their own milk to keep a baby alive; they are used to being independent today, much less reliant upon each other and for some, that dependency is overwhelming. Women are told that breast is best, but know at the back of their minds that if they do not breastfeed their baby will not die. One hundred years ago it would have been a different story.

Caroline hated her bosoms expanding from a size A to a D. "It just wasn't my size. It made me feel like a cow, a feeding machine, not like a woman." Lactating bosoms are not seen as being sexy. Nursing bras are never frilly or flowery. They come in sensible white rather than risqué black or red, and many women feel de-sexed and de-humanized. Monica did not like the smell or "that they'd leak everywhere and stink. I couldn't go anywhere. I had to feed Joseph once in a café. People really stared at me – I hated it." Monica weaned Joseph at six weeks, but admitted for the first time that she carried on feeding him at night for some time after. "He loved it so much and I loved it at night. It was all quiet and we were alone together."

For some, breastfeeding would be fine if they never had to go out of the house. Despite health professionals constantly stressing the advantages, breastfeeding is still greeted with mixed reaction in the outside world. John Lewis recently asked a woman to leave the restaurant of one of its stores because she was breastfeeding in public. A spokesman for the store said, "It is the case that we feel the majority of our customers would not like to see breastfeeding in public."[10]. This is from a chain-store that tries to cater for mothers and babies and has a reputation for its nursing bras. A recent poll showed that 57 per cent of men objected to breastfeeding in public despite having children in their households.[11] Bosoms to be ogled at in a newspaper are OK, but bosoms discreetly tucked behind a jumper feeding a baby, are not. And yet facilities for nursing mothers are few and far between. Women either have to feed babies in public loos or put up with disapproving looks. Faced with a howling, hungry baby and the hostility of others, many give up.

Breast is best, but for whom?

Babies require six to eight feeds a day. Each feed takes approximately forty minutes; the commitment is five-and-a-half hours a day. Breastfeeding is all very well in textbooks and theory, but it ignores the many responsibilities a mother may have. Many women have to go back to work, have other children to look after and a home to run. Sandra decided to bottlefeed her baby because she already had twin sons aged four-and-a-half to look after. "What with taking the boys back and forward to nursery and swimming lessons, I just couldn't imagine fitting in breastfeeding. I didn't want to have to breastfeed in the playground or not be able to leave home to pick them up because of having to drop everything and feed." But that did not stop her feeling guilty about not breastfeeding him. "I feel really bad that he has to fit in around the twins and our lifestyle. I keep thinking that I wouldn't be able to fit it in, but it sounds awful when I say it." Sandra felt even more guilty about not having breastfed the twins. "I felt really bad. They were premature and were at risk to infection and because they were so premature they didn't have their sucking reflex and I had to go on this electric breast pump in the special care unit which was really awful. Every time I went on the machine bits of my skin kept on coming off. I'd get an ounce of milk with all bits of my skin in it, and a lot of the time they couldn't use it. I was crying because it was so sore, but the midwife would say, 'Keep trying, you've got to keep trying. It will get better.' Then she must have gone on holiday or something, because after eight or nine days this other midwife came in and said, 'Why are you doing this? I don't know why you're bothering.' I told her that I'd feel really guilty if I gave up and if anything should happen to them I'd never forgive myself. She said, 'Forget it. They'll survive perfectly well on bottle milk.' And they did. They did very well. But I still feel I should have tried harder."

Women are told that breast milk is better nutritionally and that it keeps allergies at bay; breast milk makes for a healthier, happier and some even say more intelligent baby and that just one little sip of formula in the first few months will undo all the good of breast milk. In the 1970s bottlefeeding was all the fashion, today it is breastfeeding and pro-breastfeeding propaganda is everywhere – in hospital, health clinics, books and magazines. For women who cannot or do not want to breastfeed, the guilt can be extreme.

Harriet has three daughters, aged eight years, six-and-a-half years and ten months. Her youngest was delivered by elective section and she found breastfeeding very difficult. "The milk took ages to come in and I didn't produce much at all. I got all tense and anxious and, of course, that affected the milk. I had to put her onto formula milk. I felt a real failure, especially as she got eczema and it got worse and worse. I thought, if only I could have gone on longer, she wouldn't have got eczema." The argument that breast is the best does not wash anymore. Yet, those who find that breastfeeding is not right for them are often told by breastfeeding counsellors and health visitors to keep going, that they must not stop, and this only serves to make them feel guilty when they do. New mothers need to find out what their baby needs to physically and emotionally survive but also what they feel comfortable with. Feeling wretched about breastfeeding and guilty for giving up does nobody, least of all the baby, any favours.

3

Hospital and Home

Back to normal?

"I felt I was back to normal. I walked a mile to and from a friend's house – this was only ten days after I'd had the baby – and I felt terrible. It was only when a midwife pointed out that I had an internal wound that I understood why I had to take things easy." This was after Jenny's first baby, now aged five. After her second, now aged eighteen months, "I stayed in bed for a week and didn't get dressed for two."

The emphasis on natural delivery and birth-is-not-an-illness mentality has meant that pregnant women are no longer treated as though they were 'sick'. The approach taken is that having babies is a natural process and women should be treated as though they weren't going through anything out of the ordinary. Women are encouraged to be as active as possible when pregnant, during labour and up and about soon after. In truth, having a baby may be natural, but it is also a major stress to the body. The physical process of recovery from childbirth is very complex. It involves the breasts and skin and the respiratory, endocrine, gastrointestinal and musculoskeletal system and recovering from pregnancy and childbirth can take some time.

Women used to have a very rigid rest and relaxation period after labour. Confinement meant not only giving birth, but also resting after it. Today, women go into labour, not confinement, the relaxation period afterwards has fallen out of fashion. Women expect to be back to 'normal' soon after delivery and are discharged from hospital as soon as possible. Once at home, the amount of support and peace a new mother gets is entirely dependent on her and her circumstances. This was unheard of years ago.

Confinement: a history

Home

Women used to spend as long as four weeks in bed after labour. Confinement was literally that – being confined to home and bed in order to give birth, and staying there after to recover and recuperate. The women who attended the birth would look after the mother, take charge of the home and stay for two or three weeks. Extended bed rest and seclusion from the outside world was thought necessary both for spiritual reasons – until the 18th century the Christian church thought a woman 'unclean' from the onset of labour and for forty days after; and for health reasons – sealed windows and a warm room were thought to help prevent childbirth fever.

Even after the church changed its views on the ungodliness of new mothers, women still spent long periods in confinement. In 1792, Mrs Campbell of Barcaldine, a physician, stated, "The house is to be kept as quiet as possible for the first week, although the new mother is possibly allowed a companion to chat to. Each evening she must be helped into a chair, so the bed can be made. If she feels like moving she can, as long as someone is there. She should by no means venture out of her room before the 16th day at the soonest and not outside the house before the 22nd."[1] At the end of the 19th century, Francis Ramsbotham, a leading obstetrician, recommended that only after two weeks might a woman "begin to put her feet on the ground."[2]

Hospital

When birth moved from home to hospital, the location changed but the stress on prolonged bed rest did not. From 1948, the 'normal' post-natal mother and baby spent twelve to fourteen days in hospital or under the care of a midwife at home. The mother stayed in bed for eight days, getting up on the ninth. A midwife from the 1940s said, "For the first two days after delivery, they were not allowed more than a cup of Bovril and toast for lunch – oh dear! the restriction on food! . . . Breakfast, of course, was porridge. Until the fourth day, they were not allowed a proper meal. I think many of the fathers used to bring in pork pies and things at night, you know! On the fifth day, they were given a blanket bath. On the ninth day, they could go to the toilet. On the thirteenth day, they were allowed to see their babies bathed. On the fourteenth day they went home."[3] This was still common practice in some hospitals in the 1960s. The routine was strictly monitored. Women's feet were even checked for signs of being up and about. Prolonged bed rest was thought physically beneficial and women were told that their 'insides would drop out' if they did not rest. In fact, such inactivity was positively harmful as it was the cause of deep vein thrombosis.

The rise in hospital births put pressure on beds and many hospitals started discharging women on the ninth or tenth day and getting women out of bed earlier. What started as a wartime air raid precautionary measure became accepted practice both on practical and health grounds. Early rising meant less nursing care and fewer chest, bowel and bladder problems.

From the 1970s, speedy confinements became more and more popular. Spending days rather than weeks in hospital fitted in with the growing idea that birth was not an illness. Being bedbound for days was inappropriate after what was essentially a natural event: active birth, active confinement. It was healthier to be up and about and it made economic sense. Hospitals facing cutbacks could no longer provide hotel rest-beds and anyway, it was what mothers wanted. Hospital stays went from weeks to days to sometimes hours. Today, it varies from hospital to hospital, but on average for a first delivery, women spend two days in hospital, and twenty-four hours for a second.[4] Women who have caesareans are home in a week.

Confinement in other countries

Many societies still have long confinements and a period of seclusion after childbirth. Like this country in the Middle Ages, this is because of health reasons and because of religious superstition. In southern India, the Adivi mother stays with her baby in a hut in a 'contaminated' state for ninety days. No one is allowed to touch her and, if they do, they are outcast from the village for three months. In Somaliland, a new mother stays with her baby indoors for forty days, fearful of being possessed by evil spirits in her unprotected godless state. Sometimes confinement is a time of seclusion from men, not women. Bedouin Arab women stay at home for forty days after labour. They are not allowed to cook or do housework and are meant to rest, eat well, and celebrate with other women. As in this country before hospital births, confinement can be a time of being nurtured and supported by other women. The new mother is looked after, made to feel special and is sometimes fed with special birth foods high in calcium to make her strong and increase her milk supply.

The equivalent support in this country comes from the hospital, the midwife, the health visitor, the doctor and any friends and relations that might be around.

Confinement today

Hospitals

"I spent a couple of days in hospital. It felt a bit rushed. I would have liked to have stayed longer. I felt tired. I needed to be shown and told a bit more about the baby and what to do with it," said Dominique, whose son was born last year at St Mary's Paddington, London. In some hospitals, the shorter stays which were introduced to give women more choice have now become more or less compulsory for everyone. Pressure on beds has been intensified by the closure of small local GP units, by shortage of staff midwives, by funds being diverted to neonatal units and by a rising demand that stretches resources to breaking-point.

For some, discharge comes too soon. Catherine, aged 36, was lucky to be in a hospital which had longer stays. She spent eight days in hospital after her daughter was born two years ago and "would have felt quite panicky if they'd made me leave earlier". Even so, "I still wasn't ready to leave. I felt I wouldn't be able to cope with looking after the baby. There were basic things I wasn't sure of – how to change a nappy, how to wash her. It was so daunting, the responsibility of looking after a helpless person twenty-four hours a day."

Second-time mothers are often even more in need of recuperation. For many, a day or two in hospital is the only rest they get before going back to look after everyone else. But, for many, rest and hospital are mutually exclusive. Heather said, "I see nothing restful in being stuck in a ward with five other women and five other women's babies. Even if yours has gone quiet and isn't squeaking for anything in the middle of the night, there's always someone else's. One of the babies I was with squeaked and spluttered all night long and the mother must have had some sleeping pills as she slept right through it. I could have cheerfully thrown something at her."

Some have to be dragged out, but most are more than ready to leave. Hospitals can be stuffy, with central heating blasting even in summer, noisy with babies crying, mothers snoring and moaning, and nurses and midwives wheeling trolleys up and down and blindingly bright, with neon lights on all night. Mealtimes can be haphazard, as Scarlet found out. "I missed breakfast. No one told me when it was. I'd been in labour until 11pm the night before, had missed all the meals when I'd been in labour, was starving and no one told me when breakfast was. That really set me off. I really wanted to go home."

"I was really concerned about the hygiene standards," said Emma, aged 31, who has two children aged four and twelve months. "It was so disgusting. There were soiled dressings, sanitary towels in the showers. I told everyone after my experience to take a big bottle of disinfectant with them. I really thought I was going to get something or the baby was. All the visitors were coughing and sneezing over the baby and they were shunting in and out and having a good old gawp at me trying to breastfeed. I was mortified."

Breastfeeding often has to be learnt and women who turn to the hospital midwives for help can, as Heather did, find them "a waste of space". She said, "The only lesson I got with breastfeeding was someone coming along and stuffing a boob in the baby's mouth." Sometimes mothers get too much help and all of it contradictory. Rebecca, aged 38, had problems feeding her daughter, now aged six months. She said, "They were trying to help get the milk out and they each tried their own preferred method of holding the baby: across my lap, tucked under my arm etc. They were super and I wouldn't want to criticize them, but what with the night and day shifts, it felt like I had hundreds of midwives telling me what to do. It was all so bewildering." Some midwives are helpful and supportive, others patronizing and bossy and making new mothers, already in a highly charged emotional state, feel childlike and inadequate. Wendy admits that she was oversensitive just after her daughter was born and was easily hurt, but found, "The ward sister was very abrupt. I had a small tub of Vaseline for my lips. They'd got really sore with the gas and air and I had a tub in my bag. She bustled over and said, 'What's this fancy stuff then?' I was afraid she thought I was using it on the baby and shouldn't have. It was just the way she said it. I took it all so much to heart". Maternity wards are designed to help new mothers recuperate, but for many, the real resting starts at home.

Midwives

Community midwives used to visit each mother, as a minimum, twice a day up to post-natal day three, and then daily up to day ten. Since 1989, they are allowed to use their own judgment about the frequency of visits. They can visit for up to twenty-eight days, but it is more likely to be every two to three days if all is well, with handover to the health visitor on day ten. Short hospital stays has meant more work: more invasive tests like the Guthrie heel prick test (to test for the disease PKU); more routine checks; and sometimes as many as sixteen post-natal visits in one day. Midwives give advice, support and expert help and can be invaluable, but often mothers do not know who will call, what time they will call and if the visit does not happen to coincide with any pressing problems, they feel abandoned to battle on alone.

When they do visit, midwives have a check list to be ticked off, and can end up concentrating on the mother's tail-ends, the baby's bellybutton, stools and vaccinations. This would be fine if a mother's needs were just physical, but they are not. Childbirth has opened up a new life, and adjusting to that takes some sorting out. The birth itself can be the first hurdle and experts now recommend 'debriefing' or talking about labour with the midwife. Any sympathetic ear would do, but it is felt that the midwife, being a professional and ideally present at the labour or at least informed by the hospital, is well placed to discuss it with the mother.[4] In practice, communication between community midwife and hospital is often poor and, even if present, the midwife is not always the sympathetic ear that is needed. Hannah's midwife had 'an attitude problem'. Hannah was on the Domino Scheme, and had a fifty-two-hour-labour. "When labour started she took one look at me, and said, 'I wish I'd brought a book'. Then, after, when she came to visit, I said, 'Well, that was long and hard, wasn't it?' And she said, 'No. I don't know what you're fussing about, it wasn't so bad.' I wanted her to say, 'My God. Fifty-two hours! You did have a terrible time'."

Sometimes the chemistry works, sometimes it doesn't – it is one of the hazards of professional care. But even when the midwife and mother do get on, lack of continuity can be a problem. Mary saw four different midwives over the period. "When I went to ante-natal classes I met Clare who was supposed to be my midwife. She went away, so I had all these different people whom I'd never seen before. My baby was born in April, but it was very hot. I'd ask, 'Can I take her into the garden?' One said, 'Yes, but make sure she's wrapped up'. The next day, another would say, 'She doesn't need all these clothes on, take them off.' Then the umbilical cord started to bleed. One said, 'Put surgical spirit on it,' the other, 'No, just boiling water.' It was all very confusing, especially as I didn't know one end of the baby from the other."

Continuity of care is what most mothers (and midwives – 82 per cent in a recent survey felt unable to give the quality of care women need)[6] would ideally aim for, but pressure of work, families and lack of resources means that organizing it can be difficult.

The health visitor

The health visitor picks up where the midwife leaves off. Sometimes the hardest weeks after the birth are weeks three and four. The euphoria has died down, colic may have started, stitches may still be hurting, sleepless nights taking their toll and the realities of motherhood are hitting home. Perhaps that is why in other cultures there is a tradition of ongoing support for forty days. Here, we have the health visitor. If her caseload is heavy, she may only call once and then is available if needed. Ideally, however, she will visit once a week until the baby's first injections at six to eight weeks.

As with midwives, health visitors are supposed to tend to both baby and mother, but many mothers find that again they play second fiddle. How are you? – a fleeting question posed before she settles down to the real business of giving out information on babycare, places to go with the baby, inoculations and clinic times. Again, health visitors are professional carers. As professionals they may be highly knowledgeable about babies and mothers, but as people they may have no experience at all of looking after babies and have nothing in common with the new mother. Because having a baby is not like having a headache or a toothache, women can clash with their health visitors in a way that they would not with other professional health workers, such as doctors or dentists. New mothers are looking for someone to relate to and it somehow matters if the health visitor is much older or younger or is not herself a mother. Mary said, "My health visitor was unmarried and insisted on being called Miss Wilson. I suppose from a professional view she knew about babies, but she didn't really know what it was like to be up all night. I was 36 and having this woman coming in insisting on being called Miss Wilson was a bit off." Ann could not identify with hers either. "She was divorced, not that that makes any difference, but she had no children. And I felt when talking to her that she was making all the responses of someone who had just read it in a book. I remember when Amanda was a few weeks old, she wasn't sleeping and was crying a lot and I asked her what to do. She said, 'Well, what she needs is company. Buy her a little mirror, tie it on the side of the cot and she'll be fine.' I thought, there we are, that's easy isn't it. And I never asked her anything again."

What some new mothers really need is a professional/friend/mother. Like the women who used to attend confinements in this country and still do in other countries today, they need someone who knows them, is a mother, and an 'expert' in baby care. Catherine really needed a sympathetic ear, but got the "jolly-hockey-sticks type who said cope or else! I tried telling her that I was tired and finding it difficult and was worried about it all, but she just kept on telling me to buck up and pull myself together." For single mothers like Fatima, health visitors will never be trusted. They will always be just another potentially critical professional who 'come and tick you off and keep your kids. When I go through a bad patch with the children I'm scared of telling the health visitor, just in case they go and tell social services and they take them away."

Lucy, aged 31, found her health visitor positively upsetting. Her twin boys were born prematurely at twenty-eight weeks. They spent several weeks in special care and Lucy was told their chance of survival was "touch and go". Lucy left hospital after a couple of days. It was not long before a health visitor got in touch. "She telephoned very early in the morning, about 8am. Every time the phone went, especially that early in the morning, we thought it was the hospital with bad news. Our friends either didn't phone or said they would phone at particular times. Then all she talked to me about was contraception, jabs and teething. At that stage we didn't know whether the twins would live or die. It was all so irrelevant. It made me really angry. Then, she went on about how she wanted to bring the red book [the baby's development book] to the hospital. At the time, the red book was the last thing on my mind. But she kept on going on about it, about how she had to hand them out."

The personal touch – fine tuning the right person with the right needs, is impossible because of the lack of resources and communication. Post-natal care works on a blanket system: you get who you get and you get it whether you want it or not. Some mothers, particularly second-timers, are quite confident, quite happy to be left alone and see health visitors as interfering; others like Catherine or Fatima have very specific needs which, in an ideal world, the professionals would be aware of and react accordingly.

Six-week check

The six-week check with a GP is the only medical routine check offered once the mother is discharged from the midwife. It should include an internal examination to check the condition of the womb, vagina and muscles; a smear test if one is due; the stomach should be felt to ensure the uterus has returned to normal; any stitch scars should be inspected; breasts examined and contraception discussed. It is the last formal contact with the doctor and brings to a close the cycle of pregnancy, labour and post-natal care. Because it is a signing off, many think that the check will be thorough. Kate, aged 37, has one son, aged two. At her six-week check "All that happened was that I lay on the couch and was prodded and weighed and was asked a few questions. It was all over in three to four minutes. I don't know really what I expected, but I expected a bit more than that." Mandy said, "Considering all the looking after I got before, it was very quick. My doctor just checked my stitches and said everything had healed and was OK." In fact Mandy had piles and had wanted to talk about them, "But he didn't ask me how I felt about anything. I thought I'm not going to bring it up unless he asks. I know he's not a mind-reader, but he might have asked how things were going or something."

In Canada, the six-week check can last up to an hour. It is a formal goodbye to the mother. The pregnancy, labour and care is discussed as well as coping with motherhood and there is a well-woman check. The impetus comes from the doctor, not the mother. Just as in the ante-natal booking in session at the hospital, she is asked questions, asked if there are specific problems; the doctors do not wait to be told. For many, six weeks is too early to be signed off. It is not some magical period by which everything is healed and back to normal. Things have changed so fast and everything is so different and so focused on the care of the baby that it is often hard to even know what is really happening to your body at that stage. But the six-week check is all that is available. After that a new mother is on her own.

Home help

"My husband really kept us going," said Flora. "He used to cook at weekends, great batches of things, and would freeze them. I couldn't have survived without his support. I also had a home help from the social services [because she had twins and has multiple sclerosis] so all the shopping and housework was taken care of. I just had to look after the babies." Ideally, every new mother should be mothered so she can concentrate on her mothering. Tending to the baby's needs, going without sleep, learning how to breastfeed and recovering from the aches and pains of labour is work enough without having to do washing, ironing, hoovering, cooking and shopping. In Holland, most births take place at home and excellent post-partum care is provided by midwives in training. These mother's helpers live in for eight to ten days. They do virtually everything from cleaning to cooking to childcare. In Britain, Social Services will organize home helps if a mother has special needs, for instance three children under two. The NCT has post-natal support groups, and some health authorities have post-natal drop-in discussion groups.

Otherwise, it is down to family, friends and personal circumstances. Some fathers can take paternity leave and are invaluable; others, like Mandy's, took two weeks off, but "He wasn't much good. He expected to be looked after too. The first night I came out, I cooked the tea". Then, there are some, like Rose's husband, who could not take any time off to help. After their third son was born, "Andrew was leaving at 6am and getting back at 9pm. He couldn't even be there for the labour. I went into hospital, had him. He picked me up after breakfast and then went into work." Rachel's husband, a postman, took two days off. After that she had to look after her three children – aged four, two-and-a-half and one-and-a-half – plus her newborn, by herself. "I was offered a home help, but I wasn't keen. I don't know why. She would have been a stranger. If it had been a member of my family I would have enjoyed it, but she would have been a stranger. I didn't want that. I'd rather do it myself." Which she did, despite being severely anaemic.

Help might be needed, but not all offers, especially from the outside, are welcome. Many couples have a romantic idea of just wanting to be left alone, of having the house to themselves, a cosy, happy little family. Hannah's mother-in-law offered to come and stay for a month, "My reaction was, no. We wanted to spend the first weeks of the baby's life with just the baby. Afterwards when you're drowning beneath housework and cooking, you think, 'How stupid, why didn't I say yes.' My advice for anyone who is pregnant is to make sure they get a cleaner in three times a week for the first two months, if they can afford it, and make sure they have their meals cooked."

Women are just not prepared for how they will feel after – how tired, sore and unable to cope. Having a baby is a total life change and yet women are discharged from hospital as if they have had a minor operation, or a very mild illness. No one tells them to take it easy or if anyone tries, many, caught in the Supermum trap, dismiss it thinking, 'it won't happen to me'. Supermums can deal with anything that is flung at them – birth, sleepless nights, caesarean sections – rest is for those who cannot cope. Supermums are fictitious. Camilla said, "My husband didn't take any time off because we were completely unprepared for the devastating effect having a baby was going to have on our lives. I thought it would be easy, everything in my life had always been easy. I'd always coped with things, I'd had my own business, nothing had fazed me particularly. But having a baby was really quite dramatic. The day I brought him home we went for a walk up to the shops and I nearly fainted. I was trying to push myself too hard. Having always been a bit of a coper, I saw no reason why I shouldn't get back to normal very quickly. If I'd said to myself it's going to be a month before I feel like going out or doing anything and the house is going to be a tip, I would have felt less like I'd failed." Dominique was the same, "At the beginning I didn't realize. I wanted to do hoovering and tidying, to do things as before. I suddenly got very tired and exhausted and nearly lost my milk. My mother came and made me understand that something major had happened and I needed to convalesce. The day after I got out of hospital I had at least ten visitors and I was making tea for them all. I thought the birth had been quick, so will recovery. It was a bit more than I could handle."

It is a vicious circle: the more a woman does, the more tired she is, the less satisfying her milk becomes, the more the baby cries, the more tired she gets. Opting out by wearing a nightdress and staying in the bedroom for one week, preferably two, is one solution, but it presupposes that someone else will opt in and take over the running of the house. And this is where mothers come in.

Solid practical and emotional support is what counts in the early weeks, and who better to give that than mothers who have had children and who really understand what the early weeks are like. Unlike midwives and health visitors, they are family and have an emotional interest both in the mother and the baby – sometimes too much of an emotional interest. Both Mary's mother and mother-in-law stayed after the birth of her son. "They both wanted to be oohing and aahing over the baby and what have you, rather than cooking dinner for me. It wasn't so much that they were telling me how to look after the baby, more that it was the centre of the universe and I was left to muddle on with whatever needed to be done." Then there are generational differences that can make life complicated. Annabel's mother stayed for two weeks after the birth of her third child. "First of all she didn't like the name. Lily as far as she's concerned is a fifty-year-old cleaner. She got herself into a state about that. She didn't sleep the night before she came because she was worried about the journey. When she arrived she was alright, but as the day wore on she became progressively more ill. She had a migraine and a stomach ache and had to spend the first twenty-four hours recovering, lying down and very reluctantly hauling herself up to make a cup of tea. She would go and collect Thomas from school, but that really put her out because all these 'young mums' wanted to know how the baby was, but none of them introduced themselves to her."

A mother's mother used to be the person most likely to help. Now that more women are working outside the home and grandmothers are likely to be committed to their own jobs, help is even less readily available. And, even if mothers are free, they can be considered of dubious value. Family members are much more dispersed today and often only get together on birthdays, anniversaries and funerals. Having a normally absent mother or mother-in-law stay for a prolonged period can add to household pressure rather than ease it. There again, mothers who live closer are not always the answer either. Megan, aged 32, and her mother live in the same town. After her son was born two years ago, her mother came around and took charge of the housework, "I'm not particularly houseproud myself, so it was brilliant. But then she started making comments about the housework I wasn't doing. She came around once and I was having a nap with the baby and I'd closed the curtains and she wanted to know why I was doing that in the middle of the day with the curtains closed. She offered to look after the baby so I could do some housework rather than lying down. There was this constant pressure that I was being lazy. In fact I was just trying to catch up on some sleep." Perhaps we have romanticized the days of the extended family with its loving relations and mutual support – basic personality differences will always make life complicated.

Being prepared

The period after labour is a very neglected area. Women are not adequately prepared for how they will feel physically, rest is not emphasized enough, and support – both formal and informal – can be haphazard. Traditional confinements were by no means perfect, but at least the message got home that labour can be exhausting and take some getting over. Today, because women are back in ordinary clothes within two days, they feel they should be back to normal and up and running the home. While nobody would want to bring back the extended hospital bed rest of past generations, why throw out the baby with the bath water? There are obvious advantages to being secluded and not dealing with hundreds of visitors, of having time to tune into the baby, of being cosseted and cared for, and of having enough of the right sort of care – be it midwives, health visitors, paid help, family or friends. But very few women are actually cared for like that. True, that sort of help would be hard to organize: paternity leave would have to be compulsory, family and friends more amenable and if we are to go the way of Holland, the state more sympathetic. There is a long way to go, but women having the same attention post-natally as they do ante-natally and being told more about the after-effects of labour, the unpleasant bits to having a baby which no one tells you about, would be a start. Knowing about the force of labour pains and being prepared for labour does not usually frighten women. It allows them to become familiar with what is going to happen and therefore more in control of themselves at the time. Knowing more about piles, episiotomies and stitches would help women feel more prepared, more in control and less shocked when they find they still have to think twice about sitting down weeks after labour.

4

Your Body after the Birth

Why didn't someone tell me I would feel like this?

"Everyone thinks that when you've had the baby, it's all wonderful. You read in the books that once you've given birth and everyone's come to visit, well, that's the end of it. It's all wonderful from then on. You're not prepared for the enormous pain." Caroline is certainly not alone in the way she felt after her son was born. Most women expect to feel some pain during labour, but they also know that sooner or later it will stop, that they will have the baby and it will all be over. That is what they are led to believe. Books and magazines may hint at some 'discomfort', tiredness and soreness, but on the whole, women are told that birth is not an illness, and are encouraged to leave hospital as soon as they are able. They therefore expect to be back to, if not 100 per cent mobility soon after, as good as. After all, the books and magazines cover every possible twinge of pregnancy – how to arrange your pillows to avoid heartburn, how to sit to avoid backache and varicose veins, and what every sort of flutter and bump means. Surely there would be the same information for after the birth, if needed?

The post-natal period or puerperium (until six to eight weeks after birth when the uterus has returned to its pre-pregnant state and breastfeeding is established), is the most neglected aspect of modern maternity care. It is a time of remarkable physical and emotional change and yet the care and information which women get when pregnant is not available. The community midwife visits daily (in theory) for ten days after labour and up to twenty-eight days, if needed. The health visitor takes over from her, and often only visits once. And then there is the six-week check with a GP. Other than that, new mothers are on their own unless they seek help. Relatives and friends who had attended the mother-to-be's every need when pregnant, switch their attention onto the baby once it is born. How are you? becomes, how is the baby? The baby's welfare, the baby's feeding, the baby's sleeping becomes all-important. It is almost as if the woman was of interest when pregnant only because she was carrying the baby. Once born, she has done her bit and is relegated from centre stage to a spear-carrier in the wings.

Given the lack of information and support, it is not surprising that many feel a sense of outrage, a betrayal. "Why didn't someone tell me I would feel the way I did," said Hannah. "I was really happy to have Katie, but I was wobbling around the ward like a sumo wrestler, feeling like my fanny was hanging by my knees, thinking, is this normal? Is this what every new mother feels like?" Many women are euphoric about having a baby, but are shocked to find how low they feel physically. They expect to take any pain in their stride, but are surprised to find they can hardly sit, let alone walk. Jill, aged 41` with two children aged three and one, said, "You have to pretend that you feel fine. You're expecting and wanting everyone to say you look wonderful, the baby's wonderful and everything's terrific. It feels like letting the side down to say I'm sore and don't know what to do."

Aches and pains after labour are as inevitable as the aches and pains during it. Even the most straightforward of labours can leave women feeling bruised and sore, and for good reason. Labour is physically traumatic: the vagina and vulva have been overstretched and the pelvic floor, bottom, belly and back can take a hammering. Muscle walls may have been cut and stitched with episiotomies and caesareans, or ripped and stitched with a tear. Excessive blood loss, particularly with caesareans, may result in anaemia. Forceps deliveries can lead to bruising and swelling on buttocks and labia, and epidural deliveries are associated with backache and headaches. On top of this is the added 'discomfort' of pain from post-labour changes like the uterus contracting (afterpains) and milk 'coming in', to say nothing of the sheer exhaustion of having spent hours, sometimes days, in labour. It is not surprising that by the third day, many women weep and feel low. Ninety-five per cent of women in one study had at least one type of pain on the first day after delivery, with uterine cramps and perineal pain being the most frequent.[1] Yet there is hardly any information on post-natal pain and the incidence and treatment of 'minor' complications. Neither uterine cramps and perineal wound pain are mentioned in *Dewhurst*,[2] the standard medical postgraduate textbook.

Afterpains

After labour, the uterus and other pelvic organs reduce to their pre-pregnant state. The uterus contracts at a rate of roughly 1cm a day from approx 30 x 22 x 20 cms to 7.5 x 5 x 2.5 cms, a weight loss of 1kg to 60g. This takes about six weeks. While expanding might have caused the odd stitch or cramp, reduction or 'involution' can be much more painful, causing afterpains. Not unlike the contractions of labour, they can hurt more while breastfeeding (as this releases oxytocin which encourages the uterus to contract), or after post-natal exercise. Generally thought to be more painful the more babies you have, they can be very intense for first-timers too. Dominique, aged 28, has one son aged eleven months, and knew nothing about afterpains. "It was a big shock. It was like being back in labour. I had contractions every minute for half an hour. I wondered what was going on. I thought there might be a bit of placenta left." Her partner's son was there too. "He's only eleven years old. He saw me on the floor, like I was in labour, in awful pain. It was terrible. My brother was there too. He phoned the hospital and they explained what it was. I wished I known about them before."

Afterpains may be one of the most common post-natal pains, but many women know nothing about them. "No one told me about afterpains," said Fatima, aged 23, who has two children aged two-and-a-half years and one. She also had severe pains after her first. "I was just sitting there and suddenly started to get these strong contractions. I thought they'd left a baby in." Since afterpains often feel very much like labour itself, the relaxation and breathing techniques used in labour may help control the pain. In addition, Paracetamol may be sufficient as a painkiller, but Co-dydramol, available on prescription, is particularly effective against strong afterpains. Both drugs are best taken about half an hour prior to breastfeeding or exercise so that they are on board before the pains start. Involution of the uterus is monitored regularly by the midwives and the pains should fade after a few days. Walking upstairs backwards (to resettle organs displaced by labour) or wrapping a cloth around the belly are some old wives' remedies to help the 'falling out' feeling.

Bleeding

The contents of the uterus (lochia) are discharged and bleeding starts off bright red and goes a darker colour as time goes on. Breastfeeding can cause rushes of brighter blood as can physical exertion. Blood clots may be passed in the first few days and this can be alarming. Mary said, "It's mentioned in the books that bleeding goes on afterwards, but you're not told exactly how much. I can remember having a bath and this blood clot floated to the surface and I thought, God, what on earth is that?! I frantically rang the bell and the nurse who came in, said, 'Oh, that's a blood clot.' I thought it was a kidney or something."

The amount and length of bleeding varies from one woman to another.

Anything up to six or seven weeks is common, but many women do not know that. Jane said, "My sister told me it was like a period after childbirth, but I was still bleeding two weeks later. Then my mother saw bloodstains on the bed and she said, 'That shouldn't still be happening'". Jane's mother took her to the doctors who rushed her into hospital where they did a scan to check that everything was alright, which it was. While any worries should be checked out, if there was more post-natal information, women would be more aware of what was normal and what was not. This would help them to tell the difference between a false alarm and legitimate grounds for concern such as prolonged heavy bleeding, the passing of huge blood clots weeks after labour, or a pain in the stomach or lower back which can be a sign of infection or 'retained products' (placenta).

Maggie, aged 33, who has two sons aged three-and-a-half-years and eighteen months, said, "I bled really really heavily for about a month. I just thought it was normal. After a month, I was getting really weak and I went to the doctor about something else and mentioned the bleeding to him. They sent me to hospital there and then. I had a scan and they found they had left part of the placenta behind. I had to have a D&C [dilation and curettage]. The bleeding made me more tired than I needed to be, it really got me down. I went around saying, 'Does this normally happen?' The response was, 'Oh yes, you bleed for a bit'. But how long is a bit?"

Another rarely-mentioned source of 'discomfort' in the early weeks are sanitary towels. There are mini pads and maxi pads, but hospitals have monster pads. For women brought up on tampons and super-sheer press-on panty liners, towels can feel bulky and uncomfortable. They show through trousers and as Dominique said, "I felt more like the baby than the mother." "The hospital ones are huge, monstrous," said Julie, aged 27, who has two sons aged five and three years, "like sitting on bricks. They're not designed well as the material catches on stitches. Every time I took it off, I'd think I must be careful of my stitches. Going to the toilet was murder. I'd think, I've got to go, but I must be careful with my towel so it doesn't pull at my stitches." The irritation can be more than just mental. Allergic rashes are not uncommon. "I couldn't believe it," said Sally, aged 35, who has two children aged five and three years. "I had piles, stitches and bruising and then I developed this itchy rash the size of a 50p piece which the midwife said was a reaction to some chemical they put in the stick-on towels. By then there is nothing you can do but laugh".

Episiotomies and tears

"I had expected to be sore with stitches, but I remember being in tears for about a month after I had him because it was so painful sitting down. I had about four or five baths a day as that was the only thing that soothed it. I remember just sobbing because I thought this pain is never going to go away," said Linda. She had an episiotomy after the birth of her first son, aged eleven, and the memory of the pain is still vivid.

"Just a little cut", but the pain from episiotomies often lasts until the third month after birth and sometimes for much longer.[3] One woman wrote to AIMS (Association for the Improvement of Maternity Services) complaining about her episiotomy: "There's not a moment of the day when I'm not thinking about my scar. It hurts when I walk, it hurts when I sit down, it hurts when I'm changing the baby, it hurts when I do the washing up and, even with all the recommended lubricants, it's excruciating when we try to make love. It's more than five months now and I don't think I'm ever going to be right."[4] Wendy's episiotomy was still painful four months after birth. After twenty-five visits to various GPs and a corrective operation, the pain was blamed on heavy scar tissue which would take time to 'break down'. She was prescribed hydrocortisone cream. Hundreds of women regularly contact AIMS with episiotomy problems.

An episiotomy is a surgical incision, made at the time of delivery, to enlarge the vaginal opening so that baby can be born more easily or more quickly. An episiotomy is often also made when forceps are used to protect a premature baby's head which could be damaged by passage out of a narrow vaginal outlet. Sometimes, episiotomies are simply to prevent tears, based on the assumption that a controlled cut is better than an uncontrolled tear. Different degrees of damage may be caused by tears which happen for example with big babies or a rapid delivery.

Studies have shown that there is no difference in the degree of pain experienced by women who have an episiotomy or a tear or in the subsequent healing.[5] Some stitches heal within days, others can take weeks. It depends on the type of episiotomy or tear, how it was stitched or repaired and the skill of the person who stitched it. Catgut and polyglycolic acid are more comfortable than chromic catgut[6] and a 'continuous subcuticular suture' where all the stitching material is buried under the skin, is less painful than 'interrupted transcutaneous stitches', which causes more trauma and pressure.[7] Women who have epidurals tend to experience more pain from their episiotomy wounds than those who do not. Under an epidural the area is already numb, and there can be a tendency to stitch too tightly, not allowing for the inevitable swelling and inflammation in the hours and days after labour.[8] Infected stitches can cause pain, as can a wound which breaks down before healing.

While any long-term problems with episiotomies or tears should be seen by a doctor, the response can sometimes be less than sympathetic. One woman was told her episiotomy could not possibly hurt as there are no nerve endings in the vagina. When Camilla complained to her doctor that she no longer "came together", he said, "You're not perfect any more. You'll never be like you were when you were 17".

The 'pain' of an episiotomy or tear is not simply physical. To have the most intimate part of your body cut and stitched is not just an incision, it can feel like a mutilation, particularly if, as in Camilla's case, women are made to feel that they are big and gaping and no longer desirable or feminine. "I had no mental picture of the state I was in." said Georgia. "I couldn't remember how my vagina felt pre-birth. I felt very out of tune with myself." Women prefer to be seen by a female doctor than a male, feeling that post-episiotomy problems are not fully understood by male GPs.[9] Perhaps if men had their scrotums snipped in half and stitched and were told, "Don't worry. It heals very quickly down there", the preference would be different.

Rose, aged 33, has three sons, aged four and a half, three, and one and a half. She tore after her second son was born. "I hardly had any stitches, but was stitched up really badly and I was in complete agony for a fortnight. It can still bring tears to my eyes thinking about it. I had quite a big episiotomy first time, but it was stitched up so beautifully I had hardly any pain with it. It was so bad after the tear that I couldn't even pass water without it being sheer agony. I had to hold cold tissues against myself all the time and bathe myself with water. It made the first few weeks much more stressful than it should have been. I couldn't sit or walk properly. Everything made me feel that I was in real bad pain."

The stitching, bruising and swelling can make sitting and walking awkward. Sitting on a foam rubber ring can be helpful, but many women find that two pillows with a gap between is more comfortable. Sitting cross-legged on a bed can eliminate pressure on stitches, and bathing regularly in salt baths, or douching in a bidet, can ease pain and help prevent infection. Thirty per cent of women in one study suffered from perineal infection one month after birth.[10] Ice packs, packets of frozen peas, compresses of witch hazel or camomile tea can all soothe swelling, as can homeopathic treatments such as arnica, comfrey or aloe vera. Stitches dictate clothes – the appeal of baggy trousers is not only in their loose waists and the pain can get worse as stitches heal, dry out and shrink.

It can take time, but episiotomy pain does eventually fade. Five months after labour Jenny thought she would always have to think twice when she sat down. "My episiotomy was like a weather vane. I could predict the weather by how much it ached." A year after, she only gets the very occasional twinge if she has been standing for too long.

Caesareans

While all mothers give birth, caesarean mothers 'give birth' and have major surgery – a detail that maternity wards, organized around mothers and babies rather than convalescing patients, can overlook. The hands-off, birth-is-not-an-illness mentality, with mothers feeding and changing nappies, and the emphasis on being up and about, can seem inappropriate to someone who has gone through surgery. Jill, aged 41, has two children. She had a caesarean for her first child, now aged three. "It's a major operation but it's not seen as such. If a man goes in and has a hernia, he is supposed to take it easy and put his feet up for six weeks at least. That's a cutting through the muscle wall as well and it seems to me that the same treatment should be given to those who have had a section. Yet you're expected to be on your feet, to look after the baby and the house as soon as you're home, and all within days of surgery."

With so much stress on natural births, caesarean mothers can feel let down that their delivery was not 'normal'. Equally, 'bonding with baby' is not easy with an abdominal incision, and makes many women feel guilty because they need to mend first, bond later. Carol Weston in *From Here to Maternity*[11] wrote, "I wanted – had expected to feel unadulterated happiness. Our baby was here whole and healthy . . . I didn't even feel sorry for myself for having a section. But I did feel guilty about being so absorbed, for concentrating on my body more than the baby."

Caesarean mothers also have had a greater blood loss than a mother who delivered vaginally. Iron supplements may be prescribed, but they can lead to constipation, liquid and roughage intake needs to be increased to counteract it. Walking, but not too much, also helps to get a sluggish system going and speeds the healing process by improving circulation. By day two or three, the incision should look well healed from outside, but a strange tightening feeling inside is common as the stitches start to pull. This can last a few weeks. Supporting the incision with a hand or pillow before coughing, sneezing or laughing can make it feel more secure. Nothing heavier than the baby should be lifted for a minimum of three weeks, preferably longer (hopefully someone will be on hand to help). Itching around the incision as it starts to heal is common; vitamin E applied to the area can help relieve it.

An unexpected side-effect of having a caesarean is wind, which sometimes causes severe pain. Less debilitating, but equally unexpected, is the wonderment at just how long it takes for shaved pubic hair to grow back. Lyn, aged 26, had a caesarean for her son, now aged eleven months. She said, "It took ages for my pubic hair to come back. I kept thinking 'I wish, they'd tell me what they use, because I would use it on my bikini line'. He was born in the summer and by Christmas I still didn't have much hair. It was a bit tufty and looked stupid, but I wasn't really bothered. I did wonder when, if ever, it would come back."

Piles

Piles or haemorrhoids are enlarged veins which stick out of the anus. They can erupt during pregnancy due to constipation, pressure on the pelvic floor and increased blood volumes; or, they can make their debut after labour. Associated with heavier babies and longer second stages,[12] increased pressure on the pelvic floor and pushing, piles are a very common post-natal complaint, and yet one that can come as a total surprise. Mary said, "I didn't know much about them before. I thought only old men got them. I heard that pregnant women could get them, but only if they put on lots of weight and got constipated. I wasn't any of those things." Women's ignorance is probably a combination of lack of information and the fact that, thanks to our British lavatorial sense of humour, piles are stock joke material – the 'grapes of wrath', exploring pile ointment, etc. The butt of those jokes tend to be men; women, especially young women, are not supposed to have bottom-trouble, it is just not sexy. The truth is that women, as mothers, are especially prone to both constipation and piles; the two tend to go hand in hand – fear of pushing because of piles leads to constipation, which in turn aggravates the piles. Nobody tells women about it or talks about it, it is just 'not nice'. Only doctors who treat the stream of new mothers for piles are not surprised.

Piles can make sitting down very uncomfortable; they can ache, itch and, after a bowel movement, they sometimes bleed. Pile cream, suppositories, witch hazel, ice packs and frozen peas can ease the pain and the itching. Pelvic floor exercises help circulation and therefore reduce pain. Constipation should be avoided, as should straining. Gently pushing the veins back inside can ease the pain after each bowel movement and for sore bottoms, baby wipes are less painful than standard loo paper.

Maggie has only recently come to terms with her piles. "They were just horrendous. They still come and go. Any sort of stress starts them off. I can't eat anything hot or spicy. I tried eating curry once and that was a big mistake. They always get me down at night when the children are all sleeping and I get into bed and start to itch. I am lying there jumping about. I remember once sitting in a cold bath and I was in agony and that was the only relief available at 4am." She now has a medicine cabinet full of suppositories, haemorrhoid cream, as well as a freezer well-stocked with frozen peas.

Piles that start after delivery and are still unresolved months after the birth are a common, but unrecognized problem. Even obstetric books[13] claim that childbirth-induced piles disappear soon after the delivery. Once you get piles, you become susceptible and stand a strong chance of getting them again. However, the risk of getting them decreases with each birth. Women who do not get them after their first delivery are less prone after subsequent births.[14] Julie's piles "were minor after my first, nothing drastic, but Lukie finished them off. I remember going to the toilet and I was desperate. I remember sitting there for three-quarters of an hour with Jackie Collins, thinking I can't go, the strain is too much. A trip to the toilet is still: will I be in agony or will it be OK."

In extreme cases surgery is necessary, but usually piles are mildly irritating and with the help of creams and suppositories women learn to live with them. However, Dorothy said, "Little did I know that when I had babies I would be condemned to a lifetime of muesli and bran flakes, and would never have the indulgence of an anxiety-free trip to the loo again."

Constipation

"No one ever explained to me about constipation," said Maggie. "I didn't do anything and, after about a week, I went and I remember being stuck in the toilet for about twenty minutes thinking, this is a bit weird. I was just stuck there until I eventually got hold of my partner by shouting. He went off and rang my mother and said, 'What shall we do, she is stuck on the toilet?'" Bowels may be sluggish in the days following labour. They become less efficient anyway during pregnancy as the hormone relaxin, which softens ligaments to make delivery easier, also slows down digestion. After labour, abdominal muscles are loose and floppy and give very poor support to the intestines and bowels. This combined with the fear of rupturing stitches, can mean that the prospect of the first post-labour bowel movement can be almost as frightening as labour itself.

Gillian, aged 41, who has two children, aged six years and eight months, got herself 'in a real state'. She said, "I felt so uncomfortable, I really needed to go. It just wasn't happening. In the end, one of the ward sisters, she was marvellous, took me down to the labour ward where it was quiet. She gave me a suppository and she said, 'You stay here on your own in this room and there's a bathroom and as soon as you've been you can use the bathroom and make yourself feel better.' I did; it was marvellous. I felt so much better after." The stretching of labour, the cutting of the muscle wall, soreness and bruising makes the whole perineal area feel very strange. "I didn't have any feeling from front to back," said Scarlet, aged 21, whose daughter was born eight months ago. "If I pushed, I pushed to have a wee rather than a pooh. It was really weird. I remember thinking, this is strange, I can't remember what you have to do."

A high-fibre diet (wholemeal bread, bran cereals, fresh fruit, etc), drinking a lot of water and doing post-natal abdominal and pelvic floor exercises can all help. Supporting stitches with a soft pad of toilet paper or a sanitary towel can make pushing more comfortable. If constipation persists, the midwife should recommend the most suitable laxative. Bulk-forming preparations such as Fybogel or Lactulose, which soften stools are usually the first choice, both being mild but effective and safe to use if breastfeeding. Stimulant laxatives such as Senokot kick-start the bowels, but are best avoided if breastfeeding.

Bladder problems

After the delivery, the first passing of urine may be delayed. Some women find they have no urge to 'go' for many hours, or feel the urge but find they have 'forgotten how to do it'. This is probably due to bruising and stretching of the bladder and urethra. It normally resolves itself by the end of the first day after birth. Nearly all women experience slight incontinence after giving birth. They may find it hard to control the flow of urine or find that they leak when coughing or sneezing. This is because muscles have been damaged and stitched and are not yet working properly. Most soon get better, but some can develop stress incontinence.

Stress incontinence

As many as one in four mothers cannot cough or run without having to cross their legs.[15] Stress incontinence – leaking urine on exertion (difficulty in 'hanging on' – is a symptom of 'urge' incontinence and is experienced equally by women who have had babies and those who haven't) is a very common post-natal complaint. Nearly all mothers experience slight incontinence after giving birth (some start losing control during pregnancy). While most soon get better, some 10 per cent of new mothers[16] develop stress incontinence.

Lee started leaking urine towards the end of her pregnancy with her first child. The accidents happened when she coughed, sneezed or laughed. Lee went through a long, twenty-one hour labour with a prolonged second stage. Once she had recovered from birth, she found her problem had not disappeared. She had to wear a sanitary towel if she was going out, but it "wasn't too awful. It was something I could live with." However, the stress incontinence became worse after the birth of her second baby.

Stress incontinence can be embarrassing. Legs have to be crossed when coughing or sneezing, and the simplest movement – picking up a toy or getting up from chair – can cause a humiliating loss of control. Leakage can also happen during sex. The pelvic floor muscles support the bladder, womb and bowel, and are responsible for keeping the urethra (the tube leading from the bladder) tightly shut. Prolonged labour and the weight of the baby puts extra stress on the pelvic floor muscles and bladder problems are associated with long second stages and big babies where pelvic floor trauma can be severe.[17] As the muscles lose some of their strength and elasticity they become less effective, allowing tiny drips of urine to escape involuntarily from the urethra during physical activity. Older mothers with less firm muscles tend to be more prone to this, regardless of the extent of pelvic compression and stress during labour. Stress incontinence can be a problem even after a caesarean. The likelihood of suffering from stress incontinence increases with each pregnancy because of the pressure on the muscles which can gradually weaken.

But babies are not all to blame. The main culprit is the human anatomy. The mechanism of urinary control is not ideally suited to life on two legs. Women suffer further because the urinary mechanism can be damaged by childbirth, smoking and the menopause.

Unlike piles, stress incontinence can be prevented or cured by simple measures and pelvic floor exercises. They should be practised several times a day, and need take only a few minutes. They can be done anywhere at any time, whenever you remember. Pelvic floor exercises should in fact be done by all women, from the early teens onwards and should become second nature to ensure good control well into old age. In France, many schoolgirls are taught pelvic floor exercises and reputedly have such good tone that post-natal stress incontinence is far less common. Initially sensation around the vagina will be poor, but it will gradually return to normal. A tampon or a 'support sponge' – a new tampon-like device made from rubber with a tassel – at times of exercise and strain may help to prevent leaking by raising the neck of the bladder and padding any accidents that do occur. But this is just a temporary solution. Although stress incontinence is usually cured by correct and conscientious exercising, sometimes badly stretched internal ligaments or vaginal and urethral tissue may require a small 'repair' operation. But this is only considered if all else has failed and the operation is usually only performed on older women who have completed their families.

Engorged/sore breasts

Breast pain, unlike the other post-natal 'minor discomforts' can become more painful over the days following labour, both for breastfeeding and bottlefeeding mothers.[18] Breasts fill up with milk within 36–72 hours after birth. Prior to that the baby is suckling colostrum which contains antibodies to disease. The 'true milk' coming in is marked by the breasts enlarging and becoming harder, and is sometimes accompanied by a low-grade fever (below 101°F). This fever can last about twenty-four hours and eases once the milk begins to flow.

Both bottlefeeding and breastfeeding mothers can suffer from engorged breasts. Swelling at this time is temporary, caused not so much by large quantities of milk as by a greatly increased blood supply and excess fluid in the breast tissue. If bottlefeeding mothers wear a tight bra this can help suppress the milk flow. When breasts fill up with milk they fill up with as much space as is available. By wearing a tight bra (or as women used to do, by binding breasts) the amount of space is restricted and therefore the amount of milk produced is reduced. After a couple of days the milk is reabsorbed and the discomfort should ease.

Non-pregnant breasts are fairly predictable – they might enlarge slightly and become more tender around certain times of the month, but on the whole they are simply there. Pregnant breasts undergo several changes: they enlarge, the areola darkens and the nipple protrudes more. However, they still do not make their presence strongly felt. But lactating bosoms have a mind of their own. They can inflate to sex-kitten sizes, become rock-hard, feel very uncomfortable and spout milk at will. Stephanie, who has four children, said, "It happens every time: very engorged breasts. With the first one I didn't realize what was happening. They tell you your breasts will feel heavy, but I hardened so much when my milk came in that I was solid right up to the prominent bone in the front of my neck. They were like lumps of concrete. The pain was very intense. I couldn't even use my arms to cut up my food. I had to stand under the shower night and morning, gradually increasing the temperature to make them feel more comfortable." Packets of frozen peas or alternating hot and cold flannels can also ease the pain.

Cabbage leaves worn inside a bra can also ease the pain of engorged breasts. The coldness of (uncooked) leaves straight from the fridge can help reduce the swelling, but also it is thought that the enzymes in cabbages may help to draw out the heat, rather as dock leaves soothe a nettle sting. No particular variety is recommended, although white and red cabbages have thin leaves which are difficult to peel away, and staining can be a problem with red cabbages. Any green cabbage would do, although Savoy cabbages with their crinkly leaves and therefore greater surface areas should give maximum relief.

Because the only other bosoms women ever see are the perfect, pert, non-pregnant ones in the pages of newspapers and magazines, the sight of a real bosom doing what nature intended can, for some, be alarming. Camilla, aged 33, who has two children aged three-and-a-half and two, said, "I felt quite horrible about the engorged breasts. I had a lot of leaking and was pretty balloon-like for a couple of days, with bright blue veins sticking out. I thought I'm the world's most unattractive woman." Monica, aged 21, has one son, aged twelve months. She said, "My breasts were massive. God, it was a real joke. I thought it was awful. I couldn't stand it. On the ward everyone was having trouble with sore nipples and weren't producing enough milk. I was totally the other way, it was pouring out. It was really awful."

Breastfeeding may be natural, but for many it does not come naturally. The Madonna and child images give no hint of the two to three weeks of toe-curling latching onto sore, cracked and bleeding nipples that have to be suffered beforehand. Mother and baby have to learn the best position for sucking. If not properly 'fixed', the baby can damage the nipple after just a few minutes. But it is not just bad positioning that causes pain. The skin on the nipple is delicate and very sensitive and new babies are born with a powerful sucking instinct. The combination of the two can cause soreness, even if the baby is positioned correctly.[19] "I wasn't expecting breastfeeding to be so painful," said Alison, aged 34, whose daughter was born four and a half months ago. "I know she didn't have teeth, but she fed like a piranha, to the extent of making me bleed. It was all a bit of a shock." Sixty-five per cent of women start off breastfeeding. That figure drops to 40 per cent in the six weeks after delivery.[20] Perhaps if pre-natal information did not skate over the throbbing, bleeding nipples and sharp let-down pains, that drop-out rate would be lower.

Using different feeding positions can alleviate the discomfort as nipples recover. Exposing sore nipples to the air as much as possible helps ease pain. A plastic tea-strainer placed over nipples inside a bra is an alternative to going around permanently topless, rubbing a little breast milk into the nipples and letting it dry after feeding can also help. Nipple shields help protect the nipples and ease the pain, as can creams like Calendula, Kamillosan or Body Shop Nipple Cream. The pain can last for up to two to three weeks.

Blocked ducts

Plugged ducts are marked by a tender area or lump in the breast and are common the day after the baby, who normally feeds through the night, sleeps through. As lactating mothers soon discover, breasts are not that evolutionary. Not only does it take weeks to get them hardened to the suction of a new baby, but the supply and demand mechanism is not finely tuned. Any change in demand takes the supply a day or two to adjust. In the meantime, the breasts keep filling up, the milk has nowhere to go and the milk ducts get clogged. Plugged ducts are a common accompaniment to weaning, again because of the change in supply. And they can also be caused by a tight bra pressing on milk ducts or by lack of rest.

Ducts can be unblocked by expressing the milk, either by hand (gently stroking the painful area) or by feeding. Hot flannels can ease the pain, as can immersing bosoms in a warm bath. Any blockage should be cleared as an untreated plugged duct can lead to mastitis.

Mastitis

Annie, aged 35, who has a son aged four and twin daughters aged three, had mastitis. "It was probably the worst thing I've ever had. When it started I just thought I had flu. I didn't realize what it was. The infected area was out of vision. It's probably comparable to the worst flu I've ever had, and it came on so quickly." Mastitis is a breast infection which can occur when an engorged breast becomes infected. Poor diet, lack of rest, emotional stress, or a weakened immune system can also lead to breast infection. It is marked by inflammation, soreness, redness, or excess heat anywhere on the breast and is accompanied by fever. The pain is a throbbing, burning sensation and feeding the baby from the infected bosom can be agony. Nevertheless it is essential to continue feeding through the infection, as stopping will only cause more of a blockage and make matters worse. A course of antibiotics should be started immediately and the baby should feed from the infected side first as the initial sucking is stronger and will keep the milk flowing. Drink plenty of liquids, rest, eat well and keep the milk flowing by feeding the baby more often or by expressing. Use a variety of feeding positions to ensure that all the milk ducts are being used.

Backache

Post-natal back problems are very common. Backache can start during pregnancy because hormones weaken pregnant women's skeletal system and their backs become more prone to strain. More than half of pregnant women have some sort of back problem, and the back remains vulnerable in the weeks following delivery.

The root of back pain can be the labour itself as awkward birthing positions, particularly under epidural[21] can cause long-term stress and strain. Two years after the birth of her son, Heather is still troubled by backache. "It can get particularly bad at work. If I'm standing over someone's desk and leaning over their terminal for any length of time, I have a problem straightening up again. I feel a bit of a berk sometimes and it does get me down. I have always slept on my stomach. If I do that now for more than an hour, it's excruciating to roll over again."

Heather did not have any back problems before her children and puts it down to the 'lousy' position she was made to push in during labour. "I was on my back with my legs in the air which made it difficult to push the baby out." She thinks she strained some muscles around the rib cage in the process. While stressed positions occur in the most normal of labours, they are even more likely when the mother has had an epidural and has lost the ability to register muscle strain.

Diana used to get the pain between her shoulder blades if she had been standing for too long. "I used to call it my shopping back, but now it's the centre of my back, right where the epidural went. At first I put it down to strain on my back because of my sore tummy from my caesarean. Then I had exactly the same pain after my second. They said, 'Oh it can't be anything to do with the epidural.' But I don't believe them – it's right on the spot where the epidural needle went in." There is a powerful association between epidurals and long-term backache as a direct consequence.[22]

If backache is persistent and begins to affect your ability to cope or move, medical advice should be sought. Low backache can be due to pelvic joints stretched by labour, and the coccyx (the tail bone at the base of the spine) can be bruised and occasionally even cracked. Sally had a bad back after the birth of both of her children:" I had an awful bruised feeling when I sat down. I realized that I had fallen on my coccyx years ago and must have fractured it again with each labour. It meant getting into the right position to feed was very difficult."

Sagging feeding positions, bad posture and incorrect lifting and bending techniques contribute to back pain. Mothers have to lift and bend more anyway – feeding, changing nappies, lifting into cars, out of cots and most equipment – and the cots and changing tables are the wrong height for backs. But having good posture and knowing how to bend and lift can help. For breastfeeding, sitting on a firm, straight-backed chair, resting the baby on a pillow helps to avoid hunched shoulders and a crooked back. When bending and stretching, bend the knees and make the thighs do the work, rather than the back. Carry the baby as centrally as possible – in a sling or backpack – and avoid carrying the baby on one hip. When lying down to rest, make sure the back is not strained in any way. Lying on your back can be made easier by putting a pillow under the knees to help flatten the hollow in the spine. Lying on your front is an excellent position for relieving the pain of stitches, piles and backache. One or two pillows under the waist will make sure the pelvis is raised and the back flattened. A pillow or two under the head and shoulders will make sure enlarged breasts are free from pressure.

Headache and neckache

Headaches are less common than backache, but are also associated with bad posture – getting into awkward positions to feed the baby etc, and epidurals.[23] Occasionally when performing an epidural, the needle is inserted a bit too far into the spinal column and causes spinal fluid to leak out. This can result in a headache. Postural headaches tend to ease when lying down; lumbar (epidural) ones, will not.

Frequent headaches and migraines can last for a year or more after labour. Headaches are more common than migraines, and as with backaches, they are associated with bad posture and epidurals; however, both headaches and migraines are also connected with mental stress and strain. Younger mothers, particularly those who have more than one child, are especially prone.[24] The social and environmental pressures on any mother are huge, but they can be more intense for younger mothers who are more likely to be less well-equipped, both financially and emotionally, to cope with the adjustments of motherhood.

Neck and shoulder pain is more common after general anaesthetic. Sixty-four per cent of women in one study who had general anaesthetic complained of it.[25] Under general anaesthetic, the patient lies with the head right back. This can stretch and pull the muscles, which again, because of hormones, are more prone to strain.

Varicose veins

Varicose veins are veins in the leg (and occasionally the vulva) which become enlarged and can hurt and ache when standing. They are caused when valves along the course of the vein become defective and they usually get worse with age. A tendency to varicose veins can be hereditary and, in women who are prone, pregnancy may provoke their appearance. A combination of hormonal changes and the pressure of the enlarged womb pressing down and obstructing the flow of blood from the legs to the heart can make varicose veins worse. Once the baby is born they generally subside and, by about three months, they are usually back to where they were before. If legs feel heavy and ankles are swollen, avoid standing or sitting still for long periods, crossing legs or wearing tight popsocks. Keeping your feet up as much as possible and wearing well-fitting elastic support tights can help, as can rotating foot exercises which increase circulation. In extreme cases, varicose veins can be dealt with surgically. This can be done either by injecting drugs into segments of the relevant vein in order to obliterate it, or by having an operation which 'strips' the vein out of the leg.

Lingering 'minor' problems

The fact that women are eligible for free healthcare not only when pregnant, but for a year after, says it all. The trips to the chemist and need for pills and cream do not end with labour. Far from it. Nearly half of the 650,000 women who have babies each year will be troubled by some long-term post-natal complaint.[26] Piles, backaches, headaches, stress incontinence, extreme fatigue, depression – none are life and death, but such problems can overshadow women's lives for years. Life-threatening they are not, but painful and debilitating they can be.

Knowing that a couple of generations ago their chances of dying in childbirth would have been high, today's new mothers may feel it ungrateful to complain about a few piles. But there again, most do not. Women tend not to fuss or grumble, particularly if it is a problem with them rather than the baby. They suffer in silence, and until a recent study by Birmingham University no one really knew the full extent of post-natal problems. Aside from odd pockets of interest in areas like depression and urinary incontinence, little research has been done on health after childbirth. The more exciting life-and-death work was pre-birth. Specialists concentrated on ante-natal care and cracking maternal mortality was the main aim. The focus paid off – ante-natal care is one of the great success stories of modern medicine, but at the expense of health after childbirth. Aside from the six-week check, post-natal care and a recognition of post-natal problems is virtually non-existent, a fact that has contributed to the assumption that women go into hospital, have their babies and go away and get better – if not straight away, then certainly by six weeks. In fact, a return to normal can take months rather than weeks.

5

Exhaustion and The Blues

"The sheer exhaustion of it all. I wasn't getting any sleep," said Sophie. "Insomnia had been a problem anyway towards the end of my pregnancy. I was waking every half-hour to three-quarters of an hour. Then labour happened two weeks earlier than anticipated, and I didn't sleep at all after labour, not all of that night. I had wanted to – it was long and arduous and I was shattered – but I was too hyper. And I hadn't anticipated the crying babies or that suddenly your ears are tuned into the crying of your own baby. I was listening out for it; I didn't want to miss it. I didn't know what I was going to do if he did cry, but I just wanted to hear it."

A deep refreshing sleep that lasts for several hours, say some experts[1] is vital if healing and the process of recuperation is to start. Fatigue affects the body's capacity to heal, to get back to its pre-pregnant state and to establish breastfeeding. But, for many, deep sleep is impossible. The excitement of a new baby, the feeling of responsibility, the aches and pains and the routine of the maternity ward (the whole point of which is to physically restore women after birth) inhibits it. It is not just the noise and the lights. There was a time when midwives cared for the baby, when the cot was stationed at the foot of the mother's bed, out of sight and out of reach. Now, the importance of those early days, hours even, for the mother/baby relationship is stressed so strongly that mothers feel duty-bound to tend to their infants before they have had a chance to draw breath from labour. Ann said, "The nurses offered to take her into the nursery for the night. I'd been working for the NSPCC when I conceived Amanda and I can remember thinking I'd better not let them take her to the nursery as they'll think, 'Rejection . . .'. I was desperate for a night's sleep, but I wouldn't let her go. I should have. I was so tired."

Chronic tiredness can be due to anaemia, particularly if there was excessive blood loss during labour. Anaemia is best corrected by careful attention to diet, by eating foods rich in iron – leafy green vegetables, lean red meat, dried fruit and nuts. Iron pills, taken on prescription, may be required, but some people find them unpalatable, or experience stomach pains or constipation.

Just as the Eskimos have several words for snow, the one not being enough to describe the different types and textures, so too there should be different words for exhaustion, and in particular the sort experienced by new mothers. 'Tired' just does not do justice to the bone-deep, all-consuming fatigue that many new (and not so new) mothers experience. "I've been tired before, but not in this way," one put it.

Women expect to be tired in the early days. The effects of labour, the inevitable night feeds and adjusting to the new routine all drain energy levels. But six or eighteen months later, to still feel exhausted, to still not have an undisturbed night's sleep, can be hard to accept. A lot of babies are not sleeping through the night at six months – it is quite normal for them to still be waking up every three hours, but most mothers do not know that. They talk to friends whose babies are sleeping through and feel that they are going wrong somewhere. Harriet's children did not sleep through the night for a long time. "There is this stigma. When someone asks if your child is good, they really mean, are they sleeping through the night. I did get very paranoid. I used to say, yes, yes, they sleep. But they weren't at all. You just felt a failure, which is stupid, but you still felt it."

Harriet also felt like a 'zombie'. Sleep deprivation is a form of torture and eighteen months of night after night, never sleeping for more than a few hours at a time, takes its toll. Helen Simpson wrote, "Frances [a mother of two] pondered her tiredness. Her muscles twitched as though they had been tenderized with a steak bat. There was a bar of iron in the back of her neck, and she felt unpleasantly weightless in the cranium, a gin-drinking side-effect without the previous fun." The physical effects of lack of sleep are craggy faces, limp hair and aching muscles, the psychological effects, a complete personality change. Mother love might make many selfless and tolerant, but new mother exhaustion, like alcoholism, has a coarsening effect. It makes many bad-tempered, and unable to concentrate or string a sentence together. Jill was not getting much sleep, "But I was still doing silly things like staying up until 2am just tidying the house. I got very short-tempered and used my husband as a punch-bag."

Sleep and how to get it becomes the topmost priority. A couple of hours here, an hour there – mothers become obsessed with time and calculating how few hours of sleep they get. But it is not the quantity, it is the quality that counts. An undisturbed eight hours become the fantasy; insomnia and thinking about your day before drifting off, a distant indulgence. New mothers are virtually comatose as soon as their heads hit the pillow – that is until there is the slightest murmur from the crib. Night feeds aside, 'mothers' ears' ensure that mothers do not sleep as soundly anyway.

Post-natal exhaustion

The black misery of tiredness can be a mild form of post-natal depression. It may only last a few months, but it can nevertheless be a recognizable depression with the mother feeling physically ill, emotionally flat and miserable. Rose's second son did not sleep through the night for more than an hour at a time. "He would wake up and then be awake for half an hour, sleep for half an hour and wake up again, and keep doing that all night. When he was six months old, he settled into a pattern of sleeping for two to three hours a night. "It would work out, if I added all the bits together, to maybe three or four hours a night, but was constantly interrupted. I can remember my father asking me, when my son was four or five months old, if I had post-natal depression. I said, 'No, I'm just very tired.' But I may have done. I kept bursting into tears over really stupid things. My vocabulary dropped to Enid Blyton levels and I felt as though I was on drugs or something – completely spaced out."

Post-natal exhaustion begins either directly after the birth or develops slowly during the first month to six weeks. It lasts for six to nine months and has usually disappeared before the baby's first birthday. A woman suffering from post-natal exhaustion will have the greatest difficulty in concentrating and will generally feel that she cannot cope. Some see the root of post-natal exhaustion as being biochemical as well as a lack of sleep.[2] The changes, both physical and hormonal during and after pregnancy are enormous. During the nine months of pregnancy the womb increases from the size of a pear to an organ big enough to hold, not only the baby, but also the placenta and surrounding fluid; organs shift around the abdominal cavity to make way for the enlarging womb; the spine adjusts to cope with the altered balance; body fluid increases, making the heart, kidneys and liver work harder. Within six weeks of delivery these changes are reversed. In short, pregnancy and birth can take some getting over.

Breastfeeding

Aside from anaemia which can contribute to new mothers feeling prolonged exhaustion, breastfeeding can be to blame. Breastfeeding is high energy work. It uses up 1,000 calories a day,[3] the same as a construction worker. Unlike a pregnant mother, a nursing mother really is 'eating for two'. What she eats is not only supplying her body, but is being converted into milk to feed the baby. Yet, because of the new fatiguing lifestyle and pressure to regain her figure, new mothers often eat less than they should to feed them both. The result, particularly if breastfeeding for some time, is loss of weight and exhaustion in the mother. Flora fed her twins for seven months and, in retrospect, feels she should have stopped sooner. "I felt desperately tired at the end of that. I felt 'sucked' dry and that feeling took quite a long time to wear off."

Cure?

A well-balanced diet and a 'tonic' like Guiness can help sustain energy levels, but ultimately the only cure for exhaustion is sleep. Widely-given advice like, "sleep during the day when the baby sleeps" or "leave the household chores and concentrate on resting" might be suitable for the first few weeks, but eighteen months of unwashed dishes and unhoovered carpets would turn any home into a health-hazard. The only solution is to rely on the body's ability to adjust to less sleep, to accept that routine has to change and take the long-term view that it will pass. It may take time, but an undisturbed eight hours is not lost forever. Sarah found the sleepless nights very trying at first. "I love my sleep and at the best of times don't have much energy or stamina. But I think I've adjusted now. I really appreciate it if I get just a few hours. I go to bed early – no later than 10pm and try not to get wound up or blame myself when he wakes four hours later. Other mothers would say, 'I don't know I've got him' and I would think, 'Oh shut up.' I'm lively (or was) and I've just accepted that she takes after me." As one woman said, "I was tired for eighteen months, but I'm OK now."

Maternity blues

Temporary weepiness or a let-down feeling is very common in the days after birth. Maternity blues or third-day weeps, marked by transient tearfulness, anxiety and irrational feelings, have both an emotional and physical cause. The stress of labour, the aches and pains, the exhaustion and the hormone changes – oestrogen and progesterone which nurtured the pregnancy are being replaced by oxytocin and prolactin, the lactation hormones – can provoke a seesaw of emotions. On top of this there is the emotional adjustment to the new baby, and coming to terms with its, at times, seemingly overwhelming demands.

Alison said, "The first few days I felt on top of the world. Then everything got on top of me – constipation, pain from stitches, sore nipples and the sleepless nights were catching up on me. All I wanted was a night's uninterrupted sleep. I felt very weepy." Julie said, "I was alright until the second or third day. I was sitting in the nursery and burst into tears for no reason whatsoever. I felt like a right twit. Everyone else was so pleased with their newborns and there was I crying my eyes out. I went back to the ward and the other mums who had their babies at the same time were doing the same thing. I thought, that's OK then, this is normal." Reassurance that periods of weepiness and feelings of not being able to cope are very common can help. Sarah, aged 30, whose daughter is three months, said, "I came home on Tuesday. On Wednesday morning Mum was here and my sister-in-law, and I just went into the front room and started to cry in front of them – I felt really silly. I said, 'Oh, Mum, what have I done? I'm never going to cope.' She said, 'Have a good cry. We all felt like that. In a few months' time you'll wonder what all the fuss was about.'"

Sometimes there is not even any apparent reason for the tears. Sally said, "On day four after my first, my eyes just leaked. I wasn't unhappy, but no matter what people said to me, I cried. They shouldn't call it the blues, because you're not unhappy. It should be called the wets – your breasts are leaking and you are leaking and your eyes are leaking. It's all very bizarre, you're just not in control."

It is not only mothers who experience third day blues. Women undergoing gynaecological and other surgery can experience blues very similar to that felt by new mothers.[4] Feeling weepy is the body's way of saying, 'I've had a shock, slow down.'

Post-natal depression

Sophie was in "bucketfuls of tears" at her six-week check-up. "The doctor said, 'How are you?' and that was it. I just cracked. She is a lady doctor and has two or three children of her own and she had had post-natal depression, so had some inkling of what I'd been going through. I felt so anxious and inadequate. I had this awful nervous eczema all over my back and shoulders. I just felt like a physical and emotional wreck. I needed some help." Cathy's post-natal depression started about three months after the birth of her son. "I wasn't sleeping properly, even though I was exhausted. I couldn't do anything. I felt less inclined to go out, less inclined to make an effort over anything." She was also anxious about her son's health. "Sterilizing bottles really got to me. I wasn't sure how much you should sterilize and when you should sterilize. I remember him picking something off the floor and eating it and worrying myself sick as to whether it was poisonous or not. I rang up the health centre in such a state. It was really unlikely he could have swallowed anything really harmful. But I just got into such a completely neurotic state about it."

Four out of five women go through a miserable period after childbirth[5] and one in ten women are affected by post-natal depression.[6] Often defined as "the first psychiatric illness requiring medical treatment, occurring in a mother within six months of delivery",[7] it covers a range of symptoms from sadness to suicide and may totally change the mother's personality, behaviour and outlook. It may start at the birth following on a continuation of maternity blues, or it may develop months later and can come unexpectedly into families who have no history of psychiatric illness. It may only last a few weeks or months, or drag on for twenty years or more. "She's never been the same since the baby" can have a sad poignancy about it.

Causes

Post-natal depression has been recognized for years, but has often been put down to the foibles of the 'weaker sex' or ignored. Hippocrates attributed it to suppressed uterine discharge. Trotula, the 11th-century gynaecologist, suggested the cause was an excessively moist womb. Earlier this century American psychiatrists all but ignored it and it disappeared from the A-Z of diseases. To this day there is still much silence and mystery about post-natal depression and opinion is divided as to what causes it. Some believe the root to be the hormonal changes that take place after birth. During pregnancy, the placenta releases high levels of hormones into the system. Once the placenta is delivered these hormones are suddenly cut off and there is no more progesterone in the body until two weeks before the first period. As some women, particularly those who breastfeed, may not menstruate for a year or more after birth, the body has to adapt to considerable chemical changes. As different placentas produce different quantities of progesterone, the degree of adaptation will vary from woman to woman. Injecting progesterone or suppositories containing this natural hormone is one way of treating the depression.[8]

Carol has a son aged four. She believes her post-natal depression was largely due to hormone factors. "I had a good pregnancy and felt well and confident. But two days after I had a severe emotional breakdown. I rejected the baby, I could not recall labour or birth and was unable to cope with breastfeeding. Due to the heat of the hospital ward I couldn't eat or sleep . . . . Few of the staff were sympathetic – they had no time to listen, and any advice I had was conflicting. On reaching home I entered a manic state, not eating or sleeping for four days and nights. I was confused and filled with feverish excitement. I was admitted to a mother and baby unit at a psychiatric hospital, whereupon I was convinced there had been a nuclear war, and I attributed my panics and trembling to the effects of radiation. I suffered hallucinations." Carol was treated with drugs and a course of ECT (electro-convulsive therapy) which was "horrifying". She feels the drugs were effective in her severely disturbed state but that a preventative hormone treatment would have been better, as drugs have side-effects and withdrawal symptoms. Carol also feels that she was totally unprepared for the realities of motherhood, "how much hard work it is and also what a full-time responsibility a small baby is."

Others believe the root of post-natal depression is psychological – a human reaction to a stressful situation, which birth most certainly is.[9] Conditions similar to post-natal depression have been seen in people following earthquakes, surgery and bereavement.[10] Women get depressed after childbirth because in one way or another childbirth and motherhood turn out to be a shock for which they were inadequately prepared. Being the victim of unrealistic expectations lessens the feeling of being in control which is important if women are to feel satisfied with their lot.

Georgia suffered from depression after the birth of her son, Barney. She planned a home birth, but ended up in the special care unit of her local hospital, an experience which changed her "spiritual and emotional life". After the birth, "I was completely hyper. I would never sit down or relax. I didn't cry for a long time, a long time, which was a mistake. I had lost a lot of confidence and was endlessly anxious. But I also think I was going through a lot of things for myself – having a child does that to you doesn't it? All the stuff about the state of the world and all those major things. I think I was sieving a lot of data for myself. So it's not as simple as just worrying about the fact that he might have been brain damaged or that it had gone so differently from how I wanted and that I was responsible. It was compounded by other changes going on." Julie's depression after the birth of her second son was also connected to unfulfilled expectations. Her first child was stillborn, her oldest, aged two, had turned "evil" and her "beautiful" new baby was "too big, too heavy" and had eczema. "He was horrible. He had an odd-shaped head, flat at the bottom. He was the sort of baby you shut in the buggy with the cover over. People would look in and go, 'ugh'. Getting out with a toddler and a baby is difficult at the best of times, so I was marooned in the house and that did it – isolated with a baby who was not what I expected and a two-year old hitting the terrible twos with a vengeance. I felt tired. I could have slept for eighteen hours a day happily. I was irritable with the children, you know, if I burnt the fish fingers I'd throw the pan across the floor then burst into uncontrollable tears."

Julie felt 'lousy' for ten months and then phoned up her health visitor, threatening to hurt the children if she did not come around. "I wasn't. It's the only way to get help around here." She didn't want drugs so her health visitor suggested a local self-help group. "You have a carer who has the same problem and she is your sounding-board. You can phone her whenever you need to. She taught me how to love my baby."

An overidealized view of motherhood and birth is one of many recognized factors that can tip women into post-natal depression. Others include stillbirth (which had more to do with Julie's problems than her ugly baby), an unloving, unsupportive partner, high anxiety at the end of pregnancy, a history of two or more years of infertility, previous abortion, no close friends, poor housing, a recent move, unfamiliarity with babies, poor social support and being single, widowed or divorced.

Helen's post-natal depression started five months after the birth of her son, now aged twenty months. She had separated from her husband a few months before Sam was born. They are now divorced. "Things were getting better with Sam – he wasn't crying as much. But it suddenly hit me that I was on my own with a baby and that a miracle wasn't going to happen. It all got too much, what with the splitting up and having to move just before I had him. I think it was delayed shock. At first I was so busy with the constant feeding and pacing up and down the floor to notice. I was standing changing his nappy and I just burst into tears. I couldn't stop. I was hysterical. I couldn't breathe. I had been down for a couple of days, but I just remember changing his nappy. It was something silly, like I couldn't do it up properly and that was it – I just couldn't cope." Helen's health visitor arranged for her to have a babysitter for a couple of hours a week and her parents also helped. "I had tried to be too much of a Supermum. I wanted to do everything by myself and I didn't want people interfering. When my husband went I was so annoyed that I thought, 'I'll show you. I'll do it on my own' " Because of the myths that surround motherhood, admitting that it is hard can be difficult. "I thought it should all come naturally and I wanted people to think I was this perfect mother."

Women who feel depressed can be helped by finding a group for new mothers. Contact the local NCT, look on noticeboards at the local health centre or baby clinic, or ask the health visitor for information about groups. The NCT and health visitor should also be able to recommend a post-natal supporter who can be contacted. Talking to a friend, particularly someone who has been through it and can give a long-term view can be helpful as can going out with or without the baby as much as possible. Post-natal exercise classes, eating well and making the time to do something for yourself (rather than the washing up) when the baby sleeps can all boost self-worth. If the mood doesn't change, women should contact their GPs. Most GPs tend to prescribe anti-depressant drugs which can be very beneficial in treating post-natal depression. Sometimes it takes a while to find the right drug as there are so many types and what works for one woman does not necessarily work for another. It can take two to three weeks for the drugs to get into the system and their effect to be felt.

For those who are against taking drugs or for whom the drug therapy is not working, the GP will refer them to a psychiatrist or a psychologist. The psychiatrist or psychologist will try to help by listening to and discussing the woman's feelings, by teaching relaxation techniques and by combating feelings of guilt. In severe cases the doctor will recommend hospitalization, ideally in a mother and baby unit.

The Association for Post-natal Illness offers advice and information and one-to-one support by volunteers who are mothers and who have had the illness and recovered. The symptoms of post-natal depression are quite varied and the Association tries to match the mothers as best they can. The NCT also has information on post-natal depression.

6

The Emotional Vortex

An emotional explosion

Annabel said, "I've had my most intensely wonderful times with my children, but also my most intensely horrible." To have a baby is to experience a huge emotional explosion. Unlike the popular image, motherhood is not cute and sentimental, it is passionate, moody and intense. Love, hate, guilt, anxiety, fulfilment, boredom – mothers expect to be on an even keel, but instead swing from one emotional extreme to another. "The highs are definitely higher, the lows definitely lower than I expected," said Rose. Sara Maitland, the writer, had planned on having eight children, but stopped after two: "Sometimes I would go to pick her up feeling furious and resentful and at the sight of her I would collapse, melted by physical love and tenderness . . . Sometimes I would be playing with her quite happily when a complete and profound anger would come over me and I would want to kill her."[1] Because motherhood is given such a rosy write-up and the blacker side ignored, the conflicting mix of positive and negative emotions – love and fear, anger and depression – can be disturbing, but is nevertheless a normal part of motherhood.

Anxiety

Mechanics of care
The birth of a healthy baby does nothing to relieve pregnancy nervousness about its well-being. If anything, it creates new levels. Helen said, "I felt I should know what to do – things like changing nappies, when and how much to feed him, why he cried, when to wind him. But none of it was instinctive. I had to be told things and I found it a bit embarrassing not knowing what to do. There were a lot of second-time mums on the ward, and the other first-time mums seemed to know what they were doing. I just felt

completely useless. I didn't change his nappy until my father came in the afternoon. As soon as he came through the door I grabbed him and said, 'Dad, you've got to show me how to do this.'" Caroline had not dressed a baby before. "The first time I had to put a jump-suit on, I couldn't do it. I thought, someone should have taught me how to do this. My mother-in-law came around and said, 'Well, you roll up the legs in the same way as you do when putting on tights.' So obvious after she pointed it out. Then there were the nappies – I couldn't get them to stick. Now I get every nappy to stick, but at the beginning I was getting more wrong than right."

Women are expected to know how to look after babies; in practice, many have not even held a baby, let alone know how to change a nappy before they are faced with their own. A century ago, families were larger and most girls had experience of looking after their younger brothers and sisters and other members of the family. By the time their own children were born, they had a good idea of what to do. Today, women have to be taught how to hold a baby as well as the practical details of feeding, changing and bathing. It can come as a shock that none of it comes naturally and some women, no matter how experienced and confident they are in other areas, can be thrown into a panic by their babies. Frances said, "Every time she cried I thought there was something wrong with her – silly isn't it? I wasn't used to seeing babies cry or be sick, that made me very anxious. I didn't feel in control. I'd had a very successful career up until that point and had been in charge of events all day, every day, and suddenly there is this little scrap of humanity and you're a quivering wreck and you don't know what to do. I used to say, 'Come on Frances, you used to do this, that and the other, now look at you!'" Babies are in fact quite robust, but they can feel terrifyingly fragile. It seems impossible that something so small can keep breathing unaided. The burping, rashes, sick and screaming can be alarming to the inexperienced, and doctors and hospitals receive dozens of calls daily from new mothers convinced their children are ill. Each new task is a hurdle – the first nappy change, bath, hairwash. Kerry was worried by her daughter's nails. "I didn't know how to cut them. I took her around to my neighbour and said, 'Just hold her, I don't want to cut her little finger off.'"

Maternal anxiety, according to psychologists, is very common,[2] and lack of experience is only part of the cause. Mothers have a heightened sense of responsibility for their babies. During pregnancy a mother's main concern is with herself and her well-being[3], but once the baby is born it takes centre stage. The mother withdraws from other relationships, identifies with the baby and becomes absorbed in its well-being and development. Anxieties about health, hygiene, overfeeding, underfeeding and nappy rash are all tied up with the mother's 'primary maternal preoccupation'.

Cot death

Cot death is one of the biggest anxieties for new mothers. Camilla said, "It had been such a difficult birth and I was convinced I was never going to go through that again, so he was extra, extra precious and I was anxious all the time. If I saw a child with a runny nose or spotty face I would steer the supermarket trolley in the other direction because they said that cot death is more common if children had had a virus." The fear that their baby will die can haunt new mothers. They hover over the crib to check the baby's breathing, prod the baby if it seems to be sleeping for too long, police sleeping positions to make sure it always sleeps on its side and never on its front, and always have that anxiety at the back of their mind that their baby will be taken away from them, that death will come as birth did and the baby will disappear as dramatically as it appeared. Frances had a "dreadful, totally illogical fear that if I wasn't watching her something was going to happen. I just had to see her all the time and check that she was breathing and that everything was OK. I would put my hand on her back just to feel the breathing going up and down. It was totally illogical. My mother-in-law would say, 'For heavens sake, go out for a quarter of an hour.' But I had to have my husband with me to make sure I stayed out, which is crazy as I'm not normally that sort of person."

Mothers do not have to be pessimists to feel that if something is good it is not going to last. Frances had never planned to have children and the strength and power of her feelings for her daughter had been an unexpected surprise. "I think deep down I worried that it was all so perfect, it would be taken away from me," she said. New mothers can be so overwhelmed by their love and their babies seem so perfect that anxieties about cot death are a way of confronting their worst fear – that their baby and new-found happiness will be taken away. Scarlet said, "I was anxious because she was so perfect and I thought, this can't last. Everyone said what a beautiful baby she was, so I kept on expecting things to go wrong, kept on thinking that something is bound to go wrong."

Responsibility

"A mother gave birth to the baby, didn't she? She nurses it, doesn't she? She is, therefore, solely responsible for it."[4] In every family it is the mother who is seen and sees herself as being responsible for the baby and its welfare. She may have a partner who helps, but ultimately the buck stops with her, she has final responsibility. It is the mother who has to make decisions and choices about what is best for the child nutritionally, educationally and psychologically every hour of the day. For new mothers, who have often come from being relatively carefree, this responsibility can be overawing.

One false move and a baby can fall down the stairs or drown in a bath. New mothers often feel that they have to stay awake twenty-four hours a day just to check that everything is alright and even when they are asleep they can find themselves rummaging in the bed thinking the baby they were feeding is trapped under the blankets or suffocating under pillows, when in reality they put it back in its cot.

In the early days, Sarah would sit on the stairs waiting for her baby to wake up. "I couldn't get on with my own life. I couldn't get over the fact that she could be left alone, that I could do other things when she slept. I felt I had to be ready and waiting always." The first day alone with the baby and the first trip out with it can be terrifying. Ann first took Amanda out on a walk to the nearest village seven minutes away. "I had her in the pram and I felt very self-conscious. I'd never pushed a real baby in a real pram before. I got into the village and I know a lot of people and they were stopping me and I felt panicky thinking, I've got to get the shopping done before she wakes up, because if she cries I don't know what I'm going to do. And I went to go into the bank and I met a friend and said, really panicked, 'How am I going to get into the bank, the door is closed?' He looked at me and said, 'Well, you open it.' That to me was a terrible problem – how to handle the pram and the door."

As time goes by babies become stronger, confidence grows and the responsibility is shared with nursery schools, playgroups and school. As the baby grows the overwhelming fear generally recedes, but for most mothers a residue of almost permanent anxiety remains – "be careful when you cross the road", "always wear a vest", "never talk to strangers" and so it goes on.

The world is a dangerous place
After childbirth it is very common for the world to suddenly seem a very threatening place. New mothers have a heightened sense of the dangers in the world, a place where neither she nor her baby is safe. On a domestic level, all car drivers turn into lunatics, pavements no longer feel safe and strangers are potential child abusers; on a more global scale women become more sensitive to news. Since having children, Rachel has felt things much more intensely. "Before, like what's happening in Bosnia, I'd have thought, 'Oh, that's hard', but that would have been it. Now seeing children hurt, it really upsets me. I *know* it's terrible. I think, what if it were mine? I really cried my eyes out over the Jamie Bulger case. The little boy, he looked so like my middle one. Everyone kept on saying, 'Doesn't he look like yours?' It seems to hurt even more. He's the same age and a little bugger too. He roams off; turn your back and he's gone. It really did upset me and it also upset me to think that children so young could do something like that."

Some psychologists say that this high level of anxiety in new mothers is passed down from a time in evolution when the world was a genuinely hostile place and dangers both to baby and mother were very real. Motherhood is a primitive experience that connects us directly with distant generations, and reawakens a primitive anxiety that today is entirely out of proportion to the real dangers faced by mothers.

New motherhood can reveal the depths of a woman's unconscious mind. Her 'inner devils' – hidden fears and worries – can surface and be projected onto the outside world. Sally said, "I remember sitting in the clinic one day and hearing one mother say, 'I think I'm getting depressed, I keep on thinking about bad things.' And it was such a relief to hear someone else say it. I used to think about silly, silly things, like what would happen if I fell over holding the baby. One friend said she kept on imagining turning around and the baby's head hitting the door and she couldn't stop it, this stupid, stupid imagination." Being aware of the vulnerability of a small child reminds us of the vulnerability of all human life. After the birth of a first child, women think about death a lot more – of themselves (they often make wills) and those they love (because they feel more dependent).

Love

The Achilles' heel

Alice Thomas Ellis observed that the perfect couple is not a man and a woman, but a woman and a child. Romantic love comes nowhere near the passion some mothers have for their babies. Lyn said, "I love my husband to bits, but I wouldn't give my life for him. I would for James. I wouldn't even have to think about it for a second. It's so strong." Mothers would live for their children and die for them and even if they would do the same for a lover, they would think it over first. It is a feeling which cannot be explained to anyone who does not have children, mainly because the only words that are available are those of cutesy, sentimental greetings cards which make it sound so soppy. The corniness of the language is a far cry from the fierce tenderness a mother feels. It is not about lace or lavender, soft lights and beaming faces. "It's a very raw emotion," said Flora. "It's bound up with protectiveness, but more than that. It's a pushiness, wanting them to achieve their potential, to see them unfolding. Every single little developmental step is a triumph. It's very bizarre."

Those who do not like other children worship their own, and even those who work with children and who know their ways, can be surprised by the power of mother love. Penny was a nanny to twins before she had her children, one aged four years and twins, aged twenty-one months. "When I was a nanny, if the twins were unwell, you cuddled them and loved them – well, you thought you loved them, but I didn't when I think back. You tried to make them feel better, but at the end of the day I went home and thought, I'll just get up tomorrow and carry on. Whereas with my lot, if they're ill, I get really upset. I feel for them. I've sat down and cried with them. They're your flesh and blood."

When other babies cry, it seems only like a baby crying, but when it is your own, it seems like an accusation, a plea for help, a desperate need, a moan of complete misery. Kate said, "When Thomas cries in the night, it is a real disturbance. It really gets me in the guts – that tearing feeling when I know he's not happy."

Although different from the love for a lover, the love for a child can feel like a love affair. Mothers can feel possessed, ache when they are apart from their babies, run home to be with them again, really look forward to seeing them in the morning, put up with the drudgery because they want to make them happy, spend hours choosing just the right toy, imagine their faces when they see it and enjoy just watching them (especially when asleep). Motherhood opens up a whole new emotional dimension making many realize how empty, how lacking life was before. But it also brings a new vulnerability. Camilla said, "I had no idea I could love them so much. It's made me feel vulnerable because, if anything happened to either of them, I'd feel that my life was over. They are my Achilles' heel."

Skin-to-skin contact

Dolls are useless at preparing girls for motherhood. Not only do they not cry through the night, but cuddling a plastic Tiny Tears comes nowhere near the warmth of holding a real baby. For many the sensuousness of mothering: the baby's smell, its 'deliciousness', its 'soft marshmallowy feel', the cuddles, is one of the greatest pleasures and surprises. Amanda Craig, the writer and a reluctant mother-to-be was expecting, "a bundle of shrieks, sour milk and pooh", but was converted to the joys of motherhood by "someone whose skin is softer than rose petals, who coos like a dove and who smells better than freshly baked bread, even in a dirty nappy".[5] As Desmond Morris points out[6] babies are physically designed to hit the love button and it seems to work. Sue Peart, a Times journalist, wrote that her new daughter was "Pink and white perfection, with huge blue eyes, squidgy little thighs, an infectious giggle, breath like new-mown hay and dimples in places most of us don't even have places."[7] According to one study[8], by five months all the new mothers had fallen in love with their babies and many talked of the smiles, the noises of post-feed contentment and the clear healthy skin as some of the addictive pleasures of motherhood.

Love returned

Fatima said, "All my life all I wanted was someone to love me back. When she was tiny, she'd open her eyes and I could see the love she was going to give me. Now, just the little things they do and the way they smile . . . it's a warm feeling that they know I'm their mother and that they love me." For the first time in Fatima's life she had a sense that she alone was needed. The unconditional love of a child can bring a sense of self-worth which some women have never had before. Adult relationships can be complicated by game-playing and inhibitions, but babies are totally trusting and love implicitly. There are no conditions. For some parents it can be the first time they are loved like that, have had some acknowledgement from another human being that they are doing something right and good.

To a baby, a mother is always perfect which for most flawed grown-ups is a revelation. Julie said, "They're lying in your arms and they're content and happy, and they suddenly give you this beaming smile and you've done nothing to deserve it. Whatever you do they will love you. Jordan is now five and he can get a good hiding because he's been a little toad and five minutes later he wants a cuddle." Babies are uncritical. Any mistakes are quickly forgiven. As Heather said, "No matter how you cock it up, they still love you. Babies are born with two misconceptions about life. One that everything revolves around them, and second, that this basket case, this physical wreck who is in charge knows what she's doing. I was amazed by my son's calm acceptance of how I changed his first nappy unsupervised. It was a mucky one, particularly stuck to him. I lifted up his heels like you're supposed to and he flew up into the air. He just sort of dangled there looking at me. He didn't even look particularly surprised, he just accepted it. No matter how cack-handed I was, he just assumed that was what was supposed to be going on."

Anger and frustration

Fantasy and reality

From paintings of the Madonna and child to Laura Ashley and the Princess of Wales, there have always been strong, positive images of mothers and babies. Some psychologists say we need these pictures to encourage women to procreate, that humanity would die out if women stopped wanting babies and that rosy portrayals of motherhood help the urges along. Others say that milk and honey pictures of mothers being all good, as opposed to witches and demons being all bad, link back to a childhood need to have a fantasy world where good and evil are easily understood and put into compartments untouched by the real world and real experiences. Deep down, say the psychologists, adults still see the world in terms of fairies and demons, and divide people accordingly.

Either way, the popular image of motherhood – the not-a-hair-out-of-place, calm, cheerful, beautiful and completely organized supermum – has little to do with what it is really like. Samantha, whose son was born seven weeks ago, said, "Recently there was this ad on TV, I forget what it was for, where this new mother is looking at her baby and crying with happiness, thinking how wonderful it all is. I thought, God, what a load of crap that is." Fairy tales concentrate on living happily ever after and skip the bit about the baby not sleeping and making twenty-four hour demands. Women are told the most fulfilling thing they can do is to have children and that a home is not a home without them, but the darker side is rarely mentioned. Sarah, said, "I had this picture in my mind of happy families: children in parks, sunshine, mothers meetings and happiness. It's not like that. Anna is a very bad sleeper. She hasn't slept through [the night] yet and she's six months old. So some days she's very irritable and I'm very irritable and too tired to really appreciate being outside and I think, But motherhood's not supposed to be like this."

Because would-be mothers do not have much hands-on experience of babies, they rely on distorted popular images, media fantasies, personal dreams and rose-coloured memories from relations. There might be the odd grazed knee, but on the whole they imagine the baby playing with wooden toys quietly by their feet while they read or paint, never losing their tempers and always being able to walk away when they want. Within a week of getting the baby home the bubble bursts. A mother is eating take-outs, is still in her dressing gown at 3pm and the washing up is piling up. While most women manage to balance the needs of the child with their own, for some the difference between expectations and reality is too great. They are overawed by the responsibility, cannot cope and cannot handle their child's needs in relation to their own.

Another big shock of motherhood is that babies and toddlers, unlike dolls, are people in their own right. Far from being simple, passive recipients of a parent's fantasy, they have minds of their own, can throw tantrums, be wilful and contrary. Annabel said, "I imagined I would be able to mould them and create babies who turned into nice little children. I didn't envisage that I would have to fight and negotiate and answer constant demands and questions. Everything is a battle with them and I didn't think motherhood was going to be like that." Ann said, "I always assumed that I would be able to placate Amanda without anyone noticing. But then she started throwing herself around shops and lying on the floor screaming, and I felt so embarrassed and didn't know what to do." While most mothers-to-be do not have their head in the clouds and are aware there is a possibility of problems, they are not fully prepared for just how frustrating or difficult early motherhood can be.

Time and motion

New babies are dictators. The do not want much, but what they want, they have to have. Their needs are paramount, the mother's are second. Birth breaks all the rules of ordinary existence. Breakfast, lunch and supper become haphazard snacks, and days and nights blur into endless service to the baby. The take-over bid can be much harder than imagined and most women are amazed that their whole lives have to revolve around this tiny human being. Scarlet said, "I thought it would be like a shift, like an eight-hour shift, but it's not, it's twenty-four hours a day, and it used to irritate me that I could never have an hour off, even when she was asleep. I was drinking a cup of tea and she cried, I would have to put it down and see to her; I'd just get in the bath and she'd wake; if I sat down with a paper she'd start, You think, 'Oh, go away'. Little irritating things, not really big things, but little things, every day, every single day and night."

Magazines talk about the disruption for the first few weeks after birth, in reality the 'jet-lagged bewilderment'[9] can last through the first year and beyond.[10] Beverley's baby tended to catnap rather than have a long sleep. "Every time I wanted to put him down to go to the loo or even make a phone call, I just couldn't because he'd start crying. I would try and eat something, and as soon as I sat down he'd start crying. I couldn't do anything. If I'd had a bad night with him and I was tired, I just couldn't cope with it. There was one occasion when I was in tears when my husband came home from work."

Babies are very tuned in to their mother's feelings. When they sense that she is unwell or unhappy they have an unfailing ability to be even more demanding, they try to re-engage her and reassure themselves, and so cry even more. This may make her angry, more angry than she can ever remember before. *All* mothers get cross and frustrated. Even those who love being a mother, who are considered naturals at it and seemingly have no difficulty at all. Parents are more bad-tempered than the childless[11], it is part of the job, part of dealing with the impossible demands of babies at a time when the mother is most tired and yet wanting to do her best. Rose said, "I would have described myself as a fairly stable person, someone who never lost her temper, but in the last five years since I've had the children, I have lost my temper fairly frequently. It has made me feel that there is this bit inside me that I didn't know existed before. I remember Harold crying a lot until we eventually got womb music and a sheepskin and that helped a lot, but he used to cry from about six pm until four or five am. I can remember throwing him down on the bed, shouting, 'I hate you, I just want you to stop crying.'" A child can bring out the child in the mother. Tears and tantrums in a baby can provoke tears and tantrums in a mother.

Real mothers get cross, mothers in babycare books only get mildly agitated. The blacker side to motherhood, the rages and tempers, might be hinted at in books or popular images, but it is all made to sound very gentle and fleeting. In reality, the rage can be so strong, so overpowering it can produce unexpectedly violent thoughts. Alison found it hard to cram all that the baby needed and the housework into one day. "Things were snowballing and I didn't have a chance to clear the day. I was finding it hard enough just to manage the baby, let alone the rest of it. It got so bad that one evening when I was bathing her, I thought if I drowned her I would be free of all the responsibilities of looking after her. I felt so guilty for even thinking it – you hear about people who do these things and you think they're mad, and there I was considering it. My mind just wasn't on an even keel, what with all the crying and the exhaustion."

It can be particularly hard for single mothers who have no one to take over or act as a safety valve. Fatima, a single mother, said, "I'd been out all day and we came back in the evening and I was doing his milk and Calvin was running around crying, only a little cry. But all of a sudden I got really wound up because all week he'd been crying and this cry was getting on my nerves really badly and I found myself pacing up and down the kitchen floor, just screaming at him to stop crying. In the end I had to phone my friend and ask her to come and get him because I thought I was going to hurt him. I didn't want to hear him crying anymore. I just wanted that crying to stop."

While there is a huge difference between thought and action and only a tiny minority actually do harm their children, contrary to the popular image, moments of rage, white heat temper and total loss of control are not at all uncommon. Different women have different ways of coping with their anger. Beverly bit hard into her daughter's dummy, "the anger is taken out that way". Sophie would go for long walks. "He cried a lot and I used to get very upset about it. I didn't know what he wanted – was he hungry or just playing on my emotions? Before I knew it I'd be screaming and felt tremendously guilty about that; I still do. I keep thinking I'm an awful person, I'm an awful mother. I was really scared that sometimes I could do something awful to him. It was just the evenings, in the time just before my husband came in from work, particularly the winter, the first winter. I'd find myself walking in the fog and the dark for hours. I thought, if I'm in the view of the public I won't do anything. He usually slept when I walked him anyway. I walked miles."

At school we all learn to be 'task-orientated', to measure accomplishments in terms of finished product and to organize it in blocks of time.[12] But looking after babies is not this sort of work. Nothing that is done, stays done. Babies are fed and changed and three hours later it all needs doing again. Floors are tidied and swept, and within an hour are messy again. Trying to maintain previous standards of cleanliness can feel like shovelling a path in a snowstorm. It cannot be done and trying to do it can add to frustration. Life with a baby is untidy and, particularly in the early days, there is no obvious reward. Flora said, "Life throughout the first three months was purely stumbling from one moment to the next. I've done this, now I must do that, then do that and then that, now it's time to go to sleep . . . thank God . . . zzzz. Then they'd scream and you'd wake up, then you had to change their nappies and feed them and so on. It is a bit of a treadmill, particularly with twins, even now that they're fourteen-and-a-half months old. I do resent it a bit that life has to be so organized." Small they may be, but babies bring a lot of extra work with them. Clothes need to be washed, bottles cleaned, toys to be tidied away. Meals can no longer be skipped or eaten out, the house untouched from one week to the next – life has to be more organized, there has to be more of a routine. Rose said, "It was such a shock to be stuck in the house with a small baby. The trivia – the constant washing and ironing – and the sheer exhaustion, the relentlessness of it all." Babies cannot be fitted around the edges of life, and mothers cannot pretend that there has been no change, that life can go on as before. Lifestyle changes overnight. Days cannot be planned in the same way and life has to slip into a slower gear. Just getting the baby up and fed and ready to go out is an achievement. And as for the days of 'just nipping out' – forget it. It can be a profound shock to discover just how long it takes to get out of the house. Assembling the paraphernalia, juice, beaker with screw-lid top, flannels, wipes, nappies, change of clothes, toys, coats, buggy, and timing it all around feeds and naps, can feel like organizing a military campaign. Rose said, "Anything, like posting a letter, takes ages. By the time I've got them all in the car, driven to the post office, found a space, got them out of the car, posted the letter and come back again, it takes an hour. I think, shall I bother? No, it's not worth it. Things like that, the sense of freedom, you take for granted."

Loss of status

The message society gives to mothers is very confused. On the one hand, girls are fed from infancy with the idea that an important part of their role is to be a mother, that it is worthwhile. Yet mothers are not valued and children are not liked. Women are educated and encouraged to pursue careers, yet working mothers are made to feel that they should be at home and are given precious little help with childcare.

Far from rewarding women for providing the next generation, they are punished. They are paid approx £10 child benefit a week, not taken seriously, made to sit in draughty family rooms in pubs and dingy corners of restaurants, and condemned to wrestling buggies up and down baby-unfriendly towns and cities. It is not surprising that many greet motherhood with a lowered sense of self-worth. Rose said, "Suddenly, being a mother meant I was treated very differently by other people, especially professional people like banks or estate agents – as if I was half brain dead or something. Very patronizing." Sophie used to be a civil servant. "I was proud of what I did, now I have no identity. I'm just a mother." Samantha said, "People think I can't discuss anything other than nappies or food. I'm a fairly intelligent person. I feel like saying, I'm not just a wife and mother. I'm me as well."

Mary said, "We could probably manage without him, but we would definitely fall apart without me." But she thinks her job is underrated in everybody else's eyes, "especially the government. When I go to functions with Jeff and people say, 'Well, what do you do?', I feel bashful about saying I stay at home. They look so crestfallen as they think I will have nothing to talk about." Children are no longer valued for their help, insurance against old age or as a sign of status, and becoming a mother is seen as a second-rate activity. We live in a work culture – we work to live. Politics, economics, commerce and industry are the real stuff of adult life. What you do is more important than who you are. To admit to *just* being a mother is to admit to being a boring non-person. Some, when asked the dreaded question, "What do you do?" answer with jobs they did before children.

Our society is one of individualism and enterprise. There are no rewards for caring activities, either for the old, the sick or children. In ancient societies, mothers were revered for their ability to procreate, and birth is still one of women's unique achievements. There would be no politics, economics or industry if women were not bearing the politicians, economists and industrialists of the future. Yet motherhood is seen as a handicap, mothers are actively excluded from the real adult world and the job title 'mother' is greeted with glazed eyes and stifled yawns. It is a testimony to the strength of maternal feelings that so many women rate motherhood in spite of the fact that 'only being a mother' has not been valued since the 1960s.

Fulfilment

Biological destiny

Biologically a woman's body is structured for pregnancy and childbearing: her pelvis, her breasts, her hormones, her monthly periods – everything is focused on that event. The sense of achievement in having fulfilled this biological destiny, of creating, sustaining and giving birth to life, can be one of motherhood's big rewards. At night, Linda would go in and look at her children and think "they're all mine, all my work". The creation, from the act of intercourse, to a 7lb baby nine months later is still one of life's great mysteries and to participate in it can be one of life's most powerful experiences. To hold a child that grew as part of yourself seems a miracle. Reproduction may be natural, but by doing it, human beings achieve a feeling of being supernatural, of being more that just a simple person.

Flora and her husband planned to have children soon after they were married. She got pregnant very quickly, but lost the baby with a ruptured ectopic pregnancy. For the following eight years she was in and out of IVF clinics trying to conceive. When she finally got pregnant with twins, "It was like a miracle and that's still how it feels [the twins are now eighteen months old]. I had this deep compulsion to have a child. It was a deep ache, like a hunger; completely irrational, but tied up with the idea of posterity, of being involved in life of fulfilling a biological destiny. The selfish gene."

It might fade, but mothers never lose the sense of having borne their children single-handedly – a memory which can be very empowering. Camilla felt "very proud of myself for having gone through pregnancy and labour. I think it makes you stronger mentally. If I now have something taxing like a job interview, I can steel myself by saying, 'I've done much harder things. I've been through labour, I've produced babies, I can jolly well go into a job interview.' I think women should be proud that they have produced children. It seems like such an easy thing. I used to think that anyone could do it. It makes you a much more complete person."

Many feel more effective and efficient after having a baby. In the sporting world it is more than just a feeling: research has confirmed that women who have babies make better athletes. Tony Buzan, the founder of the Brain Foundation who has made a twenty-five-year study of athletes and all aspects of their performance, concluded that one of their reasons for success is that they are far more capable of going through barriers. They can run further and further and do not feel pain. It is not physical, it is mental, born of a new attitude of mind.

Women do not normally regard themselves as clever or congratulate themselves on a job well done. But producing a baby can bring a positive self-evaluation and sense of self-worth. Motherhood connects women with a fraternity, not only of mothers of a similar age, but all mothers. Annabel said, "I think it's really nice when you're on a bus or in a shop and other women relate to you and your child because they know what it's like, they have been there. It makes me feel part of something that is continuing and good."

Fun to be with

"I thought I would be bored and frustrated. I wasn't. I was fascinated," wrote Carol Weston when her daughter was a few months old.[13] Women count on having to make sacrifices, but they do not count on babies giving so much back and on being completely won over. Babies can, even from an early age, be surprisingly entertaining. Beverly said, "I find her very good company, which is a surprise. I imagined all babies to be boring. She isn't. She's a lot of fun. She listens and doesn't miss a thing." Babies grow and develop and learn very quickly and being a part of that process can be very satisfying. The tiniest little thing they do can be totally absorbing – their changing expressions, their movements and how they examine even the most mundane object with total concentration.

Babies might bring back the childhood tempers and tantrums, but they also bring back the childhood wonderment. Kate said, "Just showing him things has brought a new perspective on the world and people, seeing things the way he sees them. Like things in the garden, things outside. He'll find something like snails and ask, 'What are these things?' It makes me reassess and gives me pleasure in things I would normally take for granted. Even shadows – we have great games with shadows. I remember as a kid being fascinated with shadows. But you forget. It is almost like he is taking me back. It's like a rediscovery of my own excitement in toys." Babies put their parents in touch with all the things they had forgotten about – toy shops, zoos, conkers, ducks, parks, autumn leaves take on a whole new meaning, or rather, reassume the meaning they once had. By singing nursery rhymes again, reading *Thomas the Tank Engine* or just being childish, life comes full circle and new (old) dimensions are opened up.

Changed priorities

Rebecca wanted a baby because she no longer wanted to be the most important person in her life. "I needed to have someone to care for. I had been spoilt for too long. I'm the youngest in a family of five, so I never had the opportunity of looking after siblings. I became aware in recent years that I was pretty spoilt. I had married late and had had a baby late. I was used to doing what I wanted when I wanted. I never had to answer to anybody and I think I was getting into bad habits. Occasionally, I'd be a bit petulant. I felt

I needed to grow up, to have somebody who truly depended on me." Rebecca now feels more complete, more tolerant and less self-centred. A dependent person can bring life new meaning, a new focus and changed priorities. Flora used to wake up in the middle of the night worrying about work, "I'd think, Oh God, I haven't done this, am I ever going to get this finished in time and what am I going to do in this important meeting. I couldn't begin to do that now. It's just not important and even if it was, I don't have the time or the energy to worry about it." Babies can be a recipe for a better life, they can make it fuller. Parents might be angrier than the childless, but they are also less depressed and unhappy for no obvious reason.[14] What mattered before no longer matters so much. Annabel said, "I think of the sort of life we led before we had children where we would be partying or going to see films and plays all the time, and it was really important to keep up with the latest things. It all seems so peripheral now, so transitory. When you have children you are actually dealing with people who are growing and developing and that seems much more important and rewarding."

Those who are not obviously maternal can find life's reevaluation very surprising. Georgia was a 'totally anarchic person'. She used to play the sax in a street band and was very political, going on demonstrations and being involved in campaigns. Since having children, "I no longer want to perform and I haven't been to a meeting or read a paper in nearly four years. I used to dash here and there and go to every film. I rarely do that now. They've changed my life and my focus. I am now ecstatically happy just sitting at the supper table looking at the children with my heterosexual partner in my bijou house. I think this is an achievement and a joy and I'm so happy. It's so bizarre that my joy should come from being a mother and the most mundane things are the most delightful; folding nappies and the first smile and all that icky stuff is the greatest." Beverly feels completely right being a mother. "I feel that is what I was made for. I never used to look at babies and wished I had one, but the second May came into the world, all that changed."

Regret

Past life, past selves
"Although I love Amy dearly", said Celia, "I have often wished that we had never had her – possibly for the first time in my life I am in a situation from which I cannot run away if the going gets tough, which it frequently does." While there are very few mothers who consider their babies a total mistake, there are many who have periods of regret, of wistfulness for their past life

and past selves. Melanie mourns "the people we used to be before we had our son – those Sundays when we would get up for a plate of bacon and eggs and go back to bed for the rest of the day. I sometimes feel I'd give anything to go and see a movie on a Sunday afternoon."

Feelings of overwhelming sadness are a common reaction to loss of any sort, and independence is no exception. Penny said, "There are days when I would love to go out on my own, even for five minutes just to put out the washing without somebody hanging on to my trousers saying, 'Mummy, Mummy, biscuit. I would love to lie in the bath, eat a bar of chocolate or read a book. If anyone had told me that I'd be fantasizing about having a bath or eating a bar of chocolate, I'd have thought they were a bit funny." Motherhood is a rite of passage and, like any life change it is a time of great gains and great losses. Freedom, spontaneity and irresponsibility are sacrificed, and grieving for going out late, sleeping all day, idleness, backpacking to India or even getting out of the house in less than 15 minutes is very common.

Emma felt wistful for things past like lie-ins, games of squash and being able to curl up with a book. "My reading is now done furtively when I go to bed or am on the loo. I actually hid behind the door once reading the last page. I could hear them both clamouring around the house for me and I just had to finish the last page." Ann's baby had been crying and crying, "I was rocking her and I looked out of the window. The neighbours are about 70 and they were walking around the garden looking at the flowers and having a chat and I was so jealous. I thought, I must be desperate, I am envious of 70-year-olds."

Birth is a rite of passage, but it is not really treated like one. Unlike marriage, there are no rituals of celebration or support, no stag night or hen night which mark the transition and emphasize the losses and gains. In other cultures becoming a mother is celebrated. The new mother is ritually initiated into her new role. She is granted new status and respect[15] and there is some evidence to suggest that transition to parenthood is more satisfying and a little easier in these societies.[16] The only post-birth ritual for the mother in this country is the six-week check – hardly a celebration. Rituals emphasize that life has changed, and while it is impossible to imagine how things will be after a baby, many think they will be the same as before. "We're not going to let them change us," say some, only to discover that babies change everything. Annabel and her family went to the United States for a four-week holiday on a house exchange. "It wasn't a holiday for the children at all. It was quite a stupid thing to do. Tony spent the whole time saying if we didn't have the kids we could do this, that and the other and when we come back in 15 years . . ."

Life after a baby is not the same with a few minor adjustments, and accepting that can be difficult. Caroline used to read, draw, go to the theatre and do keep fit. "Now, she won't let me do anything. You have a baby and you go home and you're supposed to be happy because a child is such a wonderful addition to life and there isn't any sacrifice. You do gain, but certainly lose in other ways. Somehow I thought I would have time. I don't know what I thought, I just didn't think it would be so severe, the loss of autonomy or of self-development."

When I was young . . .

Babies age you: overnight you become the next generation and have to make that jump to being more responsible, more grown up. No matter how old, this is when adolescence really ends and many feel truly adult. Rebecca is 38, "I've come of age. I feel like a settled, happily married MOTHER, whereas before I was a young career woman, and almost at whim could go off here, there and everywhere." Jane is 25 and felt like an "old woman. I've lost some of my bubbles. I have to be responsible for another life. You can't mess your life up any more, because if you mess your life up, you mess the child's up as well. I don't take any risks anymore."

Babies turn girls into women and the light-hearted, sex'n'drugs'n' rock'n'roll part of life becomes out-of-bounds. Being a mother and being responsible for a child means not taking any risks, being irresponsible or getting into dangerous situations – there is too much to lose. Attitudes change, outlooks become more realistic as idealistic parents discover that cars, washing machines and money are useful after all and that, like it or not, they are 'tied down'. Life can feel more set, set with partners, set in homes, set in jobs – set, comfy, cosy, dull and middle-aged.

Stabs of nostalgia and getting misty-eyed about former freedom is one thing, but actually reliving it is another. Fatima's children were getting on her nerves and she longed to drop everything and be free again, so she arranged for them to stay with a friend for the night. "I thought I'd love it, but I didn't. When it came to bedtime I had to pretend they were upstairs asleep before I could go to sleep. It was just horrible having no one around calling 'Mummy' or whingeing. When it's bad all I want to do is get rid of them and never see them again, but once they're gone it isn't a home anymore, it's just a house." Nothing is the same after children – not even freedom.

Protectiveness

The lioness

Beverly felt protective towards her daughter almost as soon as she was born. "In the hospital, we were next to a toilet where the window was kept open constantly and I kept thinking it would be so easy for someone to come in. The staff didn't patrol or anything, they were just in the reception where I couldn't be seen." Beverly did not sleep all that night, she was too worried someone would try to snatch her daughter. A baby is vulnerable and defenceless and it is only natural to want to protect them from danger, but the power of that feeling can take women by surprise. Rose said, "The oldest one was about two and we were at a playgroup. The other boy was the grand old age of four or something and he pushed Harold out of the Wendy house. I thought, I want to kill those children. I'd never felt this way before, so protective." "If you want to see a good punch-up, go to a One o'Clock Club." wrote Rosalind Coward,[17] because what really enrages mothers is when their child is hurt or wronged by another and the behaviour goes unpunished. Lyn's son "was pushing this tractor along and this three-year-old started bashing his hands to get him off. I looked at the boy's mum and she was just watching him. I went over to the boy and said, 'Daniel was pushing this first' and he said, 'But I want a go on it.' I said, 'Why don't you let Daniel push it a bit longer, he'll get bored soon?' He went storming off and I got this really evil look from his mother."

The root of this feeling is more than simply wanting to protect a child from danger, or wanting fair play. It is not even just sympathizing with a child's frustrations, it is feeling them as if they were your own. The bond between a mother and child can be so strong it can be difficult to acknowledge that it is a separate person. Any reaction to the child is also a reaction to the mother. The mother feels the hurt and the injustice as if it was directed against her. The pain when a child starts nursery or school comes not only from the mother having to let go, it is also her trying to protect her child from experiences she herself found painful. Rose said, "I felt desperately protective when he started nursery. He was perfectly happy and ran in and threw his coat off and said, 'See you later Mum', and I felt this real pain wondering if he would be OK, I felt even more upset when he started school recently. He is quite a tough, independent child, but to see him with all these seven- and eight-year-olds. He said, 'I feel really shy Mummy.' And I thought, 'Oh God, this is my boy.' It really gets to you."

Possessiveness

One of the strangest things about protectiveness is that it can well up even when there is no obvious threat to the baby's well-being. Lucy could not bring herself to trust anyone to look after or hold her twins "apart from my husband and he doesn't count. I can't bear people holding them or taking them away from me." Lucy is perhaps unusual in that her twins were born prematurely at twenty-eight weeks and, although they are now nine months, thinks her reluctance to 'let go' is tied up with her having to hand them over to strangers as soon as they were born. Nevertheless, extreme possessiveness is not at all uncommon. Many set out intending to be relaxed mothers who will share parenting only to find that something much more primitive and complex takes hold – an almost pathological protectiveness. Scarlet said, "I didn't like anyone else holding her apart from me and Mum. There was no way I was going to let anyone look after her or hold her. I was very frightened of her not bonding with me. I knew that I had bonded with her, but I was very frightened she wouldn't bond with me. I used to carry her in a sling everywhere, which was tiring. I remember reading somewhere that a baby knows its mother's smell by the time it is a week old and I thought, if she keeps on sitting on different people she's not going to know her mother's smell, so she had better just be with me." Motherhood can fulfil something very deep in many women, finding someone who really needs them and loves them. "I wanted them to love me, I don't just mean love me. I mean *me* alone," said one mother[18]. Sharing, even with the father, can be much harder than anticipated. Sue, whose son is sixteen weeks old, said, "When my husband plays with 'my' baby he flings him around and I feel like rushing over and taking him back. The baby loves it, he cackles with joy and yet I feel, 'no, no, no'."

Guilt

The perfect mother
Georgia said, "I felt I wasn't a good enough mother, that I wasn't doing it right. I blamed myself for feeling ratty if he cried or for crying myself and I cried whenever he cried for the first four weeks. I blamed myself for not being a complete saint and not always being cheery and energetic with him. When I got cross with him I felt inadequate because I thought I wasn't a good enough mother, because a good mother wouldn't get cross. I had this very strong image in my head." Women are bombarded with images – the ideal body, the ideal home, the ideal child – the ideal mother. A mother's duty is quite clear, to always be perfect. 'Good' mothers love breastfeeding, give birth easily, cook nutritious meals, are able to soothe their babies when they

cry, never get cross and, above all, have a boundless enthusiasm for creative play.

Cathy felt guilty because she should be "playing with them and doing creative things with them rather than shouting at them because I'm tired." Annabel felt sure she was not a good enough mother, "a pretty massive guilt to feel" as a good mother was one who "is very patient and understanding and always has a lot of time and makes models out of cardboard boxes." Sally felt anxious when she heard other mothers talk about "every day playdoh, painting, every day. I thought, Oh no, I don't do that with them." A good mother devotes herself to her children and really loves it; concentrates on their development and encourages them to realize their full potential by organizing endless stimulating and educational games.

Women want to be good mothers. They set out with the aim of giving themselves to their children selflessly, just like magazines and books say, only to find they do not enjoy their children in a way they thought they should. Heresy as it is to admit it, some find painting and playdoh a bit boring and some would rather do the cooking and cleaning instead; Caroline said, "at least the washing up doesn't answer back." Emma was 'ridden with guilt'. She said, "You are a bad mother if you put them in disposable nappies, a stupid one if you use towelling nappies. Just the pressure from the media, from ghastly magazines, from the different generation gaps – it's all pressure on this poor woman who has had this child and is trying to raise it in the best way she can. I have this monstrous book which my mother-in-law (an ex-nurse) gave me and it literally says 'at nine months your child will be . . .' and talks about potty-training in terms of you must do this and that. It can get you really worried."

The experts

"The experts are right – babies are born to be placid, contented creatures. It is only the bad mother repressing her resentment, holding the baby too tightly, too loosely, too often, too rarely, letting him cry, picking him up too soon, feeding him too much, too little, suffocating him with her love or not loving him enough – it is only the bad mother who is to blame."[19] Mothers feel guilty because the experts make them feel guilty. Intentionally or not, many books and magazines peddle the idea that mothers should always be available, always put their babies' needs first, have no needs of their own and aim towards a perfect form of relating with the baby. "A baby only wants what it needs," writes Penelope Leach. "If he gets it he is content. If he is content he demands no more until he needs more."[20] Her whole book, *Baby and Child*, is geared towards mothers and babies as units of pleasure-giving – fun for you is fun for her, and the more fun you have the fewer will be your problems. Presumably the less fun you have the more will be your problems. A mother's influence on her child is at the core of ideas on child-rearing today. Current thinking is very 'child-centred'. There is an awareness of the needs of the child which previous generations did not have. While writers like Leach focus on the child's mind, our grandmothers thought only of body and concentrated on exercise and fresh air. Influenced by Dr Frederick Truby King, mothers in the early part of this century were told that babies should not be 'spoilt', should only be fed once every four hours, should have no night feeds, should not be over-handled (a cause of indigestion), and should be given as much fresh air as possible. That Truby King based his theories on calves and was from New Zealand and therefore used to a kinder climate was neither here nor there, and women dutifully adopted his 'scientific' method, gritted their teeth through their babies' tears and aired them daily come sun, rain or snow. (Truby King's theories live on in the memories of grandmothers and mothers and surface in comments like "show the baby you are master", "let him cry it out, it's for his own good", "she's only crying because she wants attention"). The more 'natural' babies-should-lead-the-way views of Leach *et al* are in part a reaction to the perceived neglect of Truby King and his generation, but also reflect the ideal of 'early learning'. Our post-Freud generations have been made aware of the importance of the early years in terms of development, both educationally and psychologically; have been told that one false move with potty-training or the comfort blanket could result in a lifetime of emotional hangup.

What has been written about childhood in the last forty years (and more books have been written and sold on baby-care since 1945 than before) has stressed the need to recognize early development and stimulate the child. Clothing advice may be offered, but no one works themselves into a state over woolly Jaegers or healthy Aertexes anymore. Crying used to be something babies were taught not to do, now it is a worrying phenomenon that requires detailed analysis. Babies used to cry because they were wet, hungry or had wind; now, they are bored, lonely or fearful. Play used to be entertainment, it is now serious business: the right sort of attention turns babies into clever children.

While getting it right emotionally and psychologically is as important as getting it right morally and physically, the main responsibility for doing it falls on the mother. It is the mother who has to devote herself wholeheartedly to her babies to ensure a fulfilled intellectual potential and a balanced personality. It is the mother who is the child's first teacher, therapist, home manager as well as altruistic saint. Gone are the days when mothers spent their days getting the house cleaned, the shopping done, giving the child some fresh air and a bit of play. Contemporary ideals are much more exacting, drudgery and routine is not allowed. She must be providing full, stimulating attention, and one slip-up in the child's behaviour or educational failure is seen as proof that the mother's choices were wrong or that her mothering is wanting. Ann was concerned that her daughter had become a bit "smack happy". "I read a chapter in my Miriam Stoppard book which said that children learn aggressive behaviour and I thought, well, that's it then, it's me. I was with her during the day and my husband was only with her in the evenings, it had to be me, what have I done to her?" Most mothers realize that the perfect mother ideal is impossible to attain, but it does not stop them from feeling guilty.

What many forget is that while mothers and babies remain constant, advice on child-rearing, as the shift from Truby King to Leach shows, alters with the winds of social, philosophical and psychological change. Theories are theories for the moment, what is happening now will be replaced in years to come. Dr Benjamin Spock, the great childcare guru himself changed his mind several times on key points, toilet-training being one example. In the 1945 version of *The Common Sense Book on Baby and Child Care* he wrote, "I think that the best method of toilet-training is to leave bowel-training almost entirely up to your baby." By the late 1960s, he changed this to, "By the time your child is eighteen months old, I think you should begin his training even if there is no sign of readiness." Only to change his mind again in the 1970s with the view that training should take place entirely in the toddler's own time, even if it still had not happened aged three.

There are as many ways of bringing up children at any one time as there are mother and babies. Experts pay lip service to the psychological needs of children, but very little to the needs of mothers. Manuals are very useful for getting some understanding, but are not the truth. "They should be kept where they belong – as tools, not tyrants", wrote Christina Hardyment[21]. One mother of three described her use of Penelope Leach's *Mother and Child*, "For the first I read it cover to cover, for the second I dipped in and out, and for the third I used it to tap her over the head when she was naughty."

Loneliness

Out of the swim

Trisha felt very alone being stuck at home with a child. "I remember I didn't go out for weeks on end. We'd do the shopping at weekends and my husband took the car to work with him. Tom was a fine baby, he would sit and amuse himself. I remember thinking, 'I'm becoming a cabbage. I'm spending my life in front of the television.' I was expecting people to pop in, everyone visited just after I had him. But I was just left with the baby, the television and the radio." It is unrealistic to expect any one adult to look after a baby (let alone several) twenty-four hours a day, day after day, without enormous self-deprivation. In the days of the extended family, responsibility for children was shared, today it falls squarely on the mother and many new mothers are left alone to cope with their children without any help. They are deprived of adult company for six to eight hours a day, and may spend more than ten hours out of the twenty-four cleaning, washing, bathing and feeding.[22] Single mothers may have no adult to talk to for days on end. Fatima said, "I would go through whole weeks and wouldn't see anyone. Plus I wasn't on the phone and I would have to wait for someone to pop in on the offchance. The kids were around me and all I longed for was adult company and just the chance to talk normal."

Mothers bringing up their children virtually alone is a fairly recent concept. It first appeared with the rise of the Victorian middle classes which produced a growing group of women who could be supported by their newly well-off husbands. They didn't have to work outside and what with the servants, cooks, parlour maids and nursemaids there was precious little to do inside, other than mother. Motherhood became a vocation and a mother's job was to cultivate and discipline her children, "as a skillful gardener suits the seed to the soil".[23] Phrases emerged like 'the warm sun of motherhood' (1869) and 'true motherhood' (1875).[24]

Other trends have increased the separation and isolation of motherhood in our time. Husbands are away at work all day and often hardly see their children except at weekends. There is little or no everyday contact with extended families. A decline in community life and an increase in privacy means that mothers and babies are shut into isolated units of four walls. Friends no longer have babies at roughly the same time. Megan had only one friend who had a baby and she lived about a mile away, "None of the others were at the same stage as me, not working, at home with a small baby." Television has taken over as the main entertainment, and again mothers and children are shut away with it; *Watch with Mother* said it all – mothers and babies stay at home and sit together. And work has become all-important. People are tied to work, not home, and mothers who have been working can find home a very lonely place. Diana, who has one daughter aged eighteen months, felt very tearful in the early months. "I suppose it was being at home and not talking to anyone. I have always been in a job where I am with lots of people. I just found myself sitting there with the baby with tears in my eyes, thinking, Oh God, why am I doing this to myself." Loneliness is not just being stuck at home with a baby, it is feeling out of the swim of things.

Mother/baby groups

Meeting up with other mothers through mother and toddler groups set up by organizations like the National Childbirth Trust or 'Meet a Mum' can make a big difference to some women. Rose moved soon after the birth of her second son. "I knew no one. The only adults I spoke to were the ones in Waitrose." She joined an NCT group, "the reason for any remaining sanity I have. Sitting down with loads of other mums drinking coffee and talking about potty-training, nappies and the colour of pooh had filled me with horror, but then I went and realized how wonderful it was. You realize that someone else is going through exactly the same as you. It is very supportive." But mother and baby groups do not suit everyone. Mary found that the baby was too much of a focus, "You never find anyone who is interested in any of the things you're interested in, apart from the baby." Emma is not into "the NCT sort of thing at all." She said, "They're all like big girl guides who ask what your husband does. I know women who trot off every day of the week to some group or other. I can't bear them."

Motherhood today

Becoming a mother today is probably more difficult than ever before. In the past, mothers may have led arduous lives with their large unplanned families and lack of labour-saving gadgets, but there was an unselfconsciousness and a freedom from self-questioning which modern mothers no longer have. Motherhood is full of uncertainty and contradictions. Becoming a mother is no longer inevitable and automatic, it can be controlled; it no longer brings status, but instead turns women into faceless non-adults. Bringing up children is no longer a case of simply providing physical and moral care, mothers have to 'create a nurturing environment', 'develop a child's self-esteem', provide quality and listening time. Mothers are not told what to expect, yet are expected to know intuitively what to do and, more often than not are left to do it alone. They are bombarded with images of the perfect mother and the perfect baby, and carry the burden not only of child-rearing, but of being scapegoats for society's problems. In return for the difficulties, the passions and the anxieties, mothers get an indefinable kind of pleasure, a depth of satisfaction which for most, despite everything, is enough. For huge numbers of women, having children is the most satisfying and rewarding experience of their lives. A testimony to motherhood if there ever was one.

7

Body Imperfect

Just after Scarlet gave birth, she thought, "Thank God, I've got my body back. I'm human again. I felt so light, I felt about eight stone. I kept thinking, I've lost so much weight, I'm so thin, but I wasn't at all." After months of elasticated waists and baggy tops, losing sight of feet and pubic hair and getting stuck in the bath, a pregnant woman's fantasies turn to the moment of shedding the bump and reclaiming their former bodies. "I felt as light and as floaty as a feather", said Lee after her baby was born. "I felt about six stone. Then I looked in the mirror." She found that the reward for months of growing a baby was a stomach that looked like a "pickled balloon". Some women stride out of hospital wearing their size 10 jeans, but most cannot fit into pre-pregnancy pants, let alone the clothes they wore nine months before. The only women's bodies who snap back into shape after childbirth are those media celebrities, and that has more to do with personal trainers than elasticity. For the rest of us, who have only nature and five minutes here and there to do the odd sit-up, it can take as long as eighteen months for muscles stretched by pregnancy to regain their strength and for clothes to feel comfortable again.

A pregnant body goes through many changes. Abdominal muscles 'unzip' down the front, allowing the bump to expand. The average woman has 17sq ft of skin on her body, which stretches to 18.5sq ft by the ninth month of pregnancy. The distance from breastbone to pubis stretches from 13in to around 20in; waists increase from around 26in to 46in. Extra weight is laid down as reserves for breastfeeding, ligaments stretch, and the rib cage and pelvis expand. Samantha said, "I wasn't naive, I did expect to be saggy and baggy, but not this saggy and baggy. I thought it would be a couple of months and then it would go away, and here we are five months later, and it hasn't. Then I go through the 'My husband doesn't love me' 'I don't feel attractive, I don't put make-up on' stage – it can be quite miserable." Sarah "really thought I'd have this bump, and then the baby, and then I'd be back in jeans and back to normal. It's a real shock. Whatever programme you see on television – a soap like *Home and Away* or whatever – whenever someone's had a baby, as soon as she's had it, she's back to her original size. That was the thing that really surprised me – that it takes so long." It would be less misleading if new mother actresses exchanged their strap-on bumps for strap-on pot-bellies, but paunches are not the stuff of successful careers.

It is OK to be 'fat' and pregnant. Adjectives like 'blooming', 'ripe', 'fruitful', as well as feeling special and being the centre of attention help women through the body changes. Pregnancy can be a period when many, for the first time, like their bodies and the feeling of fullness, of being fertile and special. However this makes the time after the birth, when they feel empty, flabby and spent, all the more difficult.

Weight gain

In the first few days after giving birth, most women lose a stone – the weight of the baby, the placenta and amniotic fluid. An extra 2-3lbs is lost during the next week in excess fluid and extra blood volume. The uterus gradually shrinks from 2.2lbs to about 2-3oz during the first six weeks. But most women still find they weigh more than they did before. They are supposed to. At least 5lbs of fat is laid down for breastfeeding and is not meant to disappear overnight. But that does not stop women from getting depressed about being heavier. "My body shape has changed," said Jane. "I feel like a whale – so much fatter. I still can't get back into my jeans because I'm two stone heavier than I was. I never had a good self-image as I've always been plump, now it's even worse." In some cultures the 'rolls' of motherhood are respected and treated as a sign of maturity. Here they are 'middle-aged spread' or 'spare tyres'.

In our 'fat is ugly' culture, many grow up believing that their shape is the most important thing about being female, so losing it can be terrifying. The time it takes to regain a pre-pregnancy weight depends on how much was gained, but there is no reason why the weight gain has to be a permanent fixture, although sometimes the rib cage and pelvis which widen during pregnancy can stay wider after birth. Breastfeeding and the endless jobs involved in being a mother burns much of the extra weight up, but many find that even when they get back to their original weight it is distributed differently. Helen had her "skinny legs back, but I've still got a flabby tummy." Loss of muscle tone because of stretching and the abdominal muscles separating means that stomachs are necessarily more round and wrinkled than before.

Exercise will help to tone slack and stretched muscles and bring the abdominal muscles back to their former strength and tautness. However, the wrong exercise can do actual damage. Jogging and high-impact exercises can make weakened pelvic floor muscles even weaker, and for at least six weeks after the birth, ligaments are still relaxed and the back prone to injury.

Finding the time and energy to exercise and getting motivated are common problems for new mothers. Birth is in itself strenuous and exhausting, and rest and relaxation are as important as exercise in the early stages. Women who have been up all night and feel exhausted should put sit-ups after a rest. Overdoing things does more harm than good.

Weight loss

While some new mothers try to lose weight, others try to put it on. Georgia "ate and ate and ate, but Barney was draining me through my breasts. I lost a lot of weight and strength." Lyn, whose son is now eleven months old, said, "As soon as I had him I was only half a stone above the weight I was when I first became pregnant. By the time I stopped feeding him at eight months, I was six and half stone and looked it. I had been eating like a pig, but he was taking it out of me. I couldn't keep up." Breastfeeding burns up a 1000 calories a day and some mothers quickly burn through reserves. Their energy and vitality drain into the visibly swelling bodies of their babies, leaving them feeling like boiled chickens.

Georgia felt she was simply treading water. "I ate like a horse and drank about two pints of water in the night, but I just wasn't getting anywhere. I felt so miserable. I hated that feeling of being exhausted, of not being able to run for the bus. A few close friends have since said, 'You look dreadful in the photos' and they're right." Flora felt much older after having her twins and losing 12lbs while breastfeeding was part of that. "I felt sucked dry and so tired I was hobbling around the place like a ninety-year-old, practically clinging to furniture to stop me falling over."

Cutting down on feeds or weaning the baby are two solutions. But above all, feeding yourself good food, possibly combined with vitamins and mineral supplements can make the difference between being able to cope or not in the early months after childbirth. The nutritional demands of early motherhood are very high and yet there is pressure to lose all the extra pregnancy weight as soon as possible. Far from following nutritional advice, some new mothers starve themselves to get thin.

Breasts

"It's like having a bag filled up to the top with water – that's how boobs are normally – nice and pert and solid and firm." said Helen. "You start breastfeeding and there's 120 per cent or 130 per cent in there – really swollen. Then, suddenly you stop breastfeeding and not only do you lose the extra 30 per cent, but another 30 per cent on top, so you're left with 60 per cent of what was there." Breasts are not the same after having a baby. It is not so much the actual breastfeeding that is responsible for sagging bosoms, but the preparation for breastfeeding. Breasts are neither muscle nor ligament; they are mainly fat with a small amount of glandular tissue. By the end of pregnancy, some of the fat under the skin of the breasts has been absorbed and the milk-producing glands have grown and developed, stretching supporting tissue. After birth, not all the tissue is replaced so even non-breastfeeding bosoms can sag (although non-breastfeeding nipples will not look chewed as breastfeeding ones sometimes can). A support bra is thought to help, but unlike muscle, breast tissue does not fully recover once stretched.

Lyn's bosoms are not what they were. "Instead of going out, they go down like a dog's nose. I used to look at women who had them and think, what horrid boobs, and now I've got them." As the ideal breast is pneumatic, adjusting to the deflating of early motherhood can be difficult. Lyn is still grieving over her breasts: "I am annoyed. I really liked my boobs. They were probably my best feature. Before, Jeff would only have to blink and they were there – they were my pride and joy. Now I don't really like him seeing them" Ann said, "My breasts were my best feature. I never worried about them. I think they're still the same bra size, so they're still there, but they're wider somehow and more floppy. I had a bath the other night and I looked at myself in the mirror and thought, Oh God, I feel sick." Her husband tried to reassure her by saying they looked like 'spaniel's ears' which, not surprisingly, did not help. Sex goddesses have 'melons' or 'peaches', not dog's ears.

Becoming a mother is the ultimate in womanliness, but the post-pregnancy loss of firmness can make many feel less feminine – particularly as support bras with their wide straps and sensible colours are never sexy. Ann said, "I don't ever think I'll have frills on my underwear again. They don't seem to come on anything that fits the shape I'm now in."

Although there are no exercises for the breasts themselves, it is possible to improve the strength of the pectorals, their supporting muscles. Breast-toning exercises will not prevent breasts from dropping, but they will improve posture, which is an important factor in determining the position of breasts on the chest wall.

Different-sized breasts can be another hazard of breastfeeding. Feeding from one side more than the other because of infection or preference can lead to a lack of symmetry which tends to resolve itself once breastfeeding is stopped. However, recovery can take time.

Hair

Wendy's hair came out in handfuls after her daughter was born. "I'd read somewhere that you lost a bit, but I couldn't believe how much. It wasn't until about three months after that I noticed." Two to four months after having a baby a woman's hair starts to moult. Normally, between 70 and 100 hairs are lost and replaced every day. During pregnancy, because of hormonal changes, hair loss is not as great. By the ninth month women hardly lose any hair, which is why pregnant hair tends to be thick and glossy. After birth, the excess hair which would have been shed, falls out. Breastfeeding delays the process until two to four months after weaning. In some cases, particularly after a problematic labour involving severe blood loss or distress, women can lose up to half the amount of hair on their head. Hair like any part of the body needs nutrients to sustain it and energy for it to grow. Any deficiency in the body makes hair a low priority and the nutrients are diverted elsewhere.

The frontal areas, particularly the temples, suffer from post-partum hair loss and new hair which grows back can look a bit stumpy at first. Wendy could see where her new hair was growing back. "It's like I've got a small fringe under my fringe. My Mum commented not long ago, 'The hairdresser's cutting your hair awfully funny these days.'" The thicker the hair the more noticeable the hair loss.

Lank hair is another post-natal complaint. Hair, like the mother, can look worn out. Again, hormones, stress and diet are responsible – a couple of weeks of not sleeping or skipping meals will soon register in hair.

Hormones can also make curly hair go straight after a baby. Five months after Ann's daughter was born, her thick and curly hair went straight and lifeless. "I had this flat, limp thing on my head. I couldn't do a thing with it. I had it permed in the end I was so depressed about it. You can hide stretch marks or a fat tummy, but hair you can't hide – it was just sitting there. It felt like a loss of youth." Doctors in particular underestimate the importance of hair to a woman's self-image. Celia's big problem with motherhood was just that. "The one thing I always thought was great was that I could just wash my hair and it would curl into place. The one time I didn't want to be running around sorting it out was when she was born. I still have to use heated rollers to make my hair manageable. If I had been depressed that would definitely have tipped me over the edge."

Many are driven to cut hair, thinking, wrongly, that it will help lank hair recover and grow. A trim will make hair look thicker, but it will not increase the growth rate. Provided a woman is eating well and taking care of herself, hair will recover, but it does take time.

Skin

The hormones of pregnancy affect each woman's skin differently. Greasy skin may develop dry patches once pregnant. If it was dry, the opposite may happen. For some, pregnancy can be a time of clear and blooming skin. "My skin was great during pregnancy", said Caroline. "Now it's all cloudy and spotty." Hormones which made skin bloom during pregnancy can make it dry and patchy after. Rebecca developed a red nose which her doctor said was a type of acne. "I've always had a bit of a problem with it anyway, even before I was pregnant, but after the baby it came on with a vengeance – this bright Rudolph nose and butterfly patches either side. It doesn't really get me down. It just looks a bit silly, like I've been drinking very heavily." Post-natal skin problems such as dryness, rashes, spots and patches of eczema are common and normally fade after a few months.

Some women develop dark patches of pigmented skin on their faces during pregnancy. Cholasma or the 'mask of pregnancy' – brown patches on the bridge of the nose, cheek and neck can be particularly noticeable on women with dark hair and is made worse by sunlight. Deeper pigmentation affects nearly every woman particularly in areas that are pigmented already – freckles, moles, the areolae of breasts, genitalia, the skin on the inner side of thighs, underneath eyes and in armpits may become darker too. A dark line called the Linea nigra often develops from the navel to the pubic bone. It marks the division of abdominal muscles which separate slightly to accommodate the expanding uterus. After birth pigmentation, particularly of the areolae and the Linea nigra, can remain darker for some time, but over the months it gradually fades and disappears. Spider veins are also common in pregnancy. All blood vessels in pregnancy become sensitive – rapidly dilating when hot and contracting quickly when cold. Consequently tiny broken blood vessels called spider veins may appear on the face, particularly on cheeks. They fade soon after delivery.

The same is true of stretch marks. Some can have as many as five pregnancies with no stretch marks, others have them after one. Hormones relax collagen fibres in the skin as well as ligaments. The skin's elasticity which determines just how much it can stretch before thinning and leaving marks varies from one woman to the next. Breasts, abdomen, buttocks and thighs are particularly prone. Stretch marks occur deep down in the lower layers of skin. Massaging oils and moisturisers won't prevent them, but it can help skin feel better. Stretch marks start out red, but after birth gradually fade to a pale silver.

Old, fat and frumpy

"I always felt fit and vital, now I feel old and tired," said Ann. With hair falling out, skin feeling dry, lack of sleep, collapsed bosoms, a slack belly and no time to primp and preen, women can feel that with each pregnancy, their looks hurtle five years on. The smooth pearliness of their baby's skin accentuates the grossness of their own bodies. Sentences begin, "When I was young. . ." Alison, aged 29, said, "Everyone used to say that I looked a lot younger than I really was. Now I look my age or older and it really gets to me. I think it's because people see you with two children and immediately think you are older. I don't get enough sleep, so I obviously look more tired than I did and I've put a little bit of weight on and am not so bothered with the way I look."

It is not so much that having a baby actually accelerates ageing, it is just that our society is ageist. Youth is worshipped and fresh young firm flesh is the ideal. Models retire in their mid-twenties and, rather than seeing grey hairs and wrinkles as marks of experience and maturity, women feel they are heading down a long and depressing decline. As long as youth is the epitome of physical perfection and women's bodies are seen as commodities, many women will worry about the effects of pregnancy on their bodies. Caroline thought Mother Nature cruel, "You go through all that and all you get is a knackered body. It's like you've done your bit, served your purpose, you've reproduced and you don't have to look attractive anymore – you're past it." Participating in nature's processes can leave its mark and like the salmon who die after spawning, mothers can feel relegated to the scrap-heap. They become more self-conscious of their 'imperfect' bodies and dread having to expose them in public. Caroline said, "I used to casually strip off with my friends and go swimming or to the sauna, and I don't feel I can do that now, because of my sagging breasts and pot belly. I feel my body is not as in good shape as theirs now." Samantha used to be proud of her body: "I didn't really show it off, but I knew it was there. I used to swim and do kinetics and yoga, and it was very important to me to have a nice figure. Now it's awful. It's the worst thing about being a mother."

A new mother's confidence in her attractiveness can be severely dented. The days of silk blouses and sheer tights are gone. She no longer has her 'blooming' pregnant body, but neither does she have her old one back. She feels as if she is in limbo or worse, that she looks like 'a mother' and mothers have a poor body image. For Camilla, 'a mother' was someone who "walked around Sainsbury's with ten children and they're all fat and their hair all greasy." Melissa described a mother as "overweight, not interested in clothes, hair a mess, no make-up, lack of self-esteem." Lyn said, "Uniform: the black moccasin shoes, leggings or M&S navy blue trousers, big jumper – ugh! They're like peas in a pod, you can spot them a mile away – 30 going on 50, as if all the youth and fun had been taken out of them. All have the same hair style, either shoulder-length or short. No sense of adventure, just boring and prim."

For many, mother equals fat, frumpy and downtrodden, which is why Lyn rebelled. "Not so much at being one as being seen as one," she said. Just after her son was born, she had her long hair cut shot because it was getting in the way. She did not want to look 'mumsy', so she dyed it red. Wrestling with the image of mother and adapting it to suit personal tastes is part of trying to resolve the tension between still being the same person, but also knowing that life has changed. Buying new clothes after birth or changing a hair style is partly practical, but is also tied up with looking (or not wanting to look) the part, it is taking on a new identity.

Younger mothers in particular can find squaring the image of being a mother with how they used to be confusing. When Monica, aged 21, was pregnant she put on a lot of weight and wore 'frumpy' dresses and tried to look old. "I don't know why, perhaps it was because I was a bit embarrassed about being so young and pregnant." After her son was born she decided that she wanted to be young again. She lost four and half stone and is now thinner than ever. Being a mother does not have to mean looking 'old'. Fatima, aged 23, was out shopping with her two children when she bumped into a girl she had met at a nightclub. "She said, 'Whose kids are these?' I said, 'Mine'. She said, 'Get lost, you've got no kids.' Then the oldest wanted something off me and she called me Mummy and she looked at me in amazement. She couldn't believe I was going out and all." Not looking the part made Fatima feel proud, but also guilty. "I thought that maybe I should look like a Mum. Like someone who doesn't mess around, who doesn't wear make-up or care about how they look." The image of the frumpy, fat mother is for some a powerful reminder of how they do not want to be. Helen was keen not to let herself go. She said, "I didn't want to look run down or like I couldn't cope. If I was to leave the house looking a complete mess I wouldn't feel confident, so I wouldn't cope anyway. Camilla felt that going out with unwashed hair or getting fat was a sign that a woman had given up. "I don't think it's necessary. It's not all to do with lack of time, it's to do with lack of self-esteem. I don't want to let the fact that I've got two children get me down or stop me from looking attractive. It's important to me, it's a measure of how well I'm coping."

Body beautiful

"I think that being a mother is a very majestic, fine thing," said Catrina. "It doesn't mean being downtrodden, it is a privilege." For some, the body changes do not matter. They are a consequence of being a mother and being a mother means having a baby and having a baby means a world of pleasure. Feeling old is part of the patterns of life: mother and child, youth and maturity. Catrina felt better about her body than ever before because she felt better about herself: "I have a greater sense of my role in life, both as a woman and a mother. I feel more confident and assured." Frances did not "give a damn" whether her hair was unwashed or her breasts were beginning to sag. "For the first time in my life I don't care what people think of me. I was never an attractive teenager. I was gauche and shy and not at all like the images of teenagers going out and having a good time, boyfriends and things like that. In my 20s I was shy as well. There was always these images of how a female should be and I never felt I fitted into them, except perhaps when I was doing well at work in the 80s, when there was the cult of the career woman. Now I've had my baby none of that seems to matter. My body has done what it's supposed to do, it has produced a baby and I feel proud of that." For Georgia, motherhood meant feeling comfortable with looking softer and more feminine, "Before I was a political being and as such I was an asexual being – I had very short, almost shaved hair. After having Barney I let my hair grow, partly because I didn't want to go and have my hair cut every two months, but also because I felt more girlie, more female."

Creating life can be so much more important than vanity. Babies can be far more important than new clothes or stretch marks. Priorities change. Flora used to enjoy window-shopping and buying clothes. "Now I haven't bought any new clothes since I was pregnant. I'm not bothered by it. I've got lots of clothes and I can keep wearing them until they fall apart. I feel the twins should now have the attention and the clothes. There is a sense of passing on, they are more important now."

8

Sex

The Wasteland

Joke: expectant father to obstetrician, "How long after the delivery, doctor, may we resume sexual intercourse?" Obstetrician: "Most men wait at least until the placenta has been delivered" A health information leaflet: "Couples used to be advised to wait until the post-natal check-up before starting to make love again, but it is now generally accepted that a couple can begin to make love earlier." [1]

It is all very misleading. While for some childbirth is a minor hiccup in their love lives, it is not at all unusual for a regular sex life not to have resumed six months after the birth. A year is still quite common. According to a survey in *She* magazine, one in four of the women with children under two who responded were only having sex once or twice a month.[2] Forty per cent of the first-time mothers seen by Ann Herreboudt, a London post-natal counsellor, have no sexual relations with their husbands for up to two years after birth.

Babies are born from sex, but are sometimes the death of it. After birth, many enter a sexual wasteland; they have no sexual fantasies, desires or erotic dreams. "It's like someone has turned off a switch and I'm waiting for it to be turned on again," said one woman. There is a growing recognition of the effects on a woman's libido of having a baby, but it is usually dealt with euphemistically. Ante-natal classes may hint at 'tiredness' and the importance of making time for husbands. Magazine columns may touch on the subject, but jolly it along and concentrate on the physical aspects: the soreness and the exhaustion. "Don't worry if post-natal sex isn't great." reassures one woman's magazine. "The vagina doesn't lubricate as well just after birth, and if you've had stitches you can feel some discomfort for ten to twelve weeks after."[3]

Women expect sex to be on hold for a few weeks while they recover from labour, but even when the stitches have healed, many still do not want to make love. They expect some discomfort but are not prepared for the total shutdown, or for how long that feeling can last. Exhaustion and soreness do play a part, but post-natal celibacy goes much deeper than the purely physical. Sex is part of something much wider, it is part of adjusting to the different roles and the complex psychological changes that women go through when they become mothers.

Soreness

Lynn had a caesarean and was "a bit frightened to have sex, what with all the stitches and my husband is quite a tall chap – 6ft. I didn't really want all that weight on me." The painful after-effects of birth interfere with sex. Forceps, stitches, painful breasts and even a 'normal' delivery can take time to recover from (see Chapter 3), and pain can be felt from penetration weeks, even months after labour. Sally went to her GP eight months after her baby was born because every time she tried to make love she felt sore and uncomfortable. "He was so reassuring. He said I still looked a bit red, but that it was quite normal and healing could sometimes take up to a year." Lee had had no stitches, but was 'sore every time we tried and so painful, I just tensed up'. This was three months after the birth. She went back to her GP suspecting that the scar from her first baby had torn internally. Her GP referred her to a consultant, who again said the soreness was common. She was given some cream which moisturized the area and it cleared up in six weeks.

But doctors are not always so sympathetic. Wendy, who contacted AIMS after 25 visits to GPs because of her sore episiotomy, told her (male) doctor that her love life was "virtually non-existent". "Your poor husband," was his response. 'We must get that sorted out then you'll start to feel normal. Get your old man to rub in some local anaesthetic cream and get him to stretch it. You can't leave him much longer, poor chap."[4] Loss of sexual interest is seen by some as a problem which women have to solve for their husband's sake.

All stitches cause soreness, but painful sex is a price some women have to pay for badly stitched episiotomies and tears. Melissa, aged 29, had a tear after the birth of her son, now seventeen months old. "When I was stitched, they didn't do it straight away and they did it too tightly. When I tried to make love, it felt like I would split. The doctor said the only way round it was to have sex and for it to hurt one more time before it healed up again." Annie's first attempts at sex were cautious and difficult. The reason was eventually diagnosed at a coil check. Her tear had been badly stitched, had not fully healed and had grown back incorrectly leaving a ridge. Annie had to go back to hospital, was recut and restitched.

Exhaustion

As far as Scarlet was concerned, sex was a valuable loss of sleeping time. "Any little bit of time I had to myself I just wanted to sleep. Any sex time, I would think, 'I just want to sleep, this is taking twenty minutes and that's twenty minutes of sleep.' And I'd get myself into a right old state about it, thinking, 'He's going to wake up in a minute and I'm only going to have ten minutes sleep'." Lack of sleep and fatigue is a big factor in loss of libido. The totally spent feeling that follows labour, the dragging tiredness of the early months and the exhaustion of answering the demands of a toddler mean that, when it comes to sleep or sex, many women nod off before they have time to even debate it.

She magazine advises mothers to "Do it anywhere – on the table, on the floor, on the dishwasher – just not in bed. Ever. Because for about two years after having a baby you fall asleep the moment your head touches the pillow."[5] Whether mothers would have enough energy to climb on the table is another matter, but many, like Heather, "have an uncanny knack of being able to crawl into bed, put my head on the pillow and fall straight to sleep." Despite heated arguments with her husband, sleep remains her top priority. "Basically, I'll say, 'Go away, I've got to get up again in a couple of hours' time. I'm going to sleep.' I'm afraid when I'm trying to work, trying to look after the kids and the rest of it, there are times when I'm going to sleep, regardless of what anyone else says." Sex becomes yet another demand, rather than a pleasure or a refreshment.

My body is my own

The birth itself can leave some women feeling violated and exposed. The medical intrusions – internal examinations, breaking the waters, caesarean or forceps, being stitched up, being prodded by nurses, doctors, midwives with "open your legs", "show me your tummy" – affect sex afterwards. Kate felt her body had been medicalized. "I felt very protective towards my body. I wanted to keep it intact. It became public property. I was manhandled by complete strangers, and then you're stitched up and afterwards the midwife comes along and pulls open your legs and takes the stitches out. I just wanted to be left alone."

Dreams of men in masks with sharp knives crowding around open legs, and memories of violent and traumatic births can haunt even the most unsqueamish of women. Having a baby means losing control: bodies are consumed by contractions, anybody can do what they want with you, and after, in a more subtle way, normal 'boundaries' are being breached by bleeding and leaking milk. There is a need to re-establish a sense of self and to rebuild boundaries around a woman's body violated both by birth and after.

Helen Simpson wrote, "For once no one was touching her. Like Holland she lay, aware of a heavy ocean at her sea wall, its weight poised to race across the low country. The baby was now three months old and she had not had more than half an hour alone since the birth in February."[6] Much of the giving of a new mother is with her body – hugs, comfort, milk. It can feel that a woman is being taken from all day, and sex is just something more to be given or taken. By the end of the day they are all kissed out and even a cuddle can feel like another demand. Rose has three boys under five. "They're very physical and climb on me a lot. They pull at me and need cuddles and their bottoms need wiping and they need to be fed and dressed. The physical demands are very high. It's as if my nerve endings have had enough and for Andrew to then come home with all the signs that he would like to go to bed, I just think, Oh no, I can't stand it. Someone else is going to be pulling at me and pawing me." A new mother can feel she has no space to herself during the day and that it is being invaded again in the evening. Someone else is making demands on her body and her time, so up go the castle gates.

Mother/lover

After birth, a woman can still think her husband is the most perfect person alive, but her body does not agree. Her body thinks the baby is. Babies bring many physical pleasures: the cuddles, the sweet smelling softness of their skin, the warmth and closeness of being next to them. And they are so helpless. All this can do strange things to a woman's sense of priorities. "Phoebe is more important than Dan," said Scarlet. "When she was born she was so tiny and vulnerable and I thought this is my baby, even though it's his as well. I'd guard her with my life. It's very intense." The passion of a new mother for her baby can be all-consuming and the love for a baby can sometimes be love enough. "This was a complete love I would die for. I didn't need any more love. I didn't feel sexy at all. I didn't have any physical desires and the baby fulfilled all the other bits – the cuddling and the touching," said Scarlet. Breastfeeding women, in particular, often feel totally satiated.

Lyn said, "Breastfeeding is comforting. It's a very nice feeling. It's not sexual at all, it's like sex without the sex."

Babies are small, pink and hairless. In comparison, men can suddenly seem big, gross and off-putting. Breasts can 'belong' to the baby and having them fondled by someone else can feel all wrong. To only want to kiss the baby and not the husband, is tied up with the intense physical and emotional involvement some women have with their babies. Boundaries blur and it is no longer clear where the baby stops and the mother begins. Resuming a sex life is part of separating from the baby and re-establishing an identity.

Reconciling the new role of mother with the old one of lover can feel strange. Beverly said, "I remember one occasion when we had sex and straight after, the baby woke up and I had to feed him and that felt very odd. You know, my husband was sort of lying there recovering and I was sitting beside him feeding the baby. It felt very strange." Frances needed space after feeding her baby at night. "I really need that transition space, even if it's just half an hour, when I've finished one role and before going on to another." It is needed in an emotional sense, but very much in a physical sense too.

In our society women tend to be viewed in two roles: whores (sex symbols) and mothers. Because a sexual mother is a 'bad' mother (until very recently in Britain prostitutes' babies were put into care), women can feel inhibited about sex after a baby. They are afraid of being disturbed and are put off by their baby's presence in a way men are not. Lucy could not even have the baby's things, let alone the baby, in the same room when she made love. Nappies, toys and clothes were an "instant turn-off". Sexual excitement can seem a potential threat to a baby: if she gets too wrapped up in her own arousal, she will not hear her baby cry; if a woman is attracted to a man, she will be putting her own needs before her child's. Women want to play it safe, to retreat, to keep on the straight and narrow. The risk-taking that is part of sex can seem out-of-bounds. Monica still felt de-sexed a year after the birth of her son. She put it down to "being grown-up now and not so young and carefree. You change, have responsibilities – house, working – you just grow up and the lack of sex seems to be a part of that."

"You never get any looks when you're out with a pram," said one woman, confirming the fact that 'good' mothers are not deemed sexy. The sexy girl who becomes a mother has to adjust, not only to the demanding role of mothering, but also to being seen as markedly less exciting than formerly. The message starts in pregnancy. While pregnancy clearly labels the woman as sexually active, mothers and mothers-to-be are not seen as being sexual. Demi Moore naked on the cover of *Vanity Fair* would have caused a sensation. Demi Moore naked and seven months pregnant caused an outrage. Sex, when it switches from seducing to producing, has to be hidden behind maternity frocks. Julie said, "Brian and me had only been married six months when I got pregnant. We were at it like a couple of rabbits. Suddenly, I was pregnant and that was it, I was untouchable. I was fat and he hated me on sight." But then, "I went through nine months of near enough celibacy and then, after, I've got this baby to feed, I've got sore nipples, I'm stitched up to the eyeballs and suddenly I'm attractive, although I'm lying there thinking I look like death."

Slim and trim is sexy and some new mothers with their flabby tummies, stretch marks and swollen (but the wrong swollen) bosoms do not feel attractive. They just do not fancy themselves anymore. Lee did not want sex because she no longer felt desirable. She had not been with her second husband long before she got pregnant. With her older children and her first husband it had not mattered, "He would accept me whatever I was like." But because she didn't feel confident about her second husband's feelings, Lee thought "I've got to get my figure back so he'll like me."

Some women feel less sexy and desirable after childbirth because they feel stretched and more 'roomy'. Pelvic floor exercises can help tighten vaginas, but mothers never quite return to their pre-pregnant state, an adjustment which is not helped by social pressure. "Making love to a mother is like waving a flag in space," goes the saying. Keep your vagina 'honeymoon fresh' urges the pro-caesarean propaganda in Brazil.[7] While the 'husband's knot' – an extra stitch sewn in the perineum after an episiotomy to restore the vaginal opening to a virginal state – is now history, women's sexuality is still seen in terms of male pleasure.

'You can help yourself by taking a long, lingering time over sex to make sure you are relaxed and lubricating properly,' advises one pregnancy and birth book.[8] As many will discover this is easier said than done. Lyn and her husband still make love, "But it's much more textbook than it used to be. You haven't got time to plan ahead and make a posh dinner and have the candles and the wine and the sexy underwear. That doesn't fit in with life at the moment. All the thrills have gone and if we're actually doing it at least that's something, better than nothing. Whereas before it was all like a game, making up ideas and thinking up things and getting the ball rolling. Now, it's let's do it quick." At a time when many feel de-sexed and unattractive, being seduced and courted again can be important, but finding the time can be hard. There is sex after birth. Lust does return, but sometimes not until after the baby is weaned, after the mother is rested, after her body is her own again.

A 'natural' shutdown

There is another way of looking at post-natal celibacy and that is as a natural, perfectly normal response which makes complete biological sense. The baby is vulnerable and dependent and needs high-intensity care. The mother's total preoccupation with it to the exclusion of all else could be behaviour that has evolved to meet that need. If breastfeeding, biologically a woman's body switches off sex. A hormone prolactin is released during breastfeeding and this inhibits the production of oestrogen, and a lack of oestrogen makes a vagina feel dry, which will affect a woman's enjoyment of intercourse.[9] Breastfeeding also inhibits ovulation and it has been suggested that the prolactin may suppress the woman's libido.[10]

Women are not designed for sex after childbirth. Sex means reproduction and the last thing a woman who has just had a baby wants is another baby. Abstinence makes reproductive sense; the wider the intervals between births, the heavier and healthier the babies (the World Health Organization recommends a gap of at least eighteen months between pregnancies).[11] Cultures like the Yoruba people of Nigeria traditionally abstain from sex for three years after childbirth, and it is claimed that the Dani people of Indonesia have a four- to six-year period of post-partum celibacy.

In our distant past we were hunter-gatherers, and as hunter-gatherers we were also a polygamous race. Women were left alone with their babies, were nurtured by other women and did not have to bother about the partners' sexual needs – The men, presumably, would be satisfying their libidos elsewhere. This is a set-up that contemporary women riddled by guilt may occasionally wish was not so distant. Rose told her husband to, "Go and have an affair, if it makes you feel better. Just don't tell me about it." Such bravado talk in a culture built on polygamy is one thing, in ours with its emphasis on Christian family life and lifelong togetherness it is a different matter. Rose added, "But I'd kill him if he did." Our bodies might still think we're hunter-gatherers, but our values tell us to be faithful spouses. Women preferring to be celibate after childbirth and men wanting to be as active as ever is a behavioural pattern that makes biological sense, but does not necessarily make for an easy life (see Chapter 7)

Better than ever

Some mothers find sex changes for the better. It might be less often, but it is more pleasurable and satisfying. Maggie has felt physically more responsive since having her babies. "I don't think there was anything actually wrong before, but it's easier now, more comfortable." Giving birth gave Georgia a feeling of power. "On the strength of having given birth and had that amazing, physical, powerful, but not at all sexual feeling, I am more confident. I feel I can be on top more, can be more feminine."

Creating a child can bring couples closer and sex can take on a new meaning, a new depth and intensity. Equally sex for sex's, rather than a baby's, sake can be liberating. Trisha said, "Now that we've had our three children and we don't intend to have any more, I would say we actually make love now rather than have sex and it's far more enjoyable."

9

Partners

For better, for worse

Sue thought the baby would cement their relationship. "We'd always been a very romantic couple and I thought the baby would be a perfect blending of each of us. In reality it's hard work. I don't feel like a couple any more, just a family group." We are told that children bring happiness, which they do, but statistics also show that, when children arrive, the relationship between the partners dips and dips, hitting rock bottom when the children reach adolescence. The relationship starts to improve once the children have left home.[1] While couples might know in principle beforehand that having a baby will mean less money, less sleep, less sex and less time for each other, they have no way of knowing just how dramatic and deep-rooted the changes will be.

Children are seen as the icing on the wedding cake, the *raison d'être* for a relationship. In some ways they are. Melissa felt more united with her husband. "I look at the baby and he's a product of our love. We made him together." Alison felt much closer to her husband, "The children have given us a common focus. We'll sit down and talk now whereas before we were always out doing something." Four years ago Frances and her husband were estranged, "I got too work-orientated and wasn't giving my fair share to the house or the marriage. Since the baby, we have refocussed more on being a family, which is much nicer." Babies can consolidate relationships, give them a new sense of purpose and commitment, and turn a couple into a family, but they also carry a price. "We never used to argue until the children were born" is a common complaint. Sandra said, "We never seem to have any time to ourselves. We argue more, and there is a stress there all the time – probably 60 to 70 per cent of it is from the children."

A baby changes the balance in a relationship, it tests the ability of the partners to adapt to their new roles and it exposes any existing weaknesses in the relationship. Babies can't be fitted around the edges of life, and couples can't pretend that there is no change and that life can go on as before. Hannah and her husband tried to keep up the "façade of happy families". She said, "I didn't tell anyone for a long time that I wasn't getting on with Charlie after the baby. Then I realized that every other mother around me was doing exactly the same thing and once one person mentioned it, they all mentioned it and then it's a great relief." Knowing that it is normal to argue after having a baby can help couples adust to being both partners and parents; as can taking the long-term view. The relationship was there before the children arrive and will still be there once the children have left.

Mother/father: adapting to roles

A life in common or a common life

The 1662 Book of Common Prayer gave the function of marriage as 'procreation' – children were its purpose. Today, we expect more. We expect mutual help, comfort and support. We want partners to be lovers and friends. We rely on each other, are expected to be everything to each other and sometimes those expectations are very much in conflict with the role of parents. Emma and her husband "only ever want to be together". She said, "We enjoy each other's company a great deal – that's why I married him. As well as being my mate, he's my best friend, he gives me everything. I enjoy talking to him, I enjoy being with him, I like all the pastimes we do together – I like to do everything with him and the children sometimes get in the way. As much as I love them, it doesn't get any easier. But it's happened over such a long time that I'm accepting it now, not willingly, but just because it's a fact." Couples who live 'a common life', who rely upon each other, have few other friends and find their identity within the marriage can find having children harder to cope with than those who live a 'life in common' – couples who have a strong identity outside the partnership and who do not depend on each other for everything. The latter are more likely to have outside support and find children less of a threat to the intimacy between them than common lifers.[2]

Birth unites, babies divide

Equality, in particular, is something that is severely tested when someone becomes a parent. In most relationships today equality is an issue. Before babies there is the façade at least that men and women are equal. Both can be earning, independent, and have time for themselves and others. Aside from obvious biological difference they are similar. The illusion continues through pregnancy. Pregnancy and birth can be a time of heightened

114

togetherness. Couples are often drawn closer together and, although it is the woman who is pregnant, there can still be a sense of going through it together. Men attend ante-natal classes and are encouraged to 'participate' in the birth. There can be a golden image of sharing – sharing the experience and sharing the responsibilities; all will be shared. Then something inextricably changes the moment women give birth. Gender differences open up; equality is blown away like a biological bomb. It does not matter how independent the woman was, or how 'new mannish' the man, as soon as babies arrive, women are cast as homemakers, men as breadwinners and the inequality and resentment starts.

Fathers, who expected to be fully involved, discover that birth for men is really a spectator sport with ringside seats. For even the most supportive, gowned-from-head to-toe, hands-on father, there is only so much he can do. And once back at home there is no obvious role. One father said, "I felt completely useless. All I did was keep out of the way of mothers, mothers-in-law and assorted midwives and health visitors, supply drinks to all and sundry and put out the rubbish. Everyone had always told me I would be a good father. But I didn't feel it, I didn't feel involved." The new man can contribute a great deal, but when it comes down to it, he is an onlooker. Another new father said, "I remember the night Liz and Alfie came out of hospital. I was still feeling high after the birth. Alfie woke up and I went to get him from the carry-cot. I handed him to Liz so she could feed him. It was then that I realized that he needed her more than me, that I would always be secondary. I felt really left out."

Men sometimes feel they lose their woman to their babies and breastfeeding confirms it. Aside from making tea and toast, changing nappies and being there, there is only so much a man can do for a breastfed baby in the early months. Disrupted nights become a woman's problem, making some women, like Hannah, "terribly angry", She said, "Charlie doesn't wake up in the night and I started to get really resentful. He said, 'Look, what can I do?' I said, 'Well, nothing, except make me a cup of tea.' But I hate tea. It was more the principle of it. I wanted him to wake up because I was waking up."

The realities of parenting are divisive, the difference between men and women open up. Young babies are very demanding and it is women who are on the front line. Both physically and psychologically a mother withdraws into herself and her baby. She changes nappies, feeds, cuddles – all of which is very time-consuming. She turns away from husband temporarily while she focuses on the baby, leaving some husbands resenting the intrusion and feeling like a spare part. In some cultures the father's envy and jealousy is diluted or preempted by ritual. Among the Arapesh Indians, a tribe that values maternal qualities in men, fathers join the mothers on the childbirth bed. Mohave Indian men ceremonially give birth to stones when their wives are in labour. These rituals help to give men a sense of purpose and a role.[3]

Parenthood does affect men, but not as dramatically as women. A man's perception of himself only changes gradually; it is simpler for men to maintain their identity – their lives at work and with friends can continue. For women, the change and immediate losses are far greater. Motherhood usually involves at the very least a break from work, which in turn means the loss of a social life and sense of identity. (Thirty years ago this would have coincided with marriage; now it coincides with parenthood, making the identity change two-fold) There is a loss of intimacy in marriage, a loss of space at home, a loss of time for oneself and a loss of financial and physical resources to cope with the demands of a baby. Lucy became 'grouchy' after a few weeks at home. "I had traded my eight-hour-a-day job for twenty-four hours a day of unpaid duty. I took care of the baby, my husband and the chores. And everyone thought staying at home was the cushy option."

The sacrifices of mothers and fathers are not equal, and evenings can highlight the difference. Fathers talk about what they have done and the people they have seen. Mothers have seen no one, talked to no one and visibly achieved very little. Carol Weston wrote, "I would send out 'come home' vibes at five pm. Not because I was starved of adult conversation, but because I was impatient to toss the baby at him and say, 'Your turn' and run – alone – into the shower or office."[4] Sue said, "I would be looking at the clock waiting for him to come home. I'd been with the baby all day and couldn't wait to hand him over the minute he walked through the door, which was unfair. He has a very stressful job and didn't want to go into baby mode."

Who does what

As soon as a baby arrives a couple starts to keep score – who looked after him/her, when and for how long. Their relationship turns into a shift system and the sense of unfairness and blame when one does more for the baby than the other becomes the biggest source of conflict.

Our mothers and fathers knew what they had to do and sharing childcare was not it. 'The Successful Wife's Pocket-book', a *Woman's Journal* pamphlet from the early 1960s, states very clearly the responsibilities of a wife. "Listen to this happy husband," it announces, "I like my wife because she listens and looks interested when I talk to her . . . is pleasant to my relations . . . is always her prettiest for me morning, noon and night . . . reads the newspapers and can talk about what she reads . . . has unfailing good manners . . . has a good sense of humour, but is never malicious . . . is gay and affectionate . . . is reliable but not consistent . . . has a mind of her own, but is never dominating and is willing to compromise when we disagree . . . is such fun to be with . . ." And as for handing over the baby in the evening, the successful wife knows that the hour at the end of the day when a husband has come home from his work often holds the secret of the success, or not, of a marriage. ". . . it must be a time of happy and relaxed quiet . . . from earliest days children must be trained to make it so . . . the tiniest should be in bed. Father will visit them; the older children reading or viewing . . ."

The days of the remote father breadwinner and the dutiful and supportive homemaking mother are long gone, or are they? Despite equality and the 'new man', despite working women and sexism, after having children couples tend to revert to traditional roles, even though they do not want to. Linda said, "We seem to have slipped into the roles that our parents had. He wanders in and says, 'What's for tea', and I think, 'I don't know, what is for tea?' I get fed up with having to think about it. If it was just me I would end up with a peanut butter sandwich, but everyone's asking me what's for tea."[5] According to a recent survey, about half the fathers with children under 12 thought it right that men had few childcare responsibilities and agreed with the fact that the husband should be the breadwinner. Men like Camilla's husband; she said, "He likes to think I'm here if he needs something doing – trousers to the cleaners, that sort of thing. He doesn't have to think when he comes in from work at lunchtime. He doesn't have to make a sandwich because I've done it and the evening supper's all ready." Before they had children, the division of labour was very different. "We were both working full-time and sharing was a recognized thing. Because I wasn't in the home, we used to spend Saturday mornings cleaning and hoovering and stuff together. Now, because I'm at home with the children, which isn't really recognized as a proper job, I get to do all the things around the house."

Babies turn women into housewives and women resent their partners for letting it happen, and not just during maternity leave. In one study, in nine out of ten couples the mother shouldered most of the responsibility for childcare and running the home, even when she had a full-time job.[6] Even if a woman works she is still seen as the prime carer. Fathers are doing more than they were twenty years ago, but mothers still do the bulk both of housework and child-rearing.

It takes fifty hours a week to look after children, and mothers do 87 per cent of it.[7] Celia's husband says he does a lot around the house, "but he doesn't really". She said, "I think the burden still falls on women, the buck stops here. I always have final responsibility to make sure the food is on the table and there are clean clothes. Husbands won't say, would you like me to put the washing on? They won't volunteer, they have to be told." Men do pivotal jobs like hoovering, but not peripheral ones like putting dishes away or dusting. They will do the shopping, but not compile the list; load the washing machine, but not sort for temperature or colours. Men do spend more time playing with their children, but they still do not take them to the doctor's or the shoe shop.[8] The new man is also conspicuously missing from the statistics on free time. Women without children have an average of forty-two hours' free time a week – with children this falls to twenty-two hours. The figure for men drops from forty-nine to forty-six hours.[9] Mary wished her husband would help more at weekends, "All he does is potter in the garden, which I regard as a hobby and I don't have time for hobbies anymore." Sandra's husband comes in from work and sits and reads the paper. "I say, 'You can't read the paper now, wait until they've gone to bed.' Only then will he help me. If I didn't say it he would just sit there and read the paper." Because men do not pull their weight, take the initiative or know what comes next, woman have to nag. "I've turned into a fishwife," said Jenny. "All I seem to do is argue with Steve about how this needs doing and that and how he's so lazy."

While couples turn into their parents when they become parents, the roles are not as clear-cut as in the days of the 'Successful Wife'. Who does what is not pre-defined, it has to be negotiated. Annabel said, "You don't know where your responsibility begins and ends. I expect Tony to play a bigger part, but it's not clear how much, because I am home two days a week. I often think it would be easier if I didn't expect anything from him. Things would be simpler if I did it all myself, but I don't. I expect a lot from him. My mother didn't expect that from my father. He went out to work and he came home and the dinner was on the table. He played his part with us, but not as much as I expect from my husband, and that's where the arguing and tension come from."

Both men and women are less locked into stereotypes and are much freer, but this means that parenting in the 1990s is full of contradictions and confusion. Negotiating and arguing is tiring and for the sake of peace and an easy life, many just get on with it. Jill had recently "changed tack completely". She had resented the extra work, had kicked and complained and nagged, but had now decided to "accept things the way they are, because the person who ends up worse off is me. I feel resentful, get myself into a state, get cross, then I don't like myself. It's not a 50/50 share and it never will be. It just seems to be the way things are. I've accepted my role more." Maggie, who felt "really pissed off that he did so little", settled for a dishwasher and the promise of recognition. "I drew up a list a while ago of what I did and what he did and I was really trying hard to balance the list out – difficult as he doesn't even pick up clothes. I thought what do I want him to do. I didn't want him to do the shopping as I would have to write out in detail where everything was, so in the end I wanted recognition and appreciation. He likes to live in a clean house and have clean clothes, but doesn't even think of the work involved. He takes it all for granted."

Maternal power
Some women can feel very protective of their 'role' and resent 'involved' fathers gate-crashing it; fights because both want to change the nappy are not uncommon. Handing over responsibility means support, but it can also mean loss of power, and feeling less of a mother. Some feel that the baby is 'theirs' and while they might want help, do not want to run the risk of undermining the special mother/baby relationship. Scarlet would not let anyone hold her baby because she was frightened if she did it would not bond with her. Mothers can feel jealous if the baby seems to prefer the father over the mother. One study revealed that 50 per cent of mothers did not like leaving their children with their fathers regularly, 38 per cent discounted the idea altogether and 18 per cent thought it a good idea – but not for them.[10] Women are critical of fathers, partly because they fail to do their job properly, but also from an even deeper-rooted belief that father is muscling in on mother's job. When Scarlet asked her husband to help with the baby, he would say, "It's your baby, if you're going to fuss over her so much and act like she's just yours, then you can do everything for her." She said "I felt like I had two children, but I did feel that she was just my baby." Maternal power is one of the few powers that women have had, and not surprisingly, one which many are reluctant to hand over.

Sex: lack of

When babies come, the sex goes. As discussed in Chapter 8, for a mixture of reasons, maternal post-natal celibacy is very common. For the couple, where sex is often heavily relied upon as a magic glue, adjusting can be very difficult. Not only is the imbalance in libidos the cause of friction – she not wanting it; he wanting it as much as ever (although sometimes the man is so traumatized by what he saw at birth that he becomes impotent – but as Michael, a first-time father, who had not had sex for ten months, explained, "It's not just a sexual thing. It's the fact that my wife puts my daughter first, second and third and that I come a poor fourth. Her disinterest in sex has become a metaphor for her disinterest in me." Babies displace men. A new father can feel jealous of his partner's love for the baby and jealous of the baby who seems closer to the mother than he is. And babies put people in touch with their own childhoods and a new father can feel like a neglected baby in need of a mother. Support and affection are needed more, support and affection received, less. One new father said, "The relationship doesn't suffer. We don't really have one."

Men tend to be patient during pregnancy as they realize there might be a risk to mother and baby, they are patient just after labour and in the early months because of soreness, stitches, losing blood and caesarean scars, but once it gets to three, four, five, six months after and there is still no sign of sexual interest, problems begin. Lyn argued a lot about sex with her husband. "He really pressurized me. The worst thing was him saying how understanding he was being, but he wasn't. 'Look,' he'd say, I'm being so understanding.' And just by saying it meant he was putting the pressure on. He would always make comments morning, noon and night. Like if something came on TV, he'd say, 'We used to do that.' I would say, 'Oh yes, we did' and then ignore it."

Fathers do not expect the shutdown and their persistent requests for explanations, because of the inability of a man to really understand what has happened, can cause resentment. Scarlet's husband used to sulk rather than argue about lack of sex. "It used to make me feel cheesed off and angry as he didn't understand, and even when I told him how I felt he still wouldn't understand. He would say, 'She's six months old now, you can't keep on harping about that forever.'" Being told 'it's nothing personal' and that feelings have not changed when all evidence is to the contrary can make men feel their partners no longer care, or that they are no longer sexually attractive.

Resolving the sexual impasse can be difficult. Julie participates in body, not mind. "I lie back and think about my shopping list"; Rose tries to preempt any pressure, "I bring up the subject and say, 'Look, I know it's been two or three weeks, but this is because of such and such.' If I let it go it becomes a big thing between us, this awful silence and it becomes a duty. Like, how long has it been, I'd better do it." For others, like Sophie, expert help seems the only option. She and her husband went to Relate. "My husband just sat back and was patient to wait. But it made me feel so sad that that part of my life had gone. Lots of parts of my life had gone, but his part made me really sad. And yet a lot of it was my own doing. If he made any move I would just recoil. I didn't want to know. I didn't think it was ever going to come back and I'm not certain if I wanted it to at one stage. Now I want to and I'm working on it. Relate was good. At least it's got us talking again."

Some women are afraid that intimacy will lead to sex, so they withdraw entirely. Experts advise couples to lower their expectations (realizing that post-natal celibacy is normal, helps) and find other non-sexual ways to nurture the relationship. If women can be reassured that they will not be rushing straight into penetrative sex they are more likely to respond to cuddles. Above all, it will pass. A couple's sexual relationship is always shifting, always changing and post-natal celibacy is just a phase like any other.

Styles of parenting

Julie argued with her husband about how their children should be brought up. "He will, for the sake of peace, when I'm not around (I work every weekend), ram sweeties down their necks, he will let them sit in front of videos all day and he won't take them out. It's a case of 'It's too much hassle, love.' I think it's nothing to put them on the bus, or walk them to see the ducks. They're out of the house, getting some fresh air. It doesn't hurt and it's an hour killed, love."

To smack or not to smack, sweets or no sweets, early to bed or late to rise – styles of parenting are a source of much disagreement. Maggie 'tapped' her son for throwing a small toy piano down the stairs and her partner, horrified, said, "You *hit* him." Parenting is a personal affair. There are no rules, it is all down to individual interpretation and habit. And one of the great discoveries of parenthood is that habits, like genes, tend to be passed down through the generations. Not only do couples tend to imitate the roles of their parents, but they can also seek to duplicate the way that they were brought up. Parents learn how to parent from their parents. Just as fingers were wagged at them, they will wag theirs at their children, and phrases and sayings ring down through the years. When it comes to the unknown, and children are a big unknown, couples retreat into what is familiar, but what is familiar to them might be totally alien to their partner.

Children raise issues rather than creating them and the exposure of differences in background and upbringing is one. Melissa's husband thought she was too strict. "I tend to be one of those people who worry about what other people think of me. If he doesn't do that, or if he walks around with his juice then people aren't going to ask me back. That was the way I was brought up myself. I had a fairly strict upbringing. His family are much more relaxed. If I change Daniel at my mum's house, I will always change him up in the bathroom, but when I go to Andrew's house, his Mum says, 'Oh, do it downstairs in the sitting room and if a bit of pooh falls into the fireplace it doesn't matter.' But I'm always thinking, Mum is watching me."

One partner may come from a family that makes a fuss over birthdays and presents; the other may regard this as pointlessly extravagant. One may believe in firm discipline, the other may bitterly disagree. Religious differences often do not surface until the birth of a baby forces decisions – to circumcise or not, Christening or Sunday School, bible reading or not? Couples can start to expect more from each other, a mother want her 'boyish', irresponsible man to grow up and be a father (like her father was) or a father feel angry that his partner is not a better cook and housekeeper (like his mother was). Parenthood is about adapting and couples usually resolve their differences either by overriding programming and knee-jerk reactions or compromise. Harriet's husband was stricter than she was because his parents were strict. "He was an only child. I'm one of four and when you have more children you tend to let them get on with it more." Harriet was quite lax with her children, but if her husband told them off, she would not contradict him. "If he says something I tend to back him up, unless I really don't agree, in which case I say to the girls, 'Go ask Daddy why you can't do it.' Once he's had a chance to think about it, he usually says, OK."

But occasionally different backgrounds can throw the relationship's balance completely out of kilter. Trisha nearly separated from her husband because they both had such different ideas on how to bring up their son. "My husband's family are a lot stricter than mine. My family are full of hugs whereas his aren't. Men are real men and women do women's things. His son was NOT going to play with dolls and NOT going to be in the kitchen, even though he does those things himself. He had to live up to his family's expectations of being a father. They wanted him to bring his son up as a fighter and a real man. I just wanted a loving, reasonably well-adjusted child that people would want to have in their homes." This was four years ago and Trisha and her husband have since worked through their differences, helped perhaps by the subsequent birth of two girls.

Going out

"Our relationship was changing," wrote Carol Weston. "Instead of going to the movies and restaurants, we were renting videos and ordering in. Instead of having sex we were having milk shakes."[11] Babies bring a change to a couple's social life. Timing feeds, the expense and availability of babysitters and the knowledge that a lazy lie-in sleeping off hangovers is out of the question means that going out becomes more complicated. Rachel and her husband used to go out three to four times a week. "Now we don't go out at all." They have four children under four. "My father has volunteered to babysit, but I would just feel so guilty. What if they all woke up, poor man.

We don't really mind. We're quite used to it now." Alison and her husband used to have a hectic social life, "But I'd tend to sit with the girls and he'd sit with the boys. Now, if we do go out together, which isn't often, we'll go out alone. We'll sit down together and talk. I feel much closer to him now." By the time babies come many couples have clocked up more than a few wild nights and are happy to exchange films for videos, and pints for cans at home. Mary and her husband did not go out until their son was twelve months old. Their first son had died from a cot death at five months. "We decided that we wouldn't go out until he was of an age when we felt happy leaving him. It was no sacrifice. The loss of my oldest had been so traumatic and, within the scope of things, a year is nothing. We just made little treats for ourselves – a bottle of cognac or champagne."

While loud clubs and bars can lose their appeal after babies, the loss of spontaneity and night after night of *The Bill* and staying up after *Newsnight* becoming a treat can make life seem boring. Beverly and her partner used to be friends, now "we're husband and wife". She said, "We used to go out a lot together, we used to have a lot of fun. We did most things together. We were very close. We never fitted into that husband and wife role, but we do now." 'Husband' and 'wife' meaning not only less fun together, but husband goes out, wife stays home. Because babysitters are expensive and sometimes hard to find, it is often easier for couples to go out separately and when it comes to who goes out in the early days, it tends to be fathers more than mothers.

From the outset it can take longer for the responsibilities of parenthood to sink into fathers. "At the drop of a hat", Samantha and her husband would go off to London for the weekend to see friends. She said, "After George was born Oliver was still for it. But I'd have to say, 'Hang on a minute, what about George?' What about George was all I seemed to be saying in the early days." Pregnancy prepares women for nights in. The bigger they get the less they want to go out, the more they stay in, the more they get used to not going out and thinking about the baby. The adjustment can take longer for men. They leave their babies every day to go to work, the baby is not dependent on them for food and the initial relationship is not so intense. George was about four months old when Samantha's husband went to a party in London. "I didn't go because of George, but he went off and had a really miserable time without me and missed me and missed George. He realized he was past all that and wanted to be at home with us." But not all husbands experience the same revelation. Megan's husband "Always compared himself with his more free-living friends who go training twice a week, play rugby on Saturday afternoons, stay out after the match and go down to the club on Sundays. I resent this."

New mothers, on the other hand, can find it very difficult to leave their babies, even if it is just for a few hours. Melissa's first trip out after Daniel was born was to the cinema with her husband. "We didn't even stay for a drink after. It felt so weird to be out. Just not having someone hanging onto the end of my nipple, or thinking, 'I've got to check that he needs feeding or changing.' Through the film I kept on saying, 'I wonder what he's doing now.' I ran home and couldn't wait to get upstairs and as I was running I could hear myself crying, really stupid. Of course, when I did get back, he didn't really want to know me." The first time Lucy and her husband went out was to a rock concert in a football stadium. The contrast with her new life in the baby-bubble could not have been greater. "I really missed him and wanted him with me. The whole set-up seemed so hard and aggressive. I felt the separation. I thought there are hundreds, thousands of people here who don't know me and they just see me and Mike as a couple and don't even know I've had a baby, that I'm a mother, yet I knew I was a completely different person. Then your body starts to tell you you should be with the baby. My breasts filled up, which made me miss the baby even more."

Spending less time together, going out separately and operating shift systems can put pressure on a relationship. Couples start to opt out, get lazy with each other and neglectful. Spending time alone together, although difficult to organize, can be important. As can taking the long-term view; as time goes by mothers find it easier to leave their babies, men adapt to the responsibilities of fatherhood and babies are only babies for a very short time.

Money

Babies are expensive. Basic equipment totals at least £500; twelve months of disposable nappies, £288; twelve months of toiletries, £168; twelve months of baby milk and food, £420.[12] Fortunately for the human race, few parents actually sit down and calculate how much it costs to have a baby, because the real cost has little to do with the money spent on equipment. The real cost is the lost earnings, normally the mother's because she opts to stay at home and look after the child, or if she does not, someone else is paid to do it in her place. And as nanny, cook, cleaner, laundress, shopper, gardener and seamstress, at the going rate a mother with a child under one should be paid £457 a week, or approximately £24,000 per annum – the same as a teacher, a civil servant or a chemist.[13] In fact, other than child benefit, she is paid nothing.

Giving up work, poor maternity pay and opting to work part-time, means that a mother's financial loss is greater than a father's, and losing out financially can equal a loss of power in the relationship. The loss of income dents not only the couple's finances, but also the woman's sense of self-worth and pride. Husbands have to be asked for money, something that Samantha finds very humiliating. "He'll just forget and I have to say, 'Can I have some money?' And that can be so degrading. Before I had George I was earning a little more than Oliver and now here I am having to ask him, it's crazy. I feel that he's always looking over my shoulder, saying 'Hang on a minute, you can't do that. That's hard-earned cash.' Whereas when it was my own, I could say, 'To hell with you.'"

Melissa did not have to go back to work and was happy to stay at home, but still worried that she no longer contributed to the household budget. "Think of it as me paying you back for your hard work," said Melissa's husband. Despite her husband's reassurances, Melissa still missed not having money, "Especially when it comes around to his birthday and I'll say, 'What do you want?' and he'll say, 'What can I afford?'" In our society where what you do is more important than who you are, money will always talk loudest. Childcare allowances, tax breaks and increases in child benefit would help ease the burden of both lost income and lost status. Until that day, money will continue to be an issue for new parents and unlike the days of the breadwinner and the homemaker, a complicated one to resolve. Women can (in theory) earn as much as men. Like their partners, women have financial commitments – the mortgage, household expenses and holidays. The financial balance in a relationship can be very even. Then babies arrive and throw the balance out. Caroline said, "When I was on maternity leave I gave up my financial independence, but my partner didn't compensate me for that. I was getting half-pay so I still had money coming in. We did make an agreement that I didn't have to contribute to the mortgage, but as far as other things – shopping, bills, etc, I still had to do my share of that. OK, I didn't have to pay the mortgage, but I was still proportionally worse off." Kerry's husband did not support her when she was on maternity leave. "Before having the baby we were financially independent with separate bank accounts, and we worked out our financial affairs quite well. After, when I was on maternity leave, I ate into a lot of my capital, while he was still earning quite a lot of money. I think he should have supported me. If the roles had been reversed I would have looked after him."

More than money, conflict over who supports whom is down to expectations, and those can be so deep-rooted that, no matter how independent or equal before, some women after a baby, look to their partners for financial support and feel resentful if they cannot provide it. Finances dictated that Harriet went back to work part-time. "I would never say anything to my husband but I do sometimes wish he earned twice as much as he does. Ideally, I would like to stay at home. So, when I'm tired I do resent him." Kate said, "I sometimes wish that things were more traditional and that I was being supported. I didn't want to go back to work after having my son and I resented the fact that someone had to do it and it had to be me, but I felt really guilty thinking it." Today's dual income families have higher expectations and raised lifestyles than the days of the breadwinner and homemaker, but also face financial pressures and confusion which were unheard of in past generations. "You stay at home, I'll earn the money" is much simpler to organize than arguing over who is going to support whom, and pay the mortgage, gas bill and buy the nappies.

It is not only women who suffer from guilt and resentment. Professional middle-class men whose wives worked after the birth of their first child have lower self-esteem and greater dissatisfaction with life than the traditional breadwinner, according to one study.[14] Real men look after their women. Lyn had to work from home in the evenings. "I do feel resentful. It's a very touchy point with him as he's doing a very good job, but doesn't get paid much for it. I'm very aware that I'm better educated than he is and I was on the same salary as him when I stopped working, so we halved our income and he doesn't like me working. He'd like to be the breadwinner. He would like to be supporting me, not because he's old-fashioned, but because he knows how much I want to just stay at home and be with Daniel and he'd desperately like to give us what we want. I try very hard not to use it against him. I haven't for a long time. He really does get very upset and I have to be very provoked to mention it as I know how much it hurts him."

10

Family and Friends

All change

Babies change not only the central relationship between the couple, but every other relationship around it. Mothers are made into grandmothers, fathers into grandfathers; old friendships are reevaluated and new ones introduced. This reassessment is a normal process that new parents go through as they sift through their old life and put it into a new perspective.

Mothers

"I get on much better with my mother now," said Wendy. "We see each other more – she looks after my daughter when I go to work. We used to argue quite a lot, but now we get on great. I suppose I now know what she went through in bringing me up." A mother's relationship with her own mother is one of the crucial factors influencing a woman's attitudes to mothering. Politics, social and economic pressure may play a part, but deep down Mum is still there. During pregnancy and early motherhood the need in a mother for her own mother is very high, this need tends to bring them closer together.[1] However daughters have viewed their mothers in the past, a new reality sweeps through their assessments – mothers are ordinary people trying to do their best. Lee said, "I now know what I put her through. My eldest is coming up to being a teenager and she mirrors what I was like: she is argumentative. So, I can appreciate mum better. I'm more tolerant. I accept her ideas more. I think she wanted what was best for me then and for my children now, something I didn't always see when I was young."

Mother love is said to be the most unselfish of loves. Most mothers accept it is their fate to love more than they will be loved. At least new mothers can comfort themselves with the thought that, although it may take 20 to 30 years, their daughters will appreciate them one day. "How could I have blamed my mother for anything with all the work and pressure she was under?" said Georgia. "I now understand what she was going through."

The short tempers, interfering concern and over-protectiveness are all understood as new mothers find themselves behaving the same way. Some women even start to feel or sound like their mothers. Parents learn to parent from their parents, and situations and expectations may vary considerably, but mothers often want to give their children what they were given – the same pleasures, environment and discipline. "Eat up your greens", "Don't leave food, think of all the millions of starving children in the world", "Sleep tight, watch the bugs don't bite" – mothers instinctively copy their own mothers, sing the same songs, hear themselves talking in the same tone of voice. Childhood memories come flooding back – what it felt like to be small, to be held, to see and feel a mother's hands, face and voice. As a mother rocks her baby in the way that she was rocked, sings the songs that she had sung, past and future merge in the present. "It's a very unifying experience," said Melissa. "I can now see why it is that when I go and stay with Mum for a week she still wants to buy me things and make me happy. I'm the same with Daniel. Every time I go to Mothercare I buy him something." Almost despite herself Fran copied her mother's ways. "My Mum had a horror of us showing her up and I can see myself being the same. I can see myself being critical of the children, expecting the same perfect behaviour and them not acting up. I think my daughter is quite well behaved, but I'm still anxious about it."

While daughters are seeing things from their mother's point of view, past periods of being offhand or cold can suddenly hit home, making daughters feel guilty and keen to make amends. Frances said, "My mother had a very difficult time. My dad is a bit of a strange personality and they had a difficult marriage. They divorced when I was about 17 or 18. When my mother really needed me around I was living in Italy and France and at that age was horribly selfish. In my 20s I was equally cavalier about ringing her up; weeks would go by and I wouldn't call. Having my daughter now, I think, Gosh, if she did that to me I would be really hurt." Turning mothers and daughters into grandmothers and mothers changes the balance in the relationship. There is a sense of coming of age, and both women can feel more equal. Mothers feel more comfortable talking about sex, or their own experiences of motherhood. They become less critical, less judgmental as their responsibilities as a mother become more low key. Annie's mother did not treat her 'like a baby' anymore. Annie said, "I was the youngest of five and there was a seven-year difference between me and the next youngest. Now, I've got married and had my family, she asks my opinion more. I feel she takes more notice of what I say."

"My mother had me down as a career woman", said Mary. "She was a bit surprised by the baby. I can remember her saying, 'I really never thought I'd see this day.' She didn't work, so my career was something she just didn't understand. I don't know if having a baby has removed any underlying friction, but it makes it easier for us to get on on a different level. I can tell her the boys are being pests and I'm sick of them, and she understands." Changing expectations and opportunities mean that daughters no longer simply repeat the experiences of their mothers. Marriage, children, work — many women make decisions that are different from those their mothers would have made, and this can mean that mother and daughter feel estranged, with neither relating to the other's life. "My mother never went to work," said Flora. "The family has always been her life, so she found it very difficult to empathize with me over work problems. She's always very keen to get discussions back to a family nature, because that's what she knows best and what she's happiest talking about. While I was unable to have children it was all a bit difficult. I didn't really want to talk about children or the best way to bring them up, or the best schools." Since the birth of Flora's twins, the relationship has become much easier. "It's now free range. Before we had areas where we were having to tread very carefully." Doing the 'right' thing in a mother's eyes can mean settling down and behaving in the 'right' way. Julie's mother 'never approved'. She said that whatever I did, I never did it right, or did it well. I left college, got pregnant, got married much against her wishes. My husband left me, I came home pregnant and got a 'told you so' again. But now I've got a husband and a home, and I'm working and have money in the bank and I'm not into wild living anymore, it's got much better. A good night out for us is a bottle of wine and a video rather than half a tin of dope in my stomach and two bottles of Scotch."

While some women want to copy their mothers totally, many experience a sense of competition. New mothers may learn how to mother from their mothers, but if that example fell short, daughters can want to do things better. Megan felt her mother was more interested in hoovering than in her. "I want to do things very differently. I want to be more relaxed about things than she was. I'd prefer to give the priority to my family rather than the house." There may be an attempt to heal old wounds. Megan wanted to give more to her daughter than to the housework because she felt neglected as a child. She wanted to make it right for herself by making it right for her daughter. Camilla's mother was not really interested in babies. "She wasn't that keen on me or my sister. She loved us dearly, but was always a career woman. I think I felt neglected. I used to come home from school and there wouldn't be anyone there, that sort of thing. It didn't bother me at the time, but looking back I think it would have been nice in the depths of winter to come back to a house with the lights on and tea on the table, but it was never like that. I want to be a cosier, more home-based mother. I want to do it differently."

Some women cope better with the transition from mother to grandmother than others. For mothers who have always been in charge, there are hard lessons to learn. The balance of power has changed: the daughter is now mistress in her own home, in charge of her own life, and grandmothers have, to a certain extent, to let go. Camilla always consulted her mother and asked for advice and support. "Whereas now, I make decisions about myself or the children, I don't turn to her. I don't see her as having a guiding, supportive role anymore, which is a bit sad for her. I think she feels she's lost her little baby."

Veiled (and not so veiled) criticism of the way their grandchildren are being brought up is the classic way mothers who find it difficult to 'let go' intrude on their daughters' lives. Rose said, "My mother has always criticized me, everything I do or wear. She has a field day with the children. She says I don't feed them properly, that I'm too strict, that I don't love them enough, that I shouldn't be going off doing things like working. Demand feeding and having them in bed is all nonsense. She's always saying, 'I never used to let you do things like that.'" Domineering mothers undermine their daughters but domineering, bossy grandmothers have less of an effect. Rose felt more confident and "less emotionally entangled" with her mother. "She still criticizes, but I don't care, it doesn't bother me. I'm doing it my way and I think I'm doing a good enough job."

Conflict between mothers and daughters does not only come from a change in the balance of power. Fashions in childcare change so quickly and today's mothers have rejected many of the methods of past generations: rigid four-hourly feeding, the daily airing, the early potty training, binding breasts, mothers not working. Some grandmothers cannot resist: "Not *still* feeding?", "What he needs is 'proper' food", "I never had a dirty nappy after you were a few weeks old", "Has she had some fresh air today?", "Going back to work, so soon?" and other 'helpful' tips are still given to new mothers through the memories of mothers and grandmothers.

While a daughter's rejection of her mother's ways might seem straightforward, the situation is often more complex. The mother/daughter relationship is a paradoxical muddle of emotions. Most new mothers both reject and copy their mothers, and are torn between wanting to do things differently, yet still needing love and approval. Because deep down, no matter how old or independent a daughter is, her mother's opinion still counts.

Absent mothers

Sophie's mother lives in Australia and, after her baby was born, she suddenly felt very close to her and wanted to be with her. She rang her from the delivery suite. "The machine only took 10p pieces so you can imagine how many it took for us to ring Australia, for her to be with us." Sophie suffered from post-natal depression after Nelly's birth and to help her out her mother spent three months with her. "I couldn't have done without her. I couldn't talk about it with my mother-in-law, she didn't like to see me crying, it frightened her. My Mum actually spoke to the post-natal depression organization and brought me literature on it. She kept telling me what a wonderful job I was doing. It was nice, it was really nice. And it was so hard when she went back. I missed her terribly. Nelly would go into her room and look for her, saying 'Where's Grandma, where's Grandma?' and I would cry."

Catrina's mother died when she was 12. "I had to rethink her, who she was and who I am." Her mother's death affected Catrina's confidence in her ability to mother herself. She was very sensitive to criticism, particularly from her mother-in-law, who "desperately wanted to sweep in and 'do'". Catrina now has three children and as time has gone by "I've missed her terribly, but now that I'm more confident, it's not so painful." Hannah's mother died two years ago and "I've never missed her more, or loved her more, to the point where I think the past couple of months I have been depressed daily. I didn't give her credit for the love or work she did as a mother and I miss those ancestral ties, cycles of mother/daughter/ granddaughter. I want to show her Katie, and say, 'Look Mum, look what I've got.'"

Fathers

While fathers are not in the front line in the same way as mothers, the daughter/father relationship still changes after having a baby. Mary appreciates her father more as a grandfather. "The boys have brought out the best in him. It's really amazing. He gives them so much time – potters with them in the garden or what have you. I don't remember him having any patience with us when we were young. I suppose because he was working he didn't have a lot of time." Women can remember their fathers as remote disciplinarians, only to discover that, as grandfathers, they are "soft, silly and daft". Freed from the stresses of work or the demands of fatherhood, grandfathers can indulge and spoil their grandchildren in a way they never did their own children. Nancy's father, on the other hand, treats her daughter in the same way as she was treated and she hates it. "I had two brothers and he always favoured them over me and I can see the same thing happening with Emily. He gives his grandsons far more attention and encourages them to be strong and tough. I want Emily to be confident and independent, yet he is always patronizing her. I don't want him to treat her in the same way as me, but I feel powerless to do anything." Fathers are as responsible as mothers for negative conditioning, for not giving their daughters enough confidence in themselves. While being a grandparent and being a parent are very different, the habits of a lifetime do not disappear with the new role.

The father/daughter relationship can be a very complicated one. Fathers can be very possessive of their daughters and resent handing them over in marriage, let alone losing them to motherhood. Trisha had always been her father's blue-eyed girl, and was very close to him until she got married. "He finds it hard that I put him after my husband. When I had my son it was yet another male taking me away. He expected me to always visit him. In the end, I said, 'Look Dad, it's easier if you come to us now' and he didn't like that at all. I think he felt pushed out."

Brothers and sisters

Any change in the relationship between brothers and sisters is often because of a difference in lifestyles. Siblings who have children feel united, those who do not are divided. Annabel used to be quite close to her brother when they were in their twenties. They liked doing the same things and would often go out together, but "since the babies he's been a complete letdown". Older, but childless he leads "a young, single sort of life in London which is all very juvenile." She said, "We moved to Norwich from London about three years ago and he has visited us once. He didn't even meet Lily until she was one, which I thought disgraceful, as he's got all the time in the world. He's always swapping girlfriends and it always depends on the girlfriend as to how much we see of him – those who like children we see a lot."

On the other hand, babies can unite siblings who have children or who are baby-friendly. Kate's sister had dismissed her as a career woman. "Now I'm more human in her eyes. She always had this idea of me as being kind of a thrusting career woman – inhuman. She was certainly surprised when I was pregnant, pleased and surprised. She also had a career, but has wanted children for some time, and has never been in a position to have one, until recently. Having children certainly seems to have eased our relationship a lot."

Not only is the pressure on to have more family get-togethers once a baby is around, families can also want to present a more united front, bury hatchets for the baby's sake. Hannah's sister had 'thrown a wobbly' before her daughter was born. "It would have been easy for me not to repair the hurt, giving birth and having Katie was far more important than a stupid quarrel about money, and now she's back in the fold." Beverly's husband had not spoken to his sister for ten years; when they were children his parents separated and he went to stay with his father and the rest of the family stayed with his mother. Then, 'She phoned up out of the blue because she had heard through mutual friends about the baby and wanted to offer her congratulations and check that everything was OK. She is in touch regularly now.'

In-laws

If babies tend to bring mothers and daughters together, they often push mothers-in-law and daughters-in-law apart. Conflicts with mothers-in-law increase after birth.[2] Heather's mother-in-law got off to a bad start by introducing her as 'my grandson's mother'; the relationship went downhill from there. "She constantly portrays me as a villain to the kids. She's always saying things like, 'What's Mummy doing now, what's that naughty, bad Mummy doing.' You can imagine what that does for my confidence.'"

A baby marks the union of two families, but it can also divide them. Genes are partly to blame. Each side wants to lay claim to their contribution with comments like "How's *my* baby" and "He looks just like his father/mother/uncle/aunt/grandmother"/ This puts the mother in a difficult position with her in-laws. The baby is partly theirs, she is not. She 'belongs' to a different family, and depending on the tenacity of her in-laws' claims, she can end up feeling like a carrier for their genes.

Sandra felt threatened by her in-laws. "They wanted to take over," she said "They'd walk in and they weren't at all interested in me. They loved it if I wasn't there and they could have him to themselves. And when I was there, they'd keep him up when he was supposed to be sleeping. They just didn't understand. I would get really tense about it. It was really unfair – they'd see him and play with him, and then they'd go off, not even thinking about what would happen when they'd gone, that he'd be really fractious and overtired. A lot of it was to do with my sister-in-law; she wasn't married then and all she wanted was to get married and have babies. She would be around every minute and it would drive me mad. She would say, 'I shall pretend this is my baby.' It made me so angry. I felt, it's not your baby, it's mine."

Irrational as it may seem, a mother can hand her baby to her mother, take advice from her mother, accept her mother's interest, but her mother-in-law is a different matter. Blood is thicker than water and blood is also easier to ignore, argue with, say 'no' to and be honest with. Being direct with a mother-in-law can be complicated, and being indirect or stewing in silence the source of 'atmospheres'. But the mother-in-law/daughter-in-law conflict is also tied up with whether the mother-in-law has been able to accept the daughter-in-law, and this has more to do with the relationship between mother and son. Trisha feels her husband's family never approved of her. "I'm a great disappointment because I'm English, not Irish. When his family came to stay they thought I was a terrible mother because I was too relaxed., If the baby dribbled I didn't rush to change his baby-gro and we'd have to wait for meals because I wasn't that organized. In Northern Ireland it's all done very differently. The children are spotless and will always be changed before the husband gets home. They wanted their son to marry an Irish girl and this is just the icing on the cake."

Scarlet's in-laws are Italian. 'She's very loud and jumpy. They're very over the top, lots of pinching of cheeks and throwing the baby in the air. Very physical and very irritating. If I had the baby in the pram she'd walk over and pick her up, even if she was asleep. She wouldn't ask me first. It used to drive me insane. She would try to tell me how to look after her, like babies shouldn't sleep on their backs.' I would say, 'No, babies sleep on their backs now.' She'd say, 'Babies choke on their backs.' She wouldn't have it any other way."

Some mothers find it hard to let go of their sons and may unconsciously resent her son's partner becoming the new mother figure and pushing her out of her place (particularly if her daughter-in-law's methods are very different from hers). Reasserting herself as a mother by offering advice is one way of compensating for a feeling of being redundant or left behind. Sophie's husband is an only child and his mother is a widow; mother and son are very close. "She didn't seem to object when we were married, just when the baby arrived and Tom was required to be at home to help me. She would make the occasional comment and make it obvious that she didn't approve of me as a mother. We've reached the stage where I neither ring her nor she rings me. She just feels I'm taking her son away from her and that she needs him more than me." A mother-in-law who allows her son's partner to be a mother to his children, and lets go of her son, finds it easier to be a mother-in-law than those who hang on to their little boy,

Lyn's father-in-law is a "real sod major", and Lyn found him very overbearing and opinionated, until after her son was born. "When he first saw Daniel he softened to me. It was almost as if he was finally proud of his son, almost as if his son had come good by producing an heir and as I was the one who was married to his son, he holds me in higher esteem. He's softer now and more mellow and accepting of my opinions." Doing the right thing by having a baby can improve relations with in-laws. Camilla choosing babies over career endeared herself to her mother-in-law who unlike her own career-minded mother was more of a "motherly mother". She said, "She treats me more like a complete woman now. She had four children, and now she's got something she can phone me about and have a woman-to-woman chat. When I was working she couldn't identify with me so much. She never had any interest in what I was doing and just saw work as a prelude to having children rather than anything serious, which annoyingly has turned out to be true."

Mothers-in-law and daughters-in-law have one fundamental thing in common – the son/husband. Beyond him, shared interests can be few and sometimes a baby will give the mother and daughter-in-law a reason to call each other, something to talk about. Sue and her mother-in-law "actually speak to each other now." She said, "We've never disliked each other, but we never seemed to have much to talk about. Me and my partner are from different backgrounds. He was brought up in a council estate and I'm from the posher part of town. His father died when he was young, so his mother brought up five children on her own. She's done really well. I can appreciate that more now. Before, we just didn't understand each other."

Friends

The world is divided into two kinds of people – those who have children and those who do not. The childless may wonder why mothers drag their children screaming on shopping trips, never go out, are unable to take their eyes off their babies for one second and can no longer hold a coherent conversation. All becomes clear after having a baby. How the world is seen after children can be very different, which is why, without enormous effort on both sides, childless friends tend to drift away.

Old friends

A new husband cannot threaten close female friendships, but the arrival of a baby can. Monica does not see her old girlfriends anymore. The first time she went out with them was to a hen night five months after her son was born. "It felt strange and didn't really appeal to me anymore. They were all getting drunk and I didn't drink. It was really boring. None of my friends had babies or anything. They were talking about boyfriends and there was me. I got the pictures of Joseph out of my handbag and started passing them around."

Friends don't necessarily have babies at the same time anymore. Thanks to contraception, family planning and careers, babies are spaced out and women become mothers at different stages. It is not at all unusual for a woman to be the only one in her group to have had a baby and for her to feel that she no longer fits in. Mental well-being is often a reflection of how comfortable people are within a circle of friends, acquaintances and colleagues, and if a way of life differs greatly it increases feelings of alienation. Life in the fast lane can be hard for mother to relate to, dinner at 9pm, and a club at 10pm being too close to bed-time. The first time Julie went out with friends she went to see a male stripper. "Which was great, but I felt fat and frumpy." Diana's first trip out was to a "fun-pub". She said, "I felt I shouldn't be there. I felt out of touch with everyone – frumpy and awful and really out of place. I thought, I ought to be at home with the baby."

Not only is there a biological difference between a mother and non-mother, but also a psychological one. A mother's main interest becomes the baby and life revolves around its demands, leaving little energy to talk about or do much else. To outsiders she had become "babyfied" and boring. The feeling of abandonment can be powerful on both sides – the child-free woman seen only when there is time, the child-bound woman misunderstood.

Some women are not interested in babies so a difference is bound to be created, but even for friends who are, it is hard for childless ones to have any idea of the demands of children. Gillian still sees her old (childless) friend, but feels more distant. "She doesn't really understand what I have to do – there's only her and her husband. We were going on holiday and I said, 'Oh, the baby isn't well, I shall have to take him to the doctor.' She said, 'You must be busy packing, surely you haven't got time to take him there?' Children always come first. That's hard for others to understand."

Mothers can try and not bore childless friends with the details of their baby's day (she slept for four hours, pooped four times and drank four ounces of formula); can try and not feed or play with their babies when they are on the phone; can enjoy not talking about nappies or teething – but they cannot pretend that things have not changed. Sally has one childless girlfriend. "It can be difficult sometimes. She is very close to the children, which is nice, but I do feel guilty when she's trying to talk on the phone and I have to call off because one of the children is crying. She had some problems and wanted a sympathetic ear and I had to just leave her.

The grass seeming greener on the other side can make the conflict worse.

Mothers envy the freedom and spontaneity of the childless women; the childless women, because of the enormous pressure on all women to have babies and the idealization of babies and motherhood, feel deviant and marginalized. It can be particularly hard for women who want babies, but cannot. Camilla's friend is infertile. "I haven't seen her for a long time, but we are still friends. She's the godmother to my son, but is terribly jealous and seems to have given up sending presents or anything like that, which is a shame. But I still speak to her on the phone. It could also bother her that I'm in a secure relationship and am seemingly happy, whereas she has a lot of problems at the moment. We had a row one day which we'd never done before. She arrived wearing those trendy sunglasses and I said, 'What do you look like' or something like that – a silly little quip. She would normally have laughed and said, 'Yes, they are a bit strange, aren't they.' But she didn't. She took complete offence and stormed off."

Couples

"I feel more relaxed with couples who have children," said Mandy, "Because they understand. If I go to someone's house who hasn't got children, and they've got all their things around, I spend all my time trying to move them. People with children are more geared up to them, and they're used to people disappearing halfway through conversations." Friends in the same boat understand that before doing anything or going anywhere, the children have to be considered. They understand that long walks over rough country with a pushchair, dropping into pubs, visiting stately homes, visiting galleries and skipping meals are out of the question.

Some friends invited Trisha and her partner to stay with them for the weekend when their son was about two. "They said that we'd have to go out for a meal at a local pub, and that they'd organized a babysitter, but they hadn't got any food in for him. They had things like half-fat milk, and when I said that I'd have to go and get some full fat milk, they couldn't understand why. I felt embarrassed, especially when I had to say, 'Can I give him something to eat please?'"

Among the childless, the child-bound can end up feeling exhausted, ostracized and frustrated. Which is why many find it is simply easier to spend time with those in the same boat. For the mother, who is busier, more tired and more home-bound than ever before, the loss of her former circle of friends and social life can be particularly hard. But there are compensations – new friends.

New friends

Young motherhood is often a time of 'discovering' female friendship and valuing its emotional and practical support. Women are often suspicious of mothers' groups and worry that they will not like them, but as Carol Weston wrote, "If they're willing to talk about the colour of your baby's shit, it doesn't matter if you like them."[3] Throughout history, women have depended on other women for support during motherhood. Today, there tends to be a home, one woman, several small children and not enough female help to share the burden. Rose said, "Whenever I've had a bad patch, one of them being hyperactive or difficult and Andrew not there to help me through, friends would say, 'Bring him over, I'll have him for the afternoon to give you a break.' We all talk about sex quite a lot – or the lack of it – it seems to be the same for most of us. We can joke which takes the tension out of it. We have a laugh, say all the men should go off for men's weekends and let us have some peace and quiet." Many are surprised by the sense of fun and freedom they have in other mothers' company. One woman said, "I feel like two people. In the daytime I get together with several other mums. We're quite a group really and we have a lot of laughs. It really helps and supports us. Then we all scatter back to our little boxes ready for the men to come home. Then I feel much older, much less full of laughter."

On the downside, new relationships with other mothers can fall victim to competitiveness. Teething, sleeping though the night, crawling, walking, talking, reading and who has the whitest nappies in the street are all seen as a gauge of a woman's ability to mother. Emma, a former teacher, remembered the competitiveness over reading. "I could hear them outside the classroom: 'Which book is he on? Oh, mine did that last year' and so on – all so unnecessary. I am sure they're all going wherever they chose, and it won't matter that one walked six months earlier than another." While nothing kills a friendship quicker between two mothers than one making the other feel like she is a 'bad' mother, not reacting can be difficult. Women are encouraged to be competitive by the media and advertising, as well as by their upbringing. And the difficulty in acknowledging a separate existence and identity from that of being a parent can lead some women to interpret other people's reactions to their children as reactions to themselves.

11

The Changing Face of the Family

Living together

"The main reason we haven't bothered getting married," said Heather, "is that neither of us are churchgoers and it just seemed meaningless. It's a form of words."

Marriage, once seen as an undertaking by a couple to bring up children has changed. For a number of reasons – feminism, changing sexual attitudes, the decline of religion – marriage is an increasingly private statement which often is not formalized. No longer associated with the bohemian and avant-garde, as in the 1960s, living together has become respectable. Not only do more and more people from all walks of life live together, but they live together for longer and, more significantly, have children. The number of children born outside marriage has doubled since the beginning of the 1980s and most of those babies are born to couples who live together. Heather said, "Children do put a different perspective on a relationship. Having children around all the time puts a great strain on everything. So, whatever the relationship, it has to be pretty sound if it's going to survive. If it isn't strong enough to begin with, then no pieces of paper are going to help patch it up." Being married is no longer the only accepted state in which to become a parent; 'illegitimate', and 'love child' are words from the past.

Marriage used to consolidate a relationship, make public a private commitment and separate the serious from the fleeting; now children do that. Monica was not living with her partner when she got pregnant. Now, they have a home, a commitment to stay together and her relationship, she says, is much closer. Maggie was not even going out regularly with her partner when she decided she wanted him to father her children. "We had been going out on and off for ten years when I decided I wanted children and he was the person I wanted to have them with. It was a bit of a struggle getting him back again. If it wasn't for the children I wouldn't be living with him, I wouldn't be living with anyone. But as I have to live with the children,

I may as well live with the father." Having children "sealed" Cathy and her partner's relationship: "We used to live in a shared house, but moved into a flat when we decided to have children. We were more partners then, now we're a family."

"We decided to get married for all the traditional reasons," wrote Nick Hornby. "We wanted to commit, we wanted to make our parents happy, my partner was six months pregnant."[2] Cohabiting might be on the increase, but most couples, 85 per cent, do eventually choose to marry and children are often the reason why. Surnames and security worry grandparents and the pressure can be on to tread the traditional path "for the sake of the children". Neither set of parents approved of Heather and her partner living together. "When I was expecting, I phoned Mum and said, 'You'd better sit down, I've got something to tell you.' She said, 'Oh, you're getting married.' 'Well, no, actually we're having a baby.' I could hear the thud as she sat on the stairs. Then, a very frosty, 'Well, most people get married first.'" Pressure to marry came from Maggie's father, but then, "He ran off with somebody my age about three years ago, had a baby and so isn't in a position to say much anymore."

How life is viewed before and after children can be surprisingly different, especially for the woman. Once she has people to feel responsible for, living with a partner may not feel responsible enough. Jenny and her partner married soon after their son was born. She said, "In the dead of night, you know you are married and that changes things right at the centre of one's being." For many, marriage is the only way of feeling truly secure, the piece of paper something to fight for should there be temptation to stray.

Legal difference

Emotionally, there might be little difference between living together and getting married, but legally, the difference could not be more clear. Marry and you acquire an automatic right to property and to financial support. Forego the vows and you could be left with nothing to show for your time together. A woman is only better off not being married to a man if she is richer than him. If a woman has the same or less money, she is better off married.

Legally, unmarrieds do not automatically acquire rights by living together; fathers of children born outside marriage have no automatic paternal rights; partners do not automatically inherit any of their other half's estate if he or she has not made a will listing them; partners may have no right to a share in the house if their name is not on the deeds, unless they can prove, among other things, that they have paid a substantial amount towards it; and neither partner has a right to claim maintenance from the other. It is true that children born outside marriage have the same rights as those born within, but unmarried fathers cannot pass on inherited titles or nationality.

Living together couples can take precautionary measures: they can draw up a 'cohabitation contract' clearly stating ownership and intention; fathers can apply to the courts for shared parental responsibility (or this can be included in a cohabitation contract); surnames can be changed by deed-poll (not strictly necessary, but some organizations, such as banks, may require formal proof); and they can make a will.

Single mothers

Sarah Keays is one, as is Mia Farrow, the Princess of Wales, the Duchess of York, Princess Caroline of Monaco, Catherine Oxenberg and Michelle Pfeiffer – they are all single mothers. One family in five is headed by a lone mother and 2.2 million children are being brought up this way, yet single mothers are all lumped together and seen as irresponsible teenagers who become pregnant just to get a council flat. In truth, the majority of single mothers once lived with or were married to the father of their children. Two-thirds of single-parent families are the result of divorce[2] and of partnerships not working out or of partners moving on to pastures new.

The realities of single parenting are undoubtedly hard. Society is centred around two-parent families – economically, legally and socially – two is the most acceptable number to bring up children. One person taking on the extra responsibility, and coping with the emotional stress and deprivations of parenthood as well as the financial hardship is not easy. Most single mothers would agree that a functioning two-parent family would be better, both for them and their children, but that is not what life has given them. Fatima, whose partner refused to live with her and their two children and in the end left altogether, complained of the relentless responsibility and loneliness. "It's hard getting out when you're on your own. I've got a regular babysitter now, but that's only happened in the last three months. Before that, weeks would go by and I wouldn't see another adult."

Not only do single mothers have to cope with the logistics of getting out, they have to reconcile their responsibilities as a mother with the demands of starting up any new relationship. Being a mother and dating men can feel strange. Helen, who separated from her husband a few weeks before their son was born had been seeing someone until about four months ago. "It was difficult for him as he'd known me when I was 16 and he'd say, 'I wish you could be the way you used to be.' And I'd say, 'Well, I can't. I've got responsibilities.' He wanted me to drop everything and be the hysterical teenager I used to be, you know, going out and getting drunk every night, and that's not me anymore. I wouldn't want it to be." Helen decided that she would rather be on her own than with someone who wanted her to be something that she was not anymore. "Sam comes first and is always going to come first."

Jane's husband left her just before the birth of her son. They had bought a home together and the pregnancy was planned. "He promised he would be there for me, would come into the hospital with me, would be there when the baby was born and would help me, and it was all one big lie." Jane suffered from depression, had to move back in with her parents and was left with a debt. "The mortgage was £1,000 in arrears just before David was born and he refused to contribute anything towards it. I was threatened with repossession. I tried to sell the house. Luckily no one wanted it because once David was born and I'd sorted myself out, I decided to take it on." Rather than go on benefit which would have made her feel 'at rock bottom', she went back to work full-time, enrolled David in a nursery and now supports him and the house. "I've come through it. It's hard, but I think it's made me stronger. I do it all for David. It's important that I have a secure home for him; I want to bring him up right."

Far from being depressed, self-pitying parasites on society, many single parents would rather work than depend on state benefits. In a recent Department of Social Security Survey, 90 per cent of single mothers said they wanted to work, and 55 per cent said they would resume work tomorrow if they could afford to. Fatima hoped to train as a youth worker: "I've applied for a grant and hopefully I'll be able to pay for a babysitter once that comes through. I've got to do something with my life so my children will look up to me. I want them to be proud of me."

Do-it-yourself mothers

When women plan to be lone parents it is often because having a child is too important to leave to the off chance of finding the ideal partner. Alexandra had always wanted children, was approaching her mid-thirties and still had not met Mr Right. "I just assumed it would happen as it did in *Bunty* and then I realized that it wouldn't. I suppose during my 20s I started to get anxious about it and that puts an enormous strain on relationships. So, when I turned 30 and I was still alone I started to get quite panic-stricken. I didn't want to leave it until the end of my 30s, so I thought I might as well get on with it."

Which she did, with the help of a friend who lived nearby and his donor sperm. The friend 'fathered' both Alexandra's daughters, but is completely uninvolved in their upbringing. As for demands of single motherhood, Alexandra has been pleasantly surprised. "I kept on waiting for it to be dreadful and it wasn't. I did get tired sometimes, but it wasn't that sort of 'how can I cope' tiredness. I suppose she was a very easy baby; she settled into a day/night pattern very easily, and didn't have any feeding problems. Everything went very smoothly. I kept on thinking, 'God, this is a complete cruise, what is going wrong?'"

Her second daughter made things more difficult, but only in terms of dividing her attention and love. Alexandra is perhaps lucky in that she works full-time and can afford a nanny – not a cheap proposition on one salary. Good childcare is probably an even higher priority for single parents and Alexandra's nanny is "quite exceptional". She said, "It's almost like having me in the house. She does the shopping and puts on the washing, and hangs it up and does the ironing – more than most partners would do." Which is why do-it-yourself mothers like Alexandra see going it alone as being positively advantageous. "Not only do I not have to cope with the resentment and hurt of having a broken relationship, but I don't have to nag or feel let down by a partner who is not pulling his weight. I honestly feel that I am not doing anything so different from what a lot of women with partners do. A lot of women with partners get very little help for one reason or another."

For Liz, aged 39, who has one son, aged four-and-half, single parenting is also easier than being in a couple. Apart from the lack of money, Liz thinks "not having a man around was actually quite advantageous." She said, "I only had to worry about myself and my baby. I certainly think I had a better experience than many friends who had partners around the whole time – they never seemed to be much help anyway. I am responsible for my son which makes things a lot easier."

12

Work

The great divide

Non-working and working women – what a misnomer. All women work. Some work for their husbands and children full-time, others go out to work as well. And those who do both, who combine work and children, are on the increase. Statistics show a steady growth in working mothers. Seventy per cent of all women with very young children, according to a recent survey, expected to continue working.[1]

On the face of it, mothers are doing what generations of women have been fighting to make possible – have a career and a family. Millions of pounds are now invested in women's education and training; mothers have been freed from the tyranny of the kitchen sink; working mothers are no longer frowned upon. Only one in five Britons now believes a woman's place is in the home.[2] "Having it all" is every modern woman's right. Or, at least that is what some assume pre-baby. Why then is the choice between home and work one of the biggest dilemmas mothers have? Why do working mothers feel so splintered and torn by anxiety and guilt?

Nothing divides mothers more than work. Both inwardly and outwardly the struggle to reconcile wanting to work, needing to work and wanting to be with the children causes a great gulf between mothers who go back to work and those who stay at home. In pregnancy, all women are sisters. Once the babies are born, they become adversaries fighting over how to be a mother and, more specifically, whether mothers should work. But both camps, whether self-righteous or defensive, are quietly afraid they are abandoning either their children or their careers. Neither choice is easy or without consequences. For most mothers work is not a simple issue.

Giving it up

"I didn't have babies to palm them off onto someone else," said Penny, who gave up her job as a nanny to stay at home with the children. "It's always been my view. Don't ask me why I became a nanny, I think it's the most horrible thing to do to a child – to give them to someone else to bring up. Yet I was a nanny. In the first family, the twins weren't planned, and financially they couldn't afford not to work. I would argue that today, there's little excuse for unplanned children. The second nannying job, the woman had no idea what to do with them. Give her a dummy and you were lucky if she put it in the right end. If the children were given a choice of either going out with Mummy or staying with me, they would always come to me. Each to their own, but I don't think it's fair. Personally, I think that my children are my responsibility."

Despite women being educated for work and independence, the majority of women still see the home and family as their priority. Seventy per cent of women with young children might expect to continue working, but 95 per cent also believed their family was their main commitment.[3] More and more mothers are working, but still only 12 per cent of mothers of young children work full-time. Fuelled by assumptions like "children need their mothers" and "*such* important years", choosing to stay at home comes out of an anxiety about the baby's welfare. Emma gave up her job as a teacher because "I have chosen to have these children and I think I can do a better job than anybody else." Emma's oldest has just started school.

The pull of motherhood can be strong. Frances was a successful financial services adviser and manager. She is now a full-time mother. She was ambitious, had hoped to become a director and had intended to go back to work after three months, but did not. "I put it all down to maternal feelings I didn't realize I had. I find motherhood satisfying in a way I never thought possible. If someone had shown me a snapshot of the future I just wouldn't have believed it. I'm amazed that I've switched over so easily. I've never once sat down and thought I wish I was back in London, in the City. The only time I think about office life is when I hear about the queues to the Blackwall Tunnel and I think, thank God, I don't have to do that anymore." Even when a mother achieves a high level of work, even when she has it all, she gives it up. Frances felt her baby was more important and more satisfying than work. While nobody would doubt the intense and often unexpected love which exists between mothers and their children, Frances' decision also reflects women's attitudes to work. Work can, it seems, be easily cast off by women, is less vital to a sense of self than it is for men. When babies come along, work is dispensable, it becomes 'unreal'. Catrina gave up her career as a television director in exchange for more time with her children. "You can't get lost bringing up children because they bring you up short all the time. You can't fudge anything because they know you are fudging it. You can't deny anything when you become a mother and therefore I think I am having to grow as a person, whereas I think, when I worked before in TV, I could happily get lost and pretend I was living." Successful women can find that values of work no longer express their 'real' concerns. Careers become shallow, babies are where the real commitment and pleasure lie.

And behind both Catrina's and Frances' decision was the feeling that they as mothers were the best people to look after their children. Frances said, "I do think I'm the best person to look after her. Intellectually speaking, I don't agree with that. I have friends who send their children to childminders and don't see why it should make that much difference. But emotionally, I really do think, Oh gosh, they are missing out on so much by not being at home. It's a real dichotomy in my head. Their children don't seem to suffer, but I could never consider doing it with my one." Catrina thought she "might balls it up", and that there is a lot to be said for professionals looking after children, but "I think there is an awful lot of conversation that happens on a daily basis between mother and child, which I wouldn't mind if I missed, but I think the child would miss."

Staying at home, however, involves sacrifices. Loss of status, income, independence and social life are not always compensated for by the pleasures of motherhood. Linda said, "I feel so dull and boring. I have no kind of conversation other than what the baby's done and what the dog's done."

Linda wanted to go back to work, but she could not afford to. From a financial point of view going back to work does not always pay. If there are other motives for working – to get out of the house or to preserve career prospects – the cost of working is of no concern, but if money is the main incentive, it is not always worthwhile. Good quality care is now available, but only for those who can pay for it. The price of live-in nannies has doubled plus a bit during the 1980s. As there are too few trained and experienced nannies for too many jobs, they are earning more than they ever have in real terms. Each rung up the nanny career ladder will add to the cost. An untrained eighteen-year-old mother's help will expect not less than £60 in London, a bit less in the country. The NNEB (National Nursery Examination Board) nanny will cost more, £90 plus for London, plus hidden costs – tax and national insurance, lighting, heating, food, telephone etc. Experienced (ie two years in a job) NNEBs may earn between £100 and £150, occasionally more in London. Nannies with less well-known qualifications are a little cheaper. Daily nannies are even more expensive – £30 to £40 a day.

Mother's helps are untrained and sometimes do the housework as well as look after the children. They charge £20 to £30 a day. Childminders are paid between £50 to £60 a week and more in London. Other than friends or relations, subsidized nurseries are the cheapest option, sometimes costing as little as £30 a week, but the lack of local authority and workplace nurseries or crèches mean that many working mothers have to turn to private nurseries, which, if run as commercial enterprises, can charge £30 plus a day. Going back to work also involves many hidden extras – clothes and shoes, and upgrading from jeans and trainers can be expensive. Lunches can be costly too and the convenience foods, which many working mothers rely upon, add extra expense. All in all, if the salary is not large enough, going back to work, particularly part-time, does not pay.

Going back

"I wanted to work to join the human race again, to get my head together", said Kerry, a former journalist who now works part-time in public relations. "I am thoroughly enjoying it. I never thought I would say I would enjoy work, but it is nice, yes, to join the human race, to realize there is a life outside coffee mornings and washing up, putting the washing out and feeding the cat." No matter how much women enjoy motherhood, for some it will never be a substitute for using their abilities creatively and to recognized effect in the outside world. Many enjoy working, enjoy the status, the social life, the money and the independence that brings. "My whole relationship with my husband is built on me being financially independent. Me losing out financially is me losing my power," said Caroline. "It wasn't so much that I wanted to go back to work, but I didn't want to be dependent. We could have lived on one salary, but in order to maintain my sanity and my financial independence and maintain the standard of living I'd got used to, I had to go back to work. I didn't want to have to ask him to buy clothes."

Women today have been encouraged to be independent, to fulfil themselves and to follow a career. To give up seventeen years of full-time education and years of work on top of that can seem a waste. "I had a life and career before children," said Heather, "when they go to school I will still have a life and career." Some industries change very quickly, and not working, even for a year or so, can mean losing touch. "Keeping a foot on the career ladder" can be important.

Some women work for their own pleasure, but most go back because they have to. Two out of three mothers would choose to stay at home with their children and not work if they could afford to do so.[4] Mothers need not be living on the breadline to have to work, simply dictated to by the mortgage or the family budget. Women's earnings are no longer pocket money, but essential money, particularly since the economic recession. Lyn would like to be a full-time mother, but they cannot live off what her husband earns, so she is forced to do accounts from home in the evenings. "We live off my money. My husband's pays the mortgage and bills. My contribution goes towards food and what have you. We are about £300 short every month and that's what I have to earn." They might not want to be at work, but many working mothers feel they are actually better mothers.[5] The change in environment, mental stimulation and social contact can be healthier for both mother and child. Lucy's job as a mental nurse gave her and her children a wider outlook on life. "As much as I like being a mother I wouldn't be as good a mother if I was with them all the time."

The return

A supermum may "take a day off from the boardroom to produce; as soon as the placenta hits the pedal-bin, she slides off the delivery table into her business suit, clips on her earrings, tosses the baby in the briefcase and drives the company car back to the office;"[6] less fictitious mothers can find returning to work quite a struggle. Organizing the right childcare, building up to separating, building down from breastfeeding, the anxiety of leaving the baby and stepping back into work, can be unexpectedly difficult. Thoughts of work can dominate and even ruin the last few weeks or months of maternity leave. Cathy, a local government officer, puts her post-natal depression down to anxieties about returning to work. "I was very worried about leaving them with a childminder. I had a nightmarish time trying to get the older one to take a bottle and formula – it took about a week. I was extremely anxious that I'd have a thirsty, starving baby crying all the time and that the childminder wouldn't be able to cope. This added to my guilt about going back. I got so depressed."

Months of baby talk, nappies, feeds and sleepless nights can affect a woman's confidence. Cathy worried about the office politics, how to talk to people and how things were done, "ordering stationery, answering the phone, you know, petty stuff, I'd forgotten how to do it." Fran, a teacher, could not sleep the night before she had to go back to work. "I was just thinking about it and how people would accept me. I felt as though I was the centre of attention, that people were looking at me thinking, well, does she look like a mum and has her body changed." Caroline, a building surveyor, got up at 6am, two hours earlier than she used to, just to get the baby and herself ready. "I felt very nervous going into the office. I'd lost all my confidence and I was much fatter and all crumpled from lifting the baby and had porridge on my shoulder. Before I felt very confident, after, totally different. I'd missed out on all the developments that had been going on – it's amazing how much changes in seven months." Wendy, a library assistant, was in tears from the moment she woke up. "I thought about what I was doing and the tears were coming. I just couldn't say goodbye. My mum said, 'Just get out and don't be silly.' I kissed the baby goodbye and the tears were streaming down my face. I got into work and if anyone asked me anything I just burst into tears." Jill's first day was "drastic". She couldn't concentrate, "I was thinking every two minutes, what's he doing" I cried and I phoned part way through the morning. I had weaned him a fortnight before and that felt strange too. I shouldn't have done it so close, but I knew I couldn't cope with pumping breasts in the loo at lunchtime. I really missed him. Being a mother at home had been so lovely and work seemed so hard and cold. I ran home as fast I could – as if ten minutes would make any difference. I was absolutely desperate to see him and it was like that for a long time."

The distance from their babies, engorged breasts and not understanding the sharp chat or the office politics can make many women feel alien on their first day back. "It's like starting a new job, but without the benefits," said Cathy. "When you start a new job, people will show you around and treat you kindly. But I got none of that." Some may be welcomed back with congratulations and fussing, but for others, at least initially, the reception can be much more chilly. Assistants who have been standing in can be frosty, and men in particular can envy women having time off for maternity leave. After all, they have been slaving away while she has been on an extended holiday and getting paid for it. It can be hard for them to welcome back colleagues without expressing their resentment in some way. Heather's first day was "horrendous". She said, "My desk was occupied by a stranger. My belongings lost, and I still haven't found some, and I was seated in the draughty corner by the door and subjected to comments like, "Ho, ho who's in the naughty corner?" and that's what it felt like. On top of that, payroll weren't notified so I missed payday."

Unsympathetic employers

Despite Opportunity 2000 and other government-sponsored drives to encourage working women, despite official company policy on job shares and flexible working hours, working mothers still have to fight against resistance and entrenched attitudes, particularly when it comes to requests for part-time work. Deep down, many employers think why should it be made easy for women to come back part-time. Why should other colleagues be inconvenienced when there are plenty of people who would do the job without fussing about job shares. Wendy's boss did not agree with mothers working. A library assistant, she returned to work and, in keeping with regional council policy, requested a job share. "He just turned around and said, 'No'. I said, 'Why not?' And he said, 'Because I want full-time workers, not part-time workers.' He felt that if somebody didn't want a full-time job they should give it to somebody who did." Wendy eventually got her job share, but only after presenting her case to the union and a long fight, and all at a time when she was missing her daughter, readjusting to work and feeling emotionally vulnerable. The right to work, the right to job share, may on paper be growing in acceptance with more companies addressing equal opportunities, but in practice many institutions still have uncompromising management structures and hierarchies and mothers still have to be grateful to employers who allow her to shorten her working hours, grateful to employers who keep her on, but delay promotion, so she has the flexibility to care for her baby.

Juggling

Working and having children are a huge burden and juggling them is a woman's problem. A man may do the cooking and cleaning, but if he has a meeting, his woman will cover for him. If she has a meeting, she has to organize the childcare. Caroline is the one who has to drop her baby off at the childminders. "He says, 'Well I have to be at work early, so I can't look after her and get her ready.' His job comes first, he earns more money than me – or that's the argument. It will be him who has to continue, or so he says. So, I have the role of making the preparations, making sure I drop her off. I found the childminder. It was my responsibility. My responsibility to pick her up." Very few working mothers get the same level of support from their male partners, both emotional and practical, that men expect from them. Most women set off to work each day with nowhere near the same domestic backup that men have. For most men, home is a safe haven at the end of the day and most women who go out to work are maintaining this haven more or less single-handedly as well as working. Successful women are either single or married to men much older than themselves, men who have already achieved, who can afford to be supportive.

Having children makes it all so much harder. Who will take the step backwards for the sake of the family? Who will take time off when the children are sick? The mother. Working mothers are constantly aware of having to be in two places at once, being two people at once, of having to juggle and feel they are not doing either particularly well. Firstly, work suffers. Most professional women who return to work after having children find they are less ambitious, see their careers on hold and are given fewer opportunities to train or develop.[7] Caroline felt her career had definitely suffered. "I can't stay late, when everyone else is staying late to impress the boss. I can't do that. Also, at work there is a culture of if you are staying late you must be working hard and if you go at 5pm you're a clock watcher. But if you have a child you have to go. I feel I am no longer perceived as a serious, ambitious person. That's the cost of having children." Long hours are equated with commitment, although there is no evidence that long hours increase productivity and working mothers cannot join in this boys' game. They cannot be flexible. To compensate, they feel they have to work doubly hard to prove they can still do it and that they have to keep their domestic and public lives in compartments. Helena Kennedy, the barrister, wrote, "The unspoken rule is never to mix the two, or evoke one in aid of the other. The image of the capable woman must never be tainted by the smell of baby powder; efficient women have that side of their lives well under control. Motherhood is like some skeleton kept in the cupboard and most of us collaborate in keeping our children invisible. We have the terrible fear that to concede that there are emotional pulls or practical complications will be used against us."[8]

As for home, there is never enough time. Working, particularly full-time, and having children is exhausting. "It's mental as well as physical," said Jill. "Your mind is constantly juggling. I leave school at 4pm to get home by 4.30pm. So, I stop one thing and the mental processes that involved, and as soon as I'm out of the door, I'm thinking, right, what are we having for tea. Then, I get home and it's the kids and sorting things out with the minder. The kids are a bit fractious because it's the end of the day and I'm trying to make the tea and not turn on the video, because that's the easy way out." Scarlet, an office administrator, said, "In the evenings there was no time to sit down and relax. I had to carry on, cook supper, I wouldn't sit down until 11pm. I thought, I can't live like this, this isn't living." Scarlet has since given up work. Because there is no let up, weekends become one big rush, shopping and housework still have to be done and there is never any time off, many full-time working mothers either feel permanently stressed and exhausted or are trying to reduce their hours at work. Working mothers have to accept that they cannot get everything done, cannot even always do their best, but that they are doing what they can.

Guilt

When women want to both follow a career and be with their children, guilt is never far away. Guilt is a working woman's biggest problem because the guilt that comes from leaving children is so deep-rooted. Admit it or not, most women feel they are the best people to care for their babies; that their attention is superior and that by leaving their children, they are running the risk of retarding their children's development: "children need their mothers" and 'good' mothers stay at home. But the idea that children need the concentrated twenty-four-hour-a-day attention of their mothers is a recent one. Motherhood as an all-excluding occupation was introduced through post-Second World War childcare literature, largely thanks to John Bowlby and his theory of 'maternal deprivation'. Bowlby stressed the crucial and irreplaceable central role played by the mother – not only in the physical well-being and progress of her children, but in their long-term emotional, social and intellectual development. Adolescent bad behaviour and neuroses were Mother's Fault, and the most damaging thing a mother could do to her small children was to deprive them of her presence even for a few hours. Mother became the only person capable, in the pre-school years, of nurturing, stimulating and teaching her children. Any substitute childcarer was very much second best. This is still the prevailing attitude. Mothers being essential has got confused with mothers being universal.

Rose was 'actively encouraged' to feel guilty by her mother and mother-in-law if she did anything that took her away from the children. "I've started training as a barrister. It requires about twenty-five hours' study a week and it's quite difficult fitting it in. I have to spend four weekends away each year, which isn't many. But my mother will say to the children, 'I feel really sorry for you. Fancy Mummy going away and leaving you. Isn't it awful.' And, 'Oh poor baby, Mummy's always working isn't she?'" Relatives can be particularly cruel to working mothers. Guilt stems not only from "mothers should be with their babies", but also from the fact that most mothers do not have the experience of mothers who worked. They are breaking away from the pattern of parents' lives and are not being a 'proper' mother. Harriet's mother did work, but "She seems to have forgotten that now. She says 'I was always at home for you', but she wasn't. She worked as a receptionist in a health centre. She makes all these comments about mothers going back to work and I feel like saying, Mum, I work too, you're getting at me. She says I look tired or says, 'You're not working another weekend?' But that's the easiest time because my husband can look after them and I think, Good, he has time with them alone."

Fathers are happy to see their children at the end of the day, but equally happy if it is just for fifteen minutes. They do not see it as a loss. Women do. There is still the underlying assumption that women have to be self-denying to help their men and children survive and prosper, that 'greed' and 'self-interest' are sinful. Some women even compete over who is the most self-denying and are highly critical of those who seem selfish. Rose was told she was "selfish to do anything for me", not by her relatives, but by a woman in her circle of friends. Friends who say they will go back to work eventually and then only part-time, friends who constantly talk about the special activities they do with their babies, and friends who never miss an opportunity to say how bad the local childminders seem. It is not only the predictable conservative lobby who make mothers feel bad about trying to "have it all", younger women do too. And some very public young women at that. Women like Kathy Gyngell, who gave up her job as a television producer for full-time motherhood and who, like any convert, has embraced her new role with a born-again vengeance. "The relationship with the mother is special and critical, and nothing else will do," she declared. "When a child's mother dies, that is a terrible tragedy. But we impose that tragedy on every child when we leave them to go to work"[9] Or Paula Yates who has not actually given up any of her jobs, but is nevertheless very vocal in her attacks on the 'selfishness' of working mothers.

"I don't feel guilty any more. I know it sounds strange, because a lot of mothers feel guilty about working. I felt more guilty about being at home and hating it. Once I started working I started enjoying my home," said one woman. It takes a brave mother to admit the inadmissible: that she would rather spend time at work than with her children. Guilt can be at its worst when mothers know what a good mother should be, but know they do not enjoy being it. Gillian did not plan to go back to work as a teacher. "When I was pregnant I planned to finish work and have this baby and I was going to be quite happy. But I soon realized I missed the company and stimulation. I got fed up with the house and the baby. I felt I needed something else, but I was really disappointed with myself for feeling like that. I'd not planned that. I'd planned to be at home and look after this baby and that was it. I expected to find it completely fulfilling. I had friends who didn't help. Friends who said, "Oh you're not going to leave him are you? You can't leave him.""

Working for financial reasons is acceptable; working for pleasure is not. Diana's friends "Made a real point of telling me they wouldn't leave their kids if they didn't have to. I thought at one point, what's wrong with me? I can leave my child, I don't love my child any less than them, but they would never consider it." Diana said it probably sounded "awful" but she did not miss them when she was at work and that when she first went back "I actually felt normal again."

Women with young children find it hard to set limits for themselves. They expect and are told to expect to be available to their children at all times. Doing anything for themselves is selfish, which is why for some work is a respite, a way of drawing a boundary and having time to themselves. "I was relieved to be back at work," said Celia, "it was a break from the children." Women at work can drink a cup of coffee, read the paper, make phone calls, can enjoy feeling stimulated and challenged and having something outside the family they can call their own. But they also feel guilty because they have their own needs as well as their children's.

Childminders and nannies

Childminders and nannies are another source of guilt and anxiety. Every mother has heard the one about the nanny who smoked dope and or made love with her boyfriend while her charges watched. Or the childminder who disappeared with the baby only to be found hours later in the police station having been arrested for stealing food and hiding it in the baby's pram and on questioning denied knowing not only the parents, but the baby too. Anxieties about how the child is being cared for in a mother's absence are very real. Some nannies and childminders are trained, but not all, and few are supervised by state bodies. Most parents, when choosing a childminder or nanny, have only their instincts to rely on and yet the minder is being entrusted with a woman's most treasured possession.

Sandra said, "It sounds stupid, but I always think about it from the baby's point of view. I always think, he's eight months old, he can't ask me what's happening. He doesn't know why I'm going to go off and leave him until 5pm. I feel so guilty about that." Kate dreaded the daily delivery to the childminder. "He hates me going. He'll grab my head and yank it around so that it's an inch away from his nose and say things like, 'Mummy, I want you to look after me today' and then absolutely howl when I say I have to go to work. It's the actual leaving of him, because you know he's unhappy." And knowing that five minutes later he will be fine does nothing to dislodge the lingering image a working mother carries with her of her child bawling his eyes out because he has been abandoned by her. Guilt, guilt and more guilt when he's picked up in the evening, crying and protesting that he does not want to come home, he wants to stay with 'Mummy' to which the minder says, "I don't know what's got into him. He's been so good all day."

The relationship between mother and minder, between two people who 'share' the care of a baby, is bound to be highly charged and confusing, for both parties. Women who work from home are different from women who choose to work outside the home. Some nannies and childminders think it is wrong for mothers to leave their babies and, voiced or not, such views can lead to misunderstandings, guilt and criticism. Minders and nannies often care with a similar intensity of feeling to the mother, at least in the short term. This is lucky for the children, but difficult for both women involved, particularly as maternity leave usually ends between three and six months, a time when mothers are still relative novices and unsure of their abilities to mother. Fears that the carer will seduce the baby away and a sense of competition with the nanny or childminder are not unusual, fears which, as most find out, are totally unfounded. Other adults may add to the richness of the baby's environment, but none will give it quite the sense of security that a mother does. A baby will always save its real intensity of love and hate, security and fears for its mother.

Working today

"Work and home is one of the most problematic areas in my life," said Sandra. "I wanted to go back, but I didn't want to go. I want to be with the children, but I don't want to be with them. I want both, but I can't have both." Work and children is a no-win situation. It not simply a case of the right to work, or of fashions, it is reconciling the difference between education, need, ambition, babies and enjoying family life; between being trained to use brains at work, but being told to use personalities on children. Working women are inevitably torn, suffer from back and forth feelings and rarely feel completely at peace with their decision.

The situation is not helped by our social system which expects everything at the same time. The late 20s and early 30s are a productive time for both careers and babies. Biology and ageism mean that delaying until a more convenient moment can mean missing out altogether. Adapting working life more to pregnancy and motherhood would also help.

If mothers felt they could take a year or so off and not be penalized by loss of earnings, position and opportunities; if there were more workplace crèches and subsidized nurseries, job shares and flexibility; more than that, if motherhood was really respected – then working mothers would have an easier time.

Conclusion

This book is about what becoming a mother is *really* like and not what women are led to believe. The medical establishment leads new mothers to think they will be physically recovered by six weeks. This number, it turns out, is not related to overall health, but principally on the time it takes for a woman's uterus to return to its pre-pregnant state. The assumption is that once a woman's reproductive system is back to normal, she herself is too. Delivery is an emotional event, but also a momentous physical stress to the body. Women ache all over; they hurt in places they never normally think about; and they are tired and need to rest. Instead they have a baby to feed, nappies to change and have to exist on little sleep. It is hard for a new mother to give her body time to heal and get strong when taking care of a new baby. On top of it all, the common post-partum ailments – piles, constipation, sore stitches, hair loss etc., are seen as temporary minor discomforts, which taken individually they are, but not when they all come at once, as they often do. Because of the traditional six-week recovery period, many are left feeling that persistent problems lie not in their bodies but their minds. They may feel weak, not quite themselves, and afraid of being seen as complainers.

In the past, women knew that recovery took longer than six weeks. An extended family and other support networks were there to help them and they often spent two weeks recovering in bed. Today, women are expected to be up and about in days and back at work within weeks (as well as taking care of a dependent child). Not only are women misled physically, but emotionally too. New mothers find that they are not full of pure love after all; their feelings are tinged with resentment. Fay Weldon described it as a "secret knowledge" and gives it as the reason why new mothers get into such a terrible state. "She finds she would rather sleep and just let the baby cry. And this is what it's like ever after; you don't sleep, because the baby needs you . . . Having children means no longer believing you're a nice person. The childless can remain convinced they are decent, civilized, pleasant human beings. It's when you have children you realize how wars start."[1]

In the interests of better serving new mothers, greater realism is needed. The traditional notion of the six-week recovery period needs to be reassessed and ante-natal classes that prepare couples for parenthood as well as birth need to be introduced. The more prepared a woman is for what she's going to have to confront, the better she will be able to deal with whatever happens. Women need to set more realistic goals for themselves post-delivery and to judge themselves more kindly. A woman who simply says she wants to have a healthy baby and to do the best she can will have an easier time than one who has set numerous specific goals for herself. Acknowledging that there are many aspects of the post-partum period which she might not feel in control of can be one of the healthiest things a woman can do. Some say that the simple fact of telling herself that she has a year to recover, get in shape and adjust relieves much of the pressure of feeling that she must be 'normal' straight away.

It is often difficult to set realistic goals when the medical establishment doesn't. And it's particularly hard in an age in which the superwoman myth equates beauty with thinness and presses for high performance at home and work. So why do we do it? Why, with the pain of childbirth, the chronic wear and tear, the sleepless nights, the need for ten pairs of hands and the total invasion of privacy, do women have babies? Because for many in spite of it all, having a baby is their greatest achievement. Not to have children is a closed door; having them opens up a wider experience. Without them we might be more even-tempered and richer, but life would be greatly impoverished. As Valerie Grove wrote, "To me, the ultimate pleasure and motivation in having children is that they satisfy one's innate curiosity about what one's children would be like."[2]

The second time around the surprises are not so great and a mother will feel more confident. You've been through it once and somehow the baby survived. You know that whatever they may be like at one stage, they will soon move on to another. Any stage is not a stage forever. And there are those who claim that the sleepless nights and teething are nothing compared with scowling adolescence. But that's another story. As I am sure that the general picture of motherhood painted by this book is not as rosy as some, it will be assumed that I was driven to write it by a particularly horrific personal experience. I love being a mother, but such is the power of the myth – the smiling baby in its mother's loving arms – and the books which deal exhaustively with babycare and child development, but draw a veil over the mother's health and feelings, that those who speak honestly run the risk of being branded 'bad'. I even worried about what my children would think of their mother writing about motherhood in less than glowing terms. I hope they will understand that this has been about trying to set the record straight.

Medical Glossary

AFTERPAINS (after birth pains) Uterine contractions due to release of the hormone oxytocin from the pituitary gland, to promote contraction or involution of the womb to its pre-pregnant size. The pains are especially stimulated by the baby suckling and are more intense after second and subsequent babies. Relaxation techniques, as used during labour, may help in controlling the pain. Otherwise analgesics such as paracetamol or codydramol (paracetamol plus hydrocodeine), taken about half an hour before breastfeeding, will help. Afterpains are only severe for the first few days post-natally and fade away completely over the next week.

BIRTHING POOL Rather like very large bathtubs, birthing pools are particularly useful when used to help relaxation during labour; sometimes, if the labour progresses normally, the baby may also be delivered in the pool. Experienced midwifery and medical staff should assess the safety of proceeding if a woman requests this mode of labour management or delivery. An optimal water temperature is used at each stage of labour and the well-being of both mother and baby is monitored at intervals.

BREAKING THE WATERS This describes the rupture of the smooth thin membranes which enclose the baby with the release of some of the surrounding amniotic fluid, either as a sudden gush or more commonly as a series of trickles. The break can occur spontaneously before the onset of labour, heralding its onset and stimulating uterine contractions, or may not occur until labour is well under way, as the cervix dilates and the baby starts to move down the birth canal.

The membranes can be ruptured artificially to induce labour or during spontaneous labour to expedite delivery. This may be achieved either by the careful insertion of a finger during vaginal examination or using a surgical instrument that looks rather like a crochet hook.

CAESAREAN SECTION This is the delivery of a baby by making a surgical incision into the abdomen and uterus to facilitate easier or more rapid birth. The procedure does carry certain risks – principally to the mother rather than to the baby – so is usually only done when there are specific medical indications. Elective caesareans, planned in advance and performed before the woman goes into labour, may be necessary because of problems with the baby or its position in the uterus; problems with the placenta (eg lying low over the cervical opening of the uterus); problems with the mother's health (eg severe heart disease) or where there is insufficient room for the baby to pass out vaginally (eg small pelvis and large baby). Emergency caesareans are performed if unforeseen problems arise usually once labour has commenced and it is necessary to expedite birth because, for example, the baby shows signs of distress or the labour is difficult and not progressing well.

The operation can be performed under epidural or general anaesthetic. The former may take some time to set up, but is usually preferable because the woman can see and hold her baby as soon as it is born so bonding is not delayed and her partner or labour companion can be with her. With an epidural, the woman should feel no pain but she will feel odd sensations of pushing and pulling and 'rummaging around'; it can also be maintained post-operatively for pain relief. After general anaesthesia women feel rather groggy over the next few days, which may be problematic particularly if she wishes to breastfeed, and there are greater risks of complications such as chest infection.

The operation itself is quick – after the incision is made, usually a bikini-line cut into the lower segment of the uterus, the baby will be delivered within about ten minutes. The placenta and membranes are then delivered and the uterus and abdomen closed, taking a further thirty to fifty minutes. Having had abdominal surgery, the woman will require pain relief and will need to recover gradually, with assistance, whilst in hospital (week or so) and for the first few weeks at home.

The old saying "Once a caesarean, always a caesarean" no longer holds; vaginal delivery may be possible in subsequent pregnancies depending, for example, on the type of incision made.

CONTRACTION The co-ordinated shortening of the muscles of the uterine wall. Contractions arrive in regular waves which initially serve to dilate the cervical opening of the womb (stage 1 of labour) and then push out through the vaginal birth canal (stage 2).

COLOSTRUM A clear yellowish fluid produced by the breasts during the later stages of pregnancy and before the onset of true milk production (lactation) after delivery. It contains serum, white blood cells and antibodies thereby providing an infant with some immunity against disease in early life.

COT DEATH Also called Sudden Infant Death Syndrome (SIDS), this is the sudden unexpected death of an infant in the absence of any identifiable cause. It is the leading 'cause' of death in infants between one month and one year of age, but it is in fact very rare.

Why cot deaths occur is as yet unknown; however ways of reducing the risks include laying babies down to sleep on their back or side rather than on their front; ensuring that an infant doesn't get too cold (when out in cold weather), nor too hot (from overwrapping – especially when coming indoors in cold weather or high room temperatures) and by avoiding exposure to tobacco smoke.

D & C (dilation and curettage) A surgical procedure done under anaesthetic to remove contents of the uterus. It is principally used for sampling of the uterine lining when diagnosing of the cause of abnormal bleeding; it may also be used for the removal of retained products of pregnancy after delivery (ie pieces of placenta or membranes) or after miscarriage, or for the termination of an early pregnancy).

The cervix is gently opened (dilated) and the contents gently scraped (curettage) or sucked away.

DOMINO SCHEME One form of antenatal care which is organized to offer continuity in care as far as possible. The central professional is the community midwife who sees a woman regularly throughout the pregnancy, either at her home or at her GP surgery (to which the midwife is usually attached). This midwife also assesses the woman when she is in early labour and will attend if working hours allow. She will deliver the baby in hospital, where an obstetrician is available if problems arise. If there are no peri-natal problems, the mother may be discharged from the hospital 6 hours after birth and post-natal care continued at home by the community midwife.

DEEP VEIN THROMBOSIS (DVT) "Clotting" of blood within a deep vein of the leg can occur in association with pregnancy, either in the antenatal period of bedrest due to some medical condition or after surgical delivery (caesarean section). A DVT may be of little consequence to the leg itself, perhaps causing some pain and swelling, but can be serious if pieces of the thrombus break off (embolize). These will be carried in the bloodstream to the lungs, where they lodge, cutting off the blood supply to part of the lungs. Small emboli may cause mild breathlessness and chest pain transiently but a massive pulmonary embolus may cause sudden collapse and require immediate life-saving treatment. Hence DVTs are treated with anti-coagulants to prevent embolism.

Anti-coagulants such as heparin thin the blood; usually the drugs are taken until a few months after delivery and their use monitored carefully by regular blood tests to avoid excessive thinning of the blood.

ECLAMPSIA This is the end-stage of a severe disease occurring in pregnancy, where a woman has fits (convulsions) and which threatens the life of both mother and baby. The preceding stage, before fits develop, is referred to as pre-eclampsia and is characterized by very high blood pressure during pregnancy in a woman whose blood pressure was previously normal, accompanied by fluid retention and the presence of protein in the urine.

Pre-eclampsia is not uncommon, but it is often asymptomatic until late in the disease so frequent screening of the blood pressure throughout pregnancy is vital.

ECT (ELECTRO-CONVULSIVE THERAPY) This is a mode of treatment used for some forms of mental illness, including severe post-natal depression. A modified and controlled fit or convulsion is produced by passing an electrical current through the brain (usually one half only). This therapy can produce a rapid and longlasting improvement of symptoms in well selected patients.

EPIDURAL A method of obtaining pain relief by anaesthetizing the nerve fibres arising in the lower back which carry the sensation of pain. Local anaesthetic is infiltrated into the spine, in the space outside the membrane (dura) that encloses the spinal cord and fluid. Epidurals may be particularly helpful when the baby's position is breech, in multiple pregnancy or premature delivery, with ineffective contractions and with forceps delivery or caesarean section.

Problems with epidurals may arise due to poor technique: for example, when the dura or blood vessels are punctured. In addition, the blood pressure may fall dramatically. Both these situations require special medical and nursing care. After delivery, there may be problems with headache (which can be severe) or urinary retention, and longer term, backache.

EPISIOTOMY A surgical incision is made in the tissues surrounding the vaginal opening (perineum) when the baby's head is well down near the outlet so that the tissues are well stretched. The aim is to enlarge the opening in a controlled manner to facilitate an easier delivery and to avoid uncontrolled tearing which may extend to the anal margin and compromise faecal continence. An episiotomy may also be performed to hasten the delivery of a baby that shows signs of distress, to protect the fragile head of a premature baby, and for instrumental deliveries (using forceps or ventouse).

However, there is little compelling evidence that the overall outcome is better with an episiotomy than when tearing occurs; the cut may not heal any better and may cause as much pain and discomfort.

Different incisions may be used – one of three types: a midline approach which heals quicker as it does not cut across the pelvic wall muscle, but has the danger of extending into the anus; the mediolateral approach (the most common) which cuts across the pelvic floor and is associated with poor healing, bleeding, pain and wound breakdown; and a 'J' shaped approach which tries to combine the previous two but is difficult to perform and stitch.

Problems with episiotomy: discomfort from stitches during healing (ice packs and salt baths may help, as may using a hairdryer to dry the perineum); bleeding; infection. Sexual intercourse may be painful long after healing is complete if the vaginal opening is made too small or if the deeper tissue layers are inadequately repaired and no longer protect the bladder.

FORCEPS These instruments assist in the delivery of a baby vaginally. There are different designs either for 'lift-out' deliveries when the baby's head is already low, for high deliveries, or for rotating the baby's head to facilitate delivery. Such assistance may be necessary because the baby shows signs of distress; because it is taking excessively long to push the baby out; or because the mother is becoming distressed or exhausted.

Forceps deliveries can only be performed if the baby's head is well down in the pelvis, the cervix is fully dilated and the pelvis is not too small: it requires an experienced doctor, adequate analgesia and usually an episiotomy. Forceps are placed around the baby's head between contractions and by gentle but firm pulling, in time with contractions, the baby can be delivered, usually over 3-4 contractions.

Complications of forceps: maternal trauma, bruising over baby's face. Some muscles of the baby's face may be paralysed temporarily after forceps deliveries, but this is thought to be caused by pressure of the pelvic bones rather than pressure of the forceps.

GAS AND AIR (ENTONOX) A mixture of nitrous oxide ("laughing gas") and oxygen in equal proportions which reduces but does not remove pain. It can be used throughout labour and is self-administered – breathed in using a mask or mouthpiece via a demand valve. For best effect, a few deep breaths of Entonox are taken at the start of a wave of contractions, so that the gas is already on board when the contraction builds to a peak, taking further deep breaths of the gas for the duration of the contraction, but stopping as the contraction fades.

Entonox can cause feelings of nausea, light-headedness or sleepiness but since it is self-administered, it can be stopped if this becomes too unpleasant. It has no harmful side-effects for mother or baby and can be used in conjunction with other methods of pain relief.

GUTHRIE TEST A screening test which examines blood to exclude a condition called phenyl ketonuria (PKU). This is a rare metabolic disease but it is important because it causes severe mental handicap unless the infant receives a special diet from an early age.

A small amount of blood is taken from the baby at six or seven days after birth by pricking the heel and collecting the blood on blotting paper. Usually the opportunity is taken to collect further drops of blood to screen for deficiency of the hormone thyroxine (hypothyroidism). In some health districts the disease Cystic Fibrosis is also screened for in this way.

HAEMORRHAGE Unexpected bleeding or haemorrhage occurring in relation to pregnancy which risks the mother's or baby's life.

HAEMORRHOIDS (PILES) Enlargement of the normal spongy veins in the walls of the anus which may bleed with defecation or cause itching, discomfort or pain. They usually arise as a consequence of prolonged constipation; in pregnancy however, they may first arise or existing piles worsen, because of additional hormonal effects on blood vessels.

A diet that is high in fibre will prevent constipation and taking regular exercise will improve the circulation, thereby reducing the risk or discomfort of piles.

INDUCTION Sometimes labour must be started artificially because of some risk to the mother or baby, such that it is safer for the infant to be delivered than for it to remain inside the uterus. Indications for the induction of labour include very elevated maternal blood pressure, poor growth of the baby due to a failing placenta, or a prolonged pregnancy – where labour hasn't started spontaneously more than one or two weeks after the expected date of delivery.

A prostaglandin tablet or pessary inserted into the vagina will prepare the cervix for labour, making it 'ripe' and may provide sufficient stimulation to initiate contractions. More usually, the hormone oxytocin (Syntocinon) is also required, given as an infusion or drip into a vein in the arm. Once an induction of labour is commenced the mother's and baby's well-being must be monitored at intervals, so the mother will be unable to move around freely during these times.

A labour which is induced *may* be prolonged – it can take some time for the cervix to ripen or the contractions to start – and the contractions *may* be more painful than with a spontaneous onset of labour, but this is certainly not the rule.

Induction is usually trouble-free, but *no* method of intervention is absolutely certain and safe. The greatest hazard is the delivery of a baby that is premature, or more so than anticipated, perhaps when the dates used to age the pregnancy were incorrect. The premature infant may require care in a Special Care Baby Unit. Another problem is that the induction may fail; a number lead to delivery by caesarean section.

INCONTINENCE OF URINE Inappropriate, involuntary passage of urine is a distressing symptom experienced by many men and women, but the type of incontinence most commonly associated with pregnancy and childbirth is **stress incontinence**. This is when leakage of urine is brought on by physical straining or sudden exertion such as sneezing, coughing, jumping or laughing (perhaps being the origin of the expression "I wet myself laughing").

The mechanism of stress incontinence is essentially related to the loss of tone in the pelvic floor muscles. Normally, these muscles ensure continence in three ways. They maintain an angle at the junction between the bladder and the urethra (the tube draining urine out of the bladder). Secondly, they ensure that the bladder neck lies well within the abdominal cavity so that any rise in pressure in the abdomen (ie during straining etc) not only squeezes the bladder but also squeezes the bladder neck, shutting it tightly. Thirdly, the muscle fibres run around the walls of the urethra; when the muscle contracts, they serve to further close off the bladder outlet. Thus lax pelvic floor muscles result in the loss of control of urine outflow. Clearly, the key to preventing and treating stress incontinence lies in exercising the pelvic floor muscles. Only if this proves to be inadequate should operative measures be considered.

Urge incontinence is another important type; in this case the person (male or female) has an urgent feeling that they must pass urine, but they do not have enough time to get to the lavatory. The person takes to going to the toilet very frequently - at the first feeling of the bladder filling up – to try to avoid wetting themselves, but this can make the problem worse. Thus urge incontinence can also have a debilitating effect, making the individual feel reluctant to go out for fear of being caught short, or outings are carefully planned around the availability of toilet amenities.

The different types of incontinence have very different causes and very different solutions; it is therefore essential that all problems of urinary incontinence are carefully assessed by a GP. Urodynamic studies may be required to establish the diagnosis and so determine the best course of treatment. Additional factors (such as urine infection, cystitis, some menstrual factors and being overweight) can contribute to the problem and may require specific treatment.

IVF (IN-VITRO FERTILIZATION) A technique of "assisted conception" whereby eggs are collected from the ovaries and fertilized outside the body. After a period of incubation and growth, viable fertilized eggs (termed zygotes) are implanted in the uterus. Thereafter the baby develops as normal.

LOCHIA A normal discharge from the uterus, consisting of its lining and blood cells, which is passed vaginally during the first weeks after delivery. It is initially red in colour (lochia rubra), then yellow (serosa) and finally white (alba).

MALPRESENTATION This is said to occur when the part of the baby that presents itself to the cervical opening of the uterus lies in such a position that it may be difficult to deliver the baby vaginally. For such deliveries, an experienced midwife or obstetrician should be present. The most common malpresentation is breech presentation, when the bottom or feet of the baby emerge first.

MASTITIS Mastitis is a breast infection which can occur when an engorged breast becomes infected. Poor diet, lack of rest, emotional stress, or a weakened immune system can also lead to breast infection. It is marked by inflammation, soreness, redness, or excess heat anywhere on the breast and is accompanied by fever. The pain is a throbbing, burning sensation and feeding the baby from the infected bosom can be agony. Nevertheless it is essential to continue feeding through the infection , as stopping will only cause more of a blockage and make matters worse. A course of antibiotics should be started immediately and the baby should feed from the infected side first as the initial sucking is stronger and will keep the milk flowing. Drink plenty of liquids, rest, eat well and keep the milk flowing by feeding the baby more often or by expressing. Use a variety of feeding positions to ensure that all the milk ducts are being used.

OBSTETRICS/OBSTETRICIAN Obstetrics is the medical speciality concerned with the care of women during pregnancy (usually from about the twelfth week of pregnancy onwards), childbirth, and about the first six weeks following birth, when the reproductive organs are recovering. An obstetrician is thus a medical doctor who is trained and experienced in this field and is usually based at a hospital. In comparison, a gynaecologist deals with conditions affecting females, particularly those affecting the reproductive system: this includes problems with fertility and early pregnancy (up to approximately thirteen weeks).

Antenatally, most women only see their obstetrician (or a member of the team) a few times; this is because most pregnancies proceed normally. However if the mother has a known medical condition, or if problems arise for the mother or baby, the antenatal care will be managed by the obstetrician more directly.

PELVIC FLOOR A sling of muscles, arranged like the figure '8', which are situated at the base of the pelvis and control the openings of the anus, vagina and urethra (from back to front). These muscles come under great strain during pregnancy and childbirth, after which their tone is usually significantly reduced. Exercising these muscles serves to minimize and repair the loss of tone which may otherwise cause problems such as leakage of urine (incontinence) or may reduce sexual enjoyment due to a more lax vaginal canal.

PERINEUM The area of skin and muscle between the vaginal and anal openings. This area may be damaged during delivery, particularly if the baby's head emerges too rapidly. The resultant tears are classified by the degree of damage caused: first degree tears are superficial, the muscle is not damaged so they may not need suturing (stitching). Second degree tears do involve the muscle and may extend to the anal sphincter if severe, so careful suturing is necessary to avoid problems with continence. Third degree tears extend into the anus and should be repaired by an experienced surgeon.

PETHIDINE A potent analgesic drug with mild sedative action commonly used to provide pain relief in labour and elsewhere. Usually it is given as an intramuscular injection and takes about fifteen minutes for the effects to be felt. It may cause the woman to feel nauseated or to vomit. In addition, because it crosses the placenta, the baby is monitored continuously and may be somewhat drowsy upon delivery.

PLACENTA PRAEVIA Adherence or implantation of the placenta in the lower segment rather than in the upper part of the uterus. This is more likely to occur if the placenta is large (eg with twins), if there are uterine abnormalities such as fibroids, or damage from previous pregnancy, surgery or caesarean section. The grade of placenta praevia can range from those which lie low but do not reach the cervical opening to those which completely cover it.

Problems may arise with bleeding during pregnancy – before or during labour, problems with delivery of the baby if the placenta obstructs the outlet, or the placenta may be abnormally adherent and difficult to remove once the baby is born.

POST-PARTUM Relating to the period of a few days immediately after birth.

POST-NATAL DEPRESSION (PND) This is loosely defined as a clinical depression starting within six to twelve months of childbirth. The symptoms are as in any clinical depression (low mood – feeling tired and empty; poor concentration; lack of interest or pleasure in life; irritability; slowness of thinking and movement; feelings of guilt and worthlessness; despair and suicidal feelings). However, the distinctive feature of PND is that there is intimate involvement with the baby and the mother may project her feelings onto the infant, incorporating it into her own identity. An anxious mother may feel resentful of her child, rejecting it or neglecting it as she becomes increasingly preoccupied and unable to cope. In severe cases, the mother may have suicidal feelings which include the child (and possibly other children).

The causes of PND are multifactoral, and include social factors, difficulties in pregnancy and childbirth, hormonal factors, but the most important is probably the occurrence of stressful life events around this time. A woman may have certain 'vulnerability factors' (eg the loss of her own mother at an early age; lack of a confiding relationship with her partner), such that she is at greater risk of having PND if she experiences 'precipitating factors' (such as a major loss or chronic financial difficulties).

The mother may seek help herself, but more commonly she is referred by a member of her family, a friend or by her midwife or health visitor. A good GP will listen carefully to her story, encouraging her to talk about her feelings. Certain features of PND respond well to treatment by anti-depressant drugs. Underlying factors of the depression may require other therapeutic approaches such as individual counselling, marriage therapy, problem solving or psychosexual counselling.

Wherever possible, the GP will try to respond to what the mother herself feels she needs, with the central aim of assisting to maintain her in her own home, so that she can care for her child or children herself. To this end, it may be appropriate to offer practical support and to co-ordinate other agencies such as home aids, community care workers and nursery or child-minding services. In extreme cases, where a mother is suicidal, has fears or fantasies of harming the baby or if she is neglecting the infant, admission to a Mother and Baby Unit is prescribed. Only rarely are mother and baby separated.

Most episodes of PND last three to six months although some continue over a year. The mother will require support throughout this time and beyond, working to rebuild lost confidence in her mothering skills.

POSTURAL HEADACHE A headache which is exacerbated by standing or sitting up and alleviated by lying flat, usually as a consequence of an epidural anaesthetic where the dura is punctured accidentally. Most resolve over a few hours (or days if severe) if the person takes plenty of fluid and rests flat in bed. Simple analgesics such as paracetamol may help.

PROLAPSE OF UTERUS The abnormal downward displacement of the uterus into the vaginal canal, caused by stretching of the supporting tissues during childbirth. The extent of uterine prolapse ranges from first degree, where the uterus is low but remains within the vagina, to third degree (procidenta), where the uterus lies completely outside the body and the vagina is turned inside out. The latter may be accompanied by prolapse of the bladder.

Prolapse is repaired surgically by shortening the supporting ligaments and narrowing the vagina and its opening (colporrhaphy).

PUERPERIUM The period after delivery during which the reproductive organs return to their pre-pregnant condition. This is usually regarded as taking six weeks, but in fact, with breastfeeding for example, can extend to the first year and beyond.

RELATE An agency of qualified counsellors who offer assistance to couples experiencing problems in their relationship.

TEAM MIDWIVES A small number of midwives (up to five or six) working together to provide 24-hour cover for any women under their care. All will meet a mother antenatally in order to establish her wishes or fears relating to labour and delivery, allowing the development of an empathetic working relationship. The mother can therefore be assured of being delivered by a midwife known to her which will promote a more relaxed and satisfactory experience of birth.

TRANSITION The period in labour when the cervix is fully dilated, just prior to the start of pushing out the baby. The woman may experience symptoms such as pronounced shivering and she may vomit; however, the transition is not always a recognizable phase in every labour.

VARICOSE VEINS Varicose veins are veins in the leg (and occasionally the vulva) which become enlarged and tortuous because the valves along the course of the vein have become defective.

Varicose veins can be painful and itchy, and the leg aches when standing, particularly towards the end of the day; they usually enlarge and become more uncomfortable with age. A tendency to varicose veins can be hereditary and, in women who are prone, pregnancy may provoke their appearance. A combination of hormonal changes and the pressure of the enlarged womb pressing down and obstructing the flow of blood from the legs to the heart can make varicose veins worse. Once the baby is born they generally subside and, by about three months, they usually return to the state they were before.

If legs feel heavy and ankles are swollen, avoid standing or sitting still for long periods; crossing legs or wearing tight popsocks also make things worse. Putting your feet up whenever possible and wearing well-fitting elastic support tights can help (department stores and large chemists now do ranges with Lycra which you could bear to wear); rotating foot exercises which increase circulation also ease symptoms. In extreme cases, if they become particularly troublesome or you find them too unsightly, varicose veins can be dealt with surgically. This can be done either by injecting drugs into segments of the relevant vein in order to obliterate it, or by having an operation which 'strips' the vein out of the leg.

VENTOUSE (Vacuum Extraction) As an alternative to forceps, a shallow cup is fitted to the baby's head by suction to assist in delivery of the baby vaginally. Ventouse is used under similar circumstances as forceps but is gentler on the mother. For the baby, the suction method commonly causes an area of swelling in the superficial tissues of the scalp which is sucked up into a 'chignon'; this gradually disappears in the first few days after birth. Much less commonly, swelling can occur in the deeper scalp tissue covering the bones; this is also spontaneously absorbed but may take weeks to resolve completely.

VESICO-VAGINAL FISTULA An abnormal connection between the bladder and vagina which can occur after a traumatic delivery and results in some uncontrollable leakage of urine via the vagina. Most fistulae close spontaneously; rarely, surgical repair is required in order to regain continence.

References

1. Birth
1. *The Midwives Tale*, Nicky Leap and Billie Hunter, Scarlet Press, 1993
2. *Inventing Motherhood: the consequences of an ideal*, Ann Dally, Burnett Books, 1982
3. *With Child: birth through the ages*, Jenny Carter and Therese Duriez, Mainstream Publishing, 1986
4. Ibid.
5. *Book of Pregnancy and Childbirth*, Sheila Kitzinger, Michael Joseph, 1989
6. *Ladies Home Journal*, May-December, 1958
7. *Ourselves as Mothers*, Sheila Kitzinger, Doubleday, 1992
8. *The American Way of Birth*, Jessica Mitford, Victor Gollancz, 1992
9. *The Experience of Childbirth*, Sheila Kitzinger, Penguin, 1981 (first published, Victor Gollancz, 1962)
10. *Journal of Reproductive and Infant Psychology*, Expected and Actual Experience of Labour and Delivery and their Relationship to Maternal Attachment, C. L. Booth and A. N. Meltzoff, 2:79-91
11. *Ibid.*
12. *Journal of Psychosomatic Obstetrics/Gynaecology*, Possible Relationship of Post-partum Psychiatric Symptoms to Childbirth Education Programmes, D. Stewart, December 1985, pp 295-301
13. *New Generation*, The Myth of Painless Childbirth, December 1984
14. Ibid.
15. *Journal of Reproductive and Infant Psychology*, Obstetric and Non-Obstetric Factors Related to Labour Pain, C. Niven and K. Gijsbers, 2:61-78
16. J. Mitford, op. cit.
17. *New Active Birth*, Janet Balaskas, Unwin, 1989
18. *The Experience of Childbirth*, S. Kitzinger, op. cit.
19. *Childbirth Unmasked*, Margaret Jowitt, Self Publishing Association, 1993
20. *Journal of Reproductive and Infant Psychology*, op. cit.
21. Ibid.

22. *Times*, 2 March, 1987
23. M. Jowitt, op. cit.
24. *Journal of Reproductive and Infant Psychology*, op. cit.
25. *Health after Childbirth: an investigation of long term health problems beginning after childbirth in 11701 women*, C. MacArthur, M. Lewis, G. Knox, University of Birmingham, 1001
26. Ibid.
27. *Parents*, National Birth Survey, April 1993

2. Revelations
1. *Guardian*, 4 September 1991
2. *Nursery World*, 2 December 1925
3. *Methods of Approach to the Problems of Behaviour*, Lorenz, New York Academic Press, no date.
4. *Maternal-Infant Bonding*, M. Klaus and J. Kennell, C. V. Mosby Co, 1976
5. *Mother-Infant Bonding: a science fiction*, Diane Eyer, Yale University Press, 1993
6. *Baby-Watching*, Desmond Morris, Jonathan Cape 1991
7. *Becoming a Mother*, Ann Oakley, Martin Robertson, 1979
8. *From Here to Maternity*, op. cit.
9. National Opinion Poll for Royal College of Midwives, 1993
10. *Times*, 22 October 1993
11. National Opinion Poll for Royal College of Midwives, 1993

3. Hospital and Home
1. *Yesterday's Babies: a history of babycare*, Diana Dick, The Bodley Head, 1987
2. Ibid.
3. *The Midwives Tale*, op. cit.
4. *Sunday Times*, Twenty-four Hours is Not Enough, Deborah Hutton, 24 April 1988
5. *Nursing Times*, Postpartum Depression/Extended Care, D. Affonso, 15 April, Vol 88, 1992
6. *Parents*, Midwife, Health Visitor and Community Nurse, June 1991.

4. Your Body after the Birth
1. *British Journal of Midwifery*, Postnatal Pain: a neglected area, G. Dewan, C. Glazener, M. Tunstall, June 1993, Vol 1, No 2
2. *Dewhurst*, Whitfield, 1990
3. *Some Women's Experience of Episiotomy*, Sheila Kitzinger and R. Walters, London, National Childbirth Trust, 1981

4. *AIMS Quarterly Journal*, Just a Small Cut, Christine Rogers, 4-5, Spring 1987

5. *BMJ*, West Berkshire Perineal Management Trials, J. Sleep, A. Grant, J. Garcia *et al*. 289/587-590, 1984

6. *British Journal of Obstetrics and Gynaecology*, Repairs of Episiotomy and Perineal Tears, A. grant, Vol 93, 417-9, May 1986

7. Ibid.

8. *British Journal of Obstetrics and Gynaecology*, Wound Pain May be Reduced by Prior Infiltration of the Episiotomy Site After Delivery Under Epidural Analgesia, G. Q. Khan *et al*, Vol 94, 341-344, April 1987

9. *New Generation*, Episiotomy and Perineal Repair, Mary Nolan, September 1989

10. *Maternal and Child Health*, Women's Illness in the Post-Natal Period, S. Field, J. Draper, M. Kerr *et al*, 60:5, 185-187, 1983

11. *From Here to Maternity: confessions of a first time mother*, Carol Weston, Little Brown and Company, 1991

12. *Health after Childbirth*, op. cit.

13. Iffy and Kaminetzky, 1981

14. *Health After Childbirth*, op. cit.

15. *Parents*, Steps to Beat Stress Incontinence, Catherine Stewen, July 1992

16. Ibid.

17. *Health after Childbirth*, op. cit.

18. *British Journal of Midwifery*, op. cit.

19. *JOGNN*, Skin Changes and Pain in the Nipple During the First Week of Lactation, M. Zeimer, J. Pigeon, May/June 1993

20. *Parents*, You're on Your Own Now, Heather Welford, June 1991

21. *Health after Childbirth*, op. cit.

22. Ibid.

23. Ibid.

24. Ibid.

25. *British Journal of Midwifery*, op. cit.

26. *Health after Childbirth*, op. cit.

5. Exhaustion and the Blues

1. *Americal Journal of Nursing*, Maternity Nursing Stops Too Soon, R. Rubin, 75 (10): 1680-1688

2. *Depression After Childbirth*, Katharina Dalton, Oxford University Press, 1980

3. *Female Cycles*, Paula Weideger, The Women's Press, London 1978

4. *Midwives Chronicle and Nursing Notes*, The Third Day Blues, V. Levy, November 1984

5. *Towards a Sociology of Childbirth: women confined*, Ann Oakley, Oxford, Martin Robinson, 1980
6. *Depression After Childbirth*, op. cit.
7. Ibid.
8. Ibid.
9. *Social Origins of Depression*, George Brown and Tirril Harris, Routledge, 1978
10. Research, AIMS

6. The Emotional Vortex

1. Sara Maitland in *Why Children?*, Stephanie Dowrick and Sybil Grundberg (eds), London Women's Press, 1980
2. *Journal of Pediatrics*, Patterns and Determinants of Maternal Attachment, K. Robson and H. A. Moss, 77, 1970
3. *The Transition to Parenthood*, (PhD) Mel Parr, 1993
4. *Becoming a Mother*, op. cit.
5. *Options*, Don't Listen to the Baby Doomers, Amanda Craig, November 1993.
6. *Baby Watching*, op. cit.
7. *Times*, Baby, Look At Us Now, Sue Peart, 23 January 1993
8. *Becoming a Mother*. op. cit.
9. *Psychological Processes of Childbearing*, Joan Raphael-Leff, Chapman and Hall, 1991
10. *The Maturation Process and Facilitating Environment*, Hogarth Press, 1965
11. Henley Centre Report quoted, *Sunday Correspondent*, The Child is Father of the Adman, Dinah Hall, 19 November 1989
12. *Occupation Housewife*, H. Z. Lopata, Oxford University Press, 1971
13. *From Here to Maternity*, op. cit.
14. Henley, Centre Report, op. cit.
15. *Health Visitor*, Birth Rate, R. Seel, 59:6 182-184, 1986
16. *Psychological Aspects of Obstetrics and Gynaecology*, (ed M. Oates), Normal Emotional Changes in Pregnancy and the Puerperium, M. Oates, Baillière Tindall, 1989
17. *Our Treacherous Hearts: why women let men get their own way*, Rosalind Coward, Faber and Faber Ltd, 1992
18. Ibid.
19. *The Mother Knot*, Jane Lazzare, Virago, 1987
20. *Baby and Child*, Penelope Leach, Penguin, 1977
21. *Dream Babies*, Christina Hardyment, Oxford University Press, 1984
22. *The Crying Baby*, Sheila Kitzinger, Harmondsworth, Penguin, 1989
23. *British Mothers' Magazine*, April 1955

24. *Inventing Motherhood*, op. cit.

8. Sex
1. *Making Love after Childbirth*, Sexual Health Information Leaflet, 1992
2. *She*, March 1991
3. *Me*, Your Body After the Baby, Paula Goodyer, August 1993
4. *AIMS Quarterly Journal*, op. cit.
5. *She*, Sex After Stitches, Amanda Craig, September 1993
6. *Heavy Weather*, Helen Simpson, published in *Granta: best of young British novelists* (2) 43, Spring 1993
7. *Guardian*, 4 February 1992
8. *Your Body, Your Baby, Your Life*, Angela Phillips, Nicky Leap and Barbara Jacobs, Pandora, 1983
9. *Becoming Orgasmic*, Julia Heiman and Joseph LoPiccolo, Piatkus, London 1988
10. *The Encyclopedia of Pregnancy and Birth*, Janet Balaskas and Yehudi Gordon, McDonald, London 1987
11. WHO: Social and Biological Effects on Perinatal Mortality, Vol 1, 1978

9. Partners
1. *To Have and To Hold*, Christopher F. Clulow, Aberdeen University Press, 1982
2. One Plus One, 1993
3. Mead 1962 and Rapoport and Rapoport, 1968, cc. p32
4. *From Here to Maternity*, op. cit.
5. British Social Attitudes Survey, 1991
6. *Dual Earner Households After Maternity Leave*, J. Brannen and P. Moss, London, Unwin Hyman, 1990
7. *Times*, Does He Deserve It?, Lee Rodwell, 17 June 1988
8. Mary Ingham Survey quoted in *Daily Telegraph*, Is This the End of the Road for the Modern Man, Martyn Harris, 22 April 1987
9. *Sunday Correspondent*, op. cit.
10. Nottingham University, quoted in *Mad About Women*, Yvonne Roberts, Virago 1992
11. *From Here to Maternity*, op. cit.
12. *Evening Standard*, What Does it Really Cost to Have a Baby. Anthea Masey, 8 July 1992
13. *Daily Mail*, The £349 Housewife, Sean Poulter, 3 February, 1993
14. Mel Parr, op. cit.

10. Family and Friends
1. Mel Parr, op. cit.
2. Ibid.
3. *From Here to Maternity*, op cit.

11. The Changing Face of the Family
1. *Elle*, Performance, Nick Hornby *et al*, February 1994
2. Quote in *Vogue*, Mother Inferior, Geraldine Bedell, January 1993

12. Work
1. *Guardian*, 25 September 1991
2. Ibid.
3. Ibid.
4. 1992 Farley Report, Snakes and Ladders – What Price Motherhood?
5. Ibid.
6. *New Generation*, I'm a Domestic Engineer Dear, What Are You? C. Bois, 1990
7. Beyond the Career Break: a study of professional and managerial women returning to work after a child, IMS Report No 223, Institute of Manpower Studies, Sussex University.
8. Helena Kennedy in *Balancing Acts*, Katherine Grieve (ed), London, Virago, 1989
9. *Guardian*, Women at War, Ros Coward, 22 March 1993

Conclusion
1. *The Compleat Woman: Marriage, Motherhood, Career: Can She Have It All*, Valerie Grove, Hogarth Press, 1987
2. Ibid.

Useful Addresses

Active Birth Movement
55 Dartmouth Park Road
London NW5 1SL.
071-267-3006

Association of Breastfeeding
Mothers
7 Maybourne Close
London SE26 6HQ
081-788-4769

AIMS (Association for
Improvements in Maternity
Services)
163 Liverpool Road
London N1 0RF
071-278-5628

Association for Post-Natal Illness
25 Jerdan Place
London SW6 1BE
071-386-0868

CRY-SIS
BM Cry-Sis
London WC1N 3XX
071-404-5011

Equal Opportunities Commission
Overseas House
Quay Street
Manchester M3 3HN
061-833-9244

Exploring Parenthood
Latimer Education Centre
194 Freston Road
London W10 6TT
081-960-1678

Freeline Social Security
(for free information on maternity
entitlements)
0800-666555

Gingerbread
35 Wellington Street
London WC2E 7BN
071-240-0953
(support for one-parent families)

Health Education Authority
Hamilton House
Mabledon Place
London WC1H 9TZ
071-387-3833

Independent Midwives' Association
63 Mount Nod Road
London SW16 2LP

Maternity Alliance
15 Britannia Street
London WC1X 9JP
071-837-1265

Meet a Mum Association
(MAMA)
5 Westbury Gardens
Luton
Bedfordshire
OU2 7DW
0582-422253

MIND (The National Association
for Mental Health)
22 Harley Street
London W1N 2ED
071-637 0741

Multiple Births Foundation
Queen Charlotte's and Chelsea
Hospital
Goldhawk Road
London W6 0XG
081-748 4666 (x5201)

National AIDS Trust
285 Euston Road
London NW1 3DN
071-383 4246

National Association of Family
Mediation and Conciliation
Services
Shaftesbury Centre
Percy Street
Swindon
Wiltshire SN2 2AZ
0793-514055

National Childbirth Trust
(NCT)
Alexandra House
Oldham Terrace
London W3 6NH
081-992 8637

National Council for One-Parent
Families
255 Kentish Town Road
London NW5 2LX
071-267 1361

National Information for Parents of
Prematures (NIPPERS)
The Sam Segal Perinatal Unit,
St Mary's Hospital
Praed Street
London W2 19Y
071-725 1487

National Network for Parents
Under Stress (OPUS)
106 Godstone Road
Whyteleafe
Surrey CR3 0EB
081-645-0469

NEWPIN (Parent/Infant Network)
Sutherland House
Sutherland Square
London SE17 3EE
071-703-6326

One Plus One (Marriage and
partnership research)
Central Middlesex Hospital
Acton Lane
London NW10 7NS
081-965-2367

PIPPIN (Parents in Partnership
Parent Infant Network)
'Derwood'
Todds Green
Stevenage
Hertfordshire SG1 2JE
0438 748478

Relate (National Headquarters)
Little Church Street
Rugby
Warwickshire
0788-573241

Royal College of Midwives
15 Mansfield Street
London W1M 0BE
071-580-6523

Twins and Multiple Births
Association
(TAMBA)
51 Thicknall Drive
Pedmore
Stourbridge
West Midlands DY9 0YH
0384 373642

Women's Health and Reproductive
Rights Centre
52 Featherstone Street
London EC1Y 8RT
071-263-6200

Working Mothers Association
77 Holloway Road
London N7 8JZ
071-700-5771

Women Returners Network
8 John Adam Street
London WC2N 6EZ
071-839-8188